HOW TO UNDERSTAND
YOUR SEXUALITY

By the same authors

How to Understand Your Gender
A Practical Guide for Exploring Who You Are
Alex Iantaffi and Meg-John Barker
Foreword by S. Bear Bergman
ISBN 978 1 78592 746 1
eISBN 978 1 78450 517 2

Hell Yeah Self-Care!
A Trauma-Informed Workbook
Alex Iantaffi and Meg-John Barker
ISBN 978 1 78775 245 0
eISBN 978 1 78775 246 7

Gender Trauma
Healing Cultural, Social, and
Historical Gendered Trauma
Alex Iantaffi
Foreword by Meg-John Barker
ISBN 978 1 78775 106 4
eISBN 978 1 78775 107 1

Life Isn't Binary
On Being Both, Beyond, and In-Between
Meg-John Barker and Alex Iantaffi
Foreword by CN Lester
ISBN 978 1 78592 479 8
eISBN 978 1 78450 864 7

HOW TO UNDERSTAND
YOUR SEXUALITY

A Practical Guide for Exploring Who You Are

MEG-JOHN BARKER AND ALEX IANTAFFI

Foreword by Erika Moen

Illustrations by Jules Scheele

Jessica Kingsley Publishers
London and Philadelphia

First published in Great Britain in 2022 by Jessica Kingsley Publishers
An Hachette Company

1

A CIP catalogue record for this title is available from the
British Library and the Library of Congress

ISBN 978 1 78775 618 2
eISBN 978 1 78775 619 9

Printed and bound in Great Britain by Clays Ltd

Jessica Kingsley Publishers' policy is to use papers that are natural,
renewable and recyclable products and made from wood grown in
sustainable forests. The logging and manufacturing processes are expected
to conform to the environmental regulations of the country of origin.

Jessica Kingsley Publishers
Carmelite House
50 Victoria Embankment
London EC4Y 0DZ

www.jkp.com

This book is dedicated to our younger selves, who could have really used a book like this, and to all the people who helped us learn more about sexuality along the way.

Contents

Foreword

This is a book that wants you to flourish. It's a book that wants to share knowledge with you so you can better understand yourself and the seven billion other people who inhabit our planet—but always at your speed, on your terms, and it understands if you don't totally agree right now or maybe ever. It just wants to let you know there are a lot more options outside of mainstream culture than you may have been exposed to yet and if you didn't know? Now you know. And if you really want to dive in deep? This book can't wait to put on flippers and plunge into the depths with you.

Wait, let me back up. What is this book about and why should you care and what qualifies me to vouch for it? *How to Understand Your Sexuality* is a comprehensive examination by Meg-John Barker and Alex Iantaffi of what sexuality is and the million different ways it can relate to you and society.

You should care because sexuality interacts, impacts, and influences you, everyone you know, and all of humankind. Whether it's positive, negative, or neutral, sexuality is a part of everyone's life. It is a key piece of the puzzle that makes up human desire, identity, repulsion, relationships, art, politics, spirituality, community... Listen, if the human experience is a table laden with a variety of delicious pies, sexuality has a finger in all of them. (That reads a lot more suggestive than it sounded in my head. But you know what? Isn't that just another example of the unexpected ways sexuality sneaks its way into nearly every aspect of human expression, including analogies?)

I'm telling you to trust Barker and Iantaffi because they know what they're talking about, and you can trust me because I'm a cartoonist. I mean, I'm a sex education cartoonist, specifically. My husband, Matthew Nolan, and I take academic and medical information about sex, sexuality, and general sex-adjacent subjects, and we translate that oftentimes dry, intimidating, abstract material into easily understandable comics. Our approach to education is to make the reader feel like they're being included in a conversation on the subject, not that they're being lectured at by an all-knowing authority figure. Sex, sexuality, and sex-adjacent subjects can be uncomfortable, shameful, scary, or genuinely distressing for some people, so we do our best to share this information with kindness, patience, empathy, and non-judgment. Plus, bad dad jokes and swears.

No wonder I like Barker and Iantaffi's work, since that's basically their approach to education as well! (Minus the bad dad jokes and swears.)

The authors explain things so patiently and kindly. Sexuality can be a very sensitive subject, especially for people who experience shame, pain, and/or any kind of oppression because of it. It's completely understandable that some people may respond to ignorant statements and questions with defensiveness or hostility when another person unintentionally (or fully intentionally) goes prodding into a painful area. While a snarky quip or a scolding may be a totally appropriate reaction in that moment, it doesn't actually replace the ignorance that caused the offensive comment in the first place.

There's nothing wrong with being ignorant! Ignorance is just a lack of knowledge, and it's the place we all start from until we learn more. Learning happens best with a kind, patient, empathic teacher who won't shame or judge you for what you don't understand. I can think of no kinder, more patient, more empathic education you could find on sexuality than this book right here. The questions that would probably get you yelled at if you asked them in public? Barker and Iantaffi are here to answer them without judgment because they really do want you to understand, or, at least, they want to open you up to a new view for you to consider.

That's the other thing that's so special about this book: Barker and Iantaffi support you learning at your own speed, at your own level, and they regularly remind you that everything they share in here may grow and change over time. They're not trying to etch the definitions and rules of sexuality into stone for generations to follow. They've made a book collecting past knowledge, current knowledge, and this makes space for the future knowledge it tells us is coming. The authors non-judgmentally say, "Let's look at this commonly accepted concept, and then we have an alternative perspective to offer."

The authors have literally built in space for people to evolve over the course of reading their book. They provide space not just for you, personally, to share your thoughts, but also for you to use them as a touchstone to return to throughout the book to see if you still agree with your initial understanding or whether you've got some different ideas now. There's no wrong answer, Barker and Iantaffi reassure you. If you do or don't change your mind, that's fine! That's okay. Your understanding is yours.

This is a book about flexibility. Flexibility of identity, labels, and concepts. It encourages you to reflect on what you already know while opening yourself up to new information that you may or may not agree with. Which is fine! It assures you. The book just wants to share what it knows with you, whether you adopt these ideas for yourself or not. The point isn't to convert you, it's to let you know how many different options there are out there.

I had physical reactions while reading *How to Understand Your Sexuality*. I "Hm!"ed at interesting points, I stopped and took deep breaths at the "slow down" pages, and I actually squawked out loud in surprised delight when I saw my own book recommended as a resource at the end of Chapter 3 (Thank you!!! I'm honored!). Some passages I nodded my head in agreement, while others I did a double take and then a re-read because some of these names and concepts were brand new to me. I re-examined the stuff I already know, I learned about some things that I didn't, and the whole way through I felt supported and respected by Barker and Iantaffi.

No matter if you're brand new to the subject of sexuality or you're a scholar (or a sex education cartoonist!), you're going to find something in here that resonates, something that surprises, and something that opens you up to an alternative perspective. Lucky you!

Erika Moen, April 2021
Portland, OR, USA

Acknowledgements

This book could not exist without the support of so many people, such as our loved ones, our wonderful editor, Andrew James, and you, our readers. Thank you for continuing to sustain our work with your care, feedback, and engagement. We are so grateful.

INTRODUCTION

Hello and welcome to our book, *How to Understand Your Sexuality*. In the pages to come we'll invite you to:

- think with us about the ways of understanding sexuality which are common out there in the world

- explore a bunch of ideas about sexuality from scholars, activists, and practitioners, which may be more useful

- most importantly, reflect on your own experience of sexuality to find out what works for you and to understand it—perhaps more deeply than you already do.

This book is part of a trilogy that we're currently in the middle of writing. The number one book in the series, *How to Understand Your Gender*, was the first full book we wrote together and came out back in 2017. This current book was written in the midst of the Covid-19 pandemic in 2020, and we hope to write the final book in the trilogy, *How to Understand Your Relationships*, in 2022. It's fine just to read one of the books in this series. But, as we'll explain, our experiences of gender, sexuality, and relationships are closely interwoven, so you may also find it useful to read them together to explore how they relate for you.

We've used a similar structure in all three books—with just a few tweaks—so it's easy to work through them in parallel, if you so wish. For example, you might want to think about the messages you received in your upbringing about gender, sexuality, and relationships, in which case you could read Chapter 3 of all three books together. Or you might want to consider your gender, sexuality, and relationship role models and support systems, in which case that's Chapter 7 of all three.

In this introduction, we'll say a little more about why this particular book is so important to us, as well as introducing ourselves, and our sense of who you, our reader, might be. We'll also talk about how you might engage with the book, and what to expect in the pages to come.

WHY THIS BOOK?

This book is super important to us as sexuality has been a huge part of both of our lives, personally, professionally, and politically. Specifically, sexuality has been a place of healing and harming for both of us, as it has for so many people. It's this "bothness" that we want to capture throughout this book: the ways in which sexuality can move us towards pleasure, aliveness, and authenticity, as well as being a site of trauma, struggle, and constraint.

Sexuality as a place of pleasure or healing: for many people, coming to an understanding of their sexuality, and owning it, is a pivotal moment in acknowledging who they are, finding community and belonging, and reaching greater self-acceptance and self-compassion. Through exploring sexual, sensual, or erotic connection, we can experience great pleasure and find deep intimacy with ourselves and others. Politically, fighting for sexual rights in solidarity with others, tuning into what makes us feel alive, and centering that in our lives can move us towards a more just world for everybody.

Sexuality as a place of danger or harm: at the same time, as the #MeToo and consent culture movements have demonstrated, non-consensual sex is a common experience in many—if not most—people's lives. Many people are marginalized in terms of their sexuality and suffer stigma, discrimination, and even violence as a result. We still live in a world where a certain, very narrow, range of sexuality is regarded as "normal," and there is a good deal of ableism, homophobia, biphobia, kinkphobia, acephobia, whorephobia, and more. There is also a very narrow range of what is deemed sexually attractive, which impacts most of us in negative ways. In addition to sexual trauma, many of us are traumatized in other ways which impact our sex lives.

We want to write a book that holds this bothness, recognizing that all of our sexualities are likely sites of pleasure and danger, of liberation and constraint, of delight and trauma. To really understand our sexualities, we need to pay equal attention to both sides of these binaries, as you might expect from two authors who also wrote a book called *Life Isn't Binary*!

Much of the material out there about sexuality is either sex-negative—focusing on danger, risk and safety, or sex-positive—insisting on the importance of having "great sex." Here we offer an alternative approach whereby we can acknowledge the complexity of all our sexualities, paying equal attention to past and present experiences of moving towards pleasure and aliveness, alongside past and present experiences of sexual struggles and trauma.

As with the other books in the series, this is the book that we wish we'd had access to ourselves when we were younger and started navigating our own sexualities!

WHO ARE YOU?

Now let's take a moment to consider who you might be, dear reader, and why you may have picked up this particular book. As we have said, we imagine that you could be someone who wants to understand your sexuality better. Or maybe your child, spouse, or friend has shared their sexuality with you, and you want to understand them better. You could be a teacher, counselor, therapist, youth worker, spiritual leader, social worker, or healthcare provider who wants to better serve your students, clients, or patients. Maybe you just like to stay up to date in the field of sexuality, and that's why you chose to read this book. Or you could have read our previous books and decided to read this one as well (thank you). Maybe someone has given it to you as a gift. Or you just picked it up on a whim because you liked the cover!

Whatever your reason for picking up this book, we do hope you'll find valuable and interesting information here that you can apply to your own life, both personal and professional (is there even a difference?). Our intention is for this book to be readable for everyone, whatever your sexuality or existing knowledge in this area. We also know that our previous book in this series, *How to Understand Your Gender*, has been used as a teaching tool everywhere, from high school classrooms to higher education institutions. If you're reading this book as a class text, we still hope you'll find information that's applicable in your own life.

When people think about sexuality, they often tend to think of other people's sexualities. If you're a professional who's picked this book up to better serve your clients, for example, you might be looking for something that helps you to understand marginalized and historically underserved populations. Just as we did in our previous book on gender, we invite you first to reflect on your own sexuality, especially if your sexuality fits in with dominant cultural expectations.

We've addressed sexuality in a very broad way through this book. We had the ambitious goal to encompass all kinds of sex and sexuality, including, but not limited to, solosexuality, asexuality, heterosexuality, ecosexuality, and queer sexualities. We've also included diverse relationship structures, although our next book, *How to Understand Your Relationships*, will focus more specifically on this topic.

We've adopted a trauma-informed lens throughout this book and we know that reading about sex and sexuality can be triggering, especially for those of us who have experienced sexual trauma. If you notice that reading this book is challenging, for whatever reason, please do pause and get the support you need. We'll keep reminding you of this throughout the book. Whoever you are, and whatever the reason you're reading this book, we invite you to be kind with yourself as you do so, and we hope you'll find some useful and interesting information here.

WHO ARE WE?

We've talked about who you might be, but who are we, the authors, to be writing such a book? We're both therapists, sex therapists, scholars, and community organizers, and we also span a range of sexualities, both between us and across our own lifespans so far. As well as being knowledgeable and experienced in these areas ourselves, we believe in drawing from—and highlighting—the work that others have done, so throughout our books you'll find references to other resources.

To help you get a better sense of who we are, and to situate our own sexualities, here are individual introductions from us both. Throughout the book, we weave in our own histories as examples, as well as drawing on other people's experiences to cover a broader range of identities, attractions, practices, and experiences. Confidentiality is very important to us, so those experiences are a composite of various people's stories. There are no direct, individual quotes, except where we talk about our own experiences.

ALEX WRITES:

Hello! We might have already met if you've read our previous books, but let me tell you a little bit about me through the lens of sexuality. I'm a trans masculine, non-binary person with white privilege who identifies as bisexual, queer, kinky, and polyamorous. I have also historically been part of lesbian community, when I first came out (more on the idea of coming out later in the book!), and, before that, I was briefly in a heteronormative marriage. I am also a survivor of sexual trauma, in both childhood and adulthood. I'm disabled and have crossed geographical and cultural borders twice, first when I moved from Italy to the UK, and then again when I moved from the UK to the US. I was brought up Catholic and I've been an openly practicing Pagan for over two decades.

I've been a parent for 17 years, at the time of writing this book, and strived to bring my child up in a sex-affirming household at a time when there was far less information than there is now on how to do so, and fewer inclusive, age-appropriate sex education materials. I've researched and published extensively on the topics of sex and sexuality, and I am a certified sex therapist, through the American Association of Sexuality Educators, Counselors, and Therapists. I'm also a family therapist, clinical supervisor, Somatic Experiencing™ practitioner, and trauma therapist. I was Editor-in-Chief for the international *Journal of Sexual and Relationship Therapy* for over a decade. Many aspects of sex and sexuality, alongside gender, disability, and relationships, have been the focus of my life professionally, and the focus of my healing and growth personally.

In some ways, it feels really vulnerable to share what is usually considered to be such personal information alongside the professional information. However, I've become increasingly convinced that challenging such binaries of personal and professional domains is vital, especially for those of us who have the capacity and privilege to do so. I was brought up to believe that the personal is indeed the political, and this belief has shaped many of my choices, and continues to do so. I'm aware that it's also risky to share this personal information about my sexuality as someone with marginalized identities and experiences. I know that some of this information can be weaponized against me, especially where I live, in what is now known as the US. In fact, I know this because it has already been used against me, in smaller and larger ways.

However, I continue to believe that living my life as openly as I am able is also its own protection. What is not secret cannot be used to shame me, although people have tried. By the time this book is published, I will be 50 years old. I owe so much to those who have come before me and have lived their sexuality openly so I could do the same. I hope to pass that gift on, as I am able, to those who come after me. I know that because of systemic issues not everyone can live their sexuality openly and safely. I dream of a day when this will no longer be the case, and sharing such information about ourselves might not be scary at all, and might even have become irrelevant.

MEG-JOHN WRITES:

Hi there. Whenever I write one of these introductions I'm struck that the things which feel important to say about myself have changed so much, from the first of these kinds of books that I wrote, and even from the most recent one! It's a good reminder of the ways in which I'm always in a process of becoming, in relation to my life, my work, and my own sexual, and related, identities. Throughout this book, we'll emphasize that our sexualities can be fluid, and that our understandings of sexuality are certainly a work in progress as we come to a deeper sense of ourselves, and as the ideas about sexuality out there in the world around us change over time.

I'm now a full-time writer, and I write mostly about topics such as gender, sexuality, relationships, and mental health. Exploring these themes has been a lifelong journey for me personally, professionally, and politically. I became aware in my twenties that the normative ways of understanding gender, sex, relationships, and mental health, in the world around me, were not great for me, or indeed for anybody else I spoke to. It became my mission to explore different ways of understanding these related topics: through the academic areas of psychology, sociology, philosophy, and more; through training as a sex and relationship therapist and working with clients in these areas; and through engaging with various activist communities, particularly bi, kink, non-monogamous, queer, and trans communities.

What else is important to say about me? I'm currently 46 years old. I'm white British with a mixed class background and I'm disabled. I'm queer, kinky, non-binary, and a relationship anarchist, and my sexuality is solosexual, with a strong emphasis on connecting different parts of myself through erotic fantasy. I've even written a couple of erotic novels which I may or may not unleash on the world at some point! I'm Buddhist and my work is particularly informed by somatic and social justice forms of Buddhism and mindfulness. I'm a survivor of both developmental trauma and sexual trauma, and this has had a major impact on my own sexual and relationship life. Like Alex, my sexuality has also been used to publicly shame me. The newspaper headline "Bisexual boffin: I'm a slut" is one that I'll never forget! I've recently spent the time of the Covid-19 pandemic doing deep work on my own trauma, supported by a wonderful therapist and amazing friends like Alex, and that work informs this book and will likely inform our next book on relationships even more.

I'm deeply passionate about getting materials out there that might help everybody to understand themselves better, and how they're impacted by the systems and structures around them. In addition to my books with Alex, I've written a number of "graphic guides" to these kinds of topics with awesome illustrator Jules Scheele (who also does the covers of these books). I've created podcasts, a book and zines with sex and relationships educator Justin Hancock, and I write blog posts, comics, and zines around topics like trauma, consent, and plurality, which you can find on my website at www. rewriting-the-rules.com.

HOW TO READ THIS BOOK?

You can read this book from start to finish, but it should also be fine to pick any chapter—or part of a chapter—that calls to you and go right to that. We've tried to write it in a way which builds knowledge through the book, so some of the basics about how sexuality works, and what words mean, are introduced up front in Chapter 1. If this area is new to you, you might want to start there.

To help you to apply what you learn through the book to your own life, you'll find the following features in all of the chapters:

— *Reflection points:* These are things to reflect on, or write some notes about, such as your own experience of a particular issue.

— *Activities:* These are invitations to do a particular exercise, like creating a mind map, drawing a simple picture, or jotting down a memory. You can do this in the book—if it belongs to you!—or in a journal or notebook.

— *Multiple experiences:* These are lists of different people's experiences of some particular aspect of sexuality, to give you a sense of the diversity that is possible, and how it actually plays out in people's lives. All of the examples given are real, in the sense that we've heard them from many people over the years, but—as mentioned before—we've fictionalized them and combined them so that no actual people are identifiable.

— *Slow-down pages:* These are invitations to pause and tune into yourself, or notice how you're responding to what you're reading about, in order to bring in your body as well as your mind, and to treat yourself kindly.

You can use these features as much or as little as you like—it's completely up to you. We hope they'll enhance your reading experience if you want to apply the learning to your own life. They might also give you something to discuss if you're exploring this book with others, for example in a book club or a class.

WHAT'S IN THIS BOOK?

The book is divided into seven chapters and each chapter includes four sections. At the end of each chapter we've also signposted other resources that are available if you want to find out more.

We start, in Chapter 1, with an introduction to what we mean by words like sex, sexuality, and erotic, and we give a broad overview of how sexuality works in terms of our identities and attractions, desires, and practices.

In Chapter 2, we explore how the world around us tends to see sexuality, and how this has been different in different places and times. We dig into how current popular understandings of sexual attractions, desires, and practices can be very limited, and how that impacts our experience of our own sexualities.

Chapter 3 begins the exploration of your own sexuality in more depth as we encourage you to think about how your upbringing influenced your understanding and experience of sexuality.

Chapter 4 continues this exploration to the present day, by looking at the current messages you receive about sexuality, how sexuality sits within other intersecting aspects of your experiences, and more.

Having explored how your sexuality developed, and the current influences on it, in Chapter 5 we spend more time considering how you experience your body, your desires, and your sexual practices now, finishing with the question of how you might—or might not—identify different aspects of your sexuality, given this.

In Chapter 6, we explore whether communicating your sexuality with others is something you want to do and—if so—how you might go about it, as well as exploring the relationship contexts in which you may want to be sexual, erotic, or sensual, and how you might do so consensually.

Finally, Chapter 7 considers the support you might get from others in relation to your sexuality, and how understanding your sexuality can be a starting point for engaging with the world in political, spiritual, creative, and other ways.

A couple of final notes before we start. First is a reminder that, throughout this book, we're using "sexuality" in its widest possible sense to encompass all of our relationships in the area of life we might think of as erotic, sensual, or sexual. We've endeavored, all the way through, to be inclusive of all sexualities and asexualites. We regard solo and partnered forms of sexuality and sensuality as equally valid, and all expressions of the erotic as legitimate so long as they're practiced consensually. For example, we've endeavoured to be inclusive of kinky and non-kinky practices, straight and queer identities, ace and aro experiences, sex that is and isn't a form of work, sex that is spiritual and not, and more, as well as questioning some of these binaries. We'll say more about all of these things over the course of the book, but this is just a heads-up that hopefully, whatever your relationship to sexuality, you will find this book helpful and the explorations accessible.

Second, as mentioned before, we highlight trauma, and the experiences of survivors, throughout this book. Many materials about sex and sexuality act as if sex and pleasure are straightforward things for people. This feels like a form of gaslighting to us, in a world where many—if not most—of us have experiences of childhood and/or adulthood sexual trauma. This focus on trauma does, however, mean that some parts of this book may be hard to engage with, particularly if you've experienced trauma yourself. We've tried to give you a heads-up, at the start of each chapter, about any content that might be tricky so that you can decide whether you want to engage with it, and—if so—how. For example, you might want to wait until you're in a good place, until you have plenty of space around it, or until you have support on hand to deal with anything tough that comes up. There's more on how to access support in Chapter 7.

Also, to support you to engage with this book kindly, and

to look after yourself around any challenging moments, we've placed reminders throughout to slow down, breathe, notice your experience, take time out if you need to, and remain curious rather than judgmental. These pages also introduce some of the practices that you might find useful in doing the kind of tuning into yourself, and self-consensual treatment, that we see as being pivotal for a good understanding of your sexuality, and a good erotic experience.

Here's your first reminder...

Take a moment to breathe...

Let's do that again.

Just breathe, at your own pace, according to your own lung capacity in this very moment in time.

Then take a few moments to reflect on why you picked this book up (or if someone gave it to you, why you decided to read it).

Set an intention for reading this book and, if you like, write it down.

If you're reading this book because you have to (maybe it's a textbook for your class), it's okay.

You can set a simple intention of just reading it.

When you feel ready, let's begin...

CHAPTER 1

WHAT IS SEXUALITY?

In this chapter, we'll start by talking about language because people often find all the terms for different sexualities disorienting. After that, we'll focus in on what the word "sexuality" itself means and how it relates to sex. Then we'll consider whether sexuality is something biological, psychological, or social (spoiler alert: it's a mixture of all of these!). Finally, we'll explore the different dimensions of sexuality which we'll return to throughout the book: how we identify our sexuality, what our sexual attraction is, what our desires are, and the sexual practices we might, or might not, engage in.

1.1 WHAT WORDS MEAN

One reason that people often find sexuality a confusing area is that there has been an explosion of labels for different sexualities in the last couple of decades.

People who had thought of sexuality as a pretty simple matter of "you're this or you're that" may now struggle to locate themselves in this vast landscape that's opened up of different terms to describe your sexual identities, the roles you take, desires you have, and so on.

Some find this personally challenging, because it opens up possibilities that had not felt available to them growing up. This may bring up a sense of grief or loss. Some feel shame and fear about "getting it wrong" when new words and concepts are so unfamiliar.

For such reasons, there has also been a cultural backlash against the "snowflake generation" who are seen as using all these labels, even though such words are certainly not restricted to young folks (we're both around 50 and use them!). The backlash presents all this new language as something silly and childish, and people who want them used as too fragile and easily offended.

One hope that we have for this book is for it to be a gentle guide through this seemingly complex territory, helping you both to explore what language might—or might not—be helpful for you, and to navigate how to communicate with others, whatever terminology they're using.

It's certainly the case that different words are used by different people, and in different contexts, so often there's not a blanket "right" term that you could use. It's more about checking in with the person or community concerned. For example, people often use an acronym like LGBTQ+ to refer to everyone who is not heterosexual and cisgender (remaining in the gender they were assigned at birth). However, there have been many different attempts to revise this acronym to be fully inclusive, such as LGBTTQQIAAP to stand for lesbian, gay, bi, trans, two spirit, queer, questioning, intersex, asexual, aromantic, and pansexual; or GSRD to stand for gender, sex, and relationship diversity.

Governments and organizations may still use the briefer form, LGBT.

For people who do not experience sexual attraction, some use the word asexual, whereas some prefer the shortened term, ace, which doesn't have "sexual" in it. Some would say they're on the ace spectrum, whereas others would prefer specific terms like gray-A or demisexual to locate themselves specifically on that spectrum. Don't worry, we'll come back to what all these different words mean over the course of the book. For now, this is just to highlight the fact that different people use different words, and that different words may be appropriate in different contexts.

So what can you do to be respectful around language?

- Check in with the person concerned about the words they use themselves and what they'd like you to use.

- Practice as much as possible using this language so you get it right with them.

- If you get it wrong, apologize and move on, rather than dwelling on the mistake.

- Check in with them if you think their terms might have changed over time.

Changing terminology

Often the backlash against new language includes an argument that it's somehow not okay to "invent new words" or to change the meaning of words over time.

It's important to remember that words are always being invented and that word meanings often change. For example, the *Oxford English Dictionary* added 650 words in its most recent update (at the time we wrote this book), including the words "craftivist" and "cookie monster!" In the past, there were two words for "you" in the English language—"thou" and "you"—but "thou" has pretty much been phased out. However, the singular "they," which has always been used for people whose gender is unknown ("Who left their bag over there?"), is now also used for non-binary folk ("Alex? Oh yes, I read their book on gender trauma").

Also, language is often reclaimed in important ways over time, particularly in the area of sexuality. Meg-John has written a whole comic book about the word "queer." This began as a word for oddness, as in the North English saying "all the world is queer except thee and me, and even thou art a little queer" (there's that old word for "you" as well!). Queer then became applied to people with same-gender attraction as a term of abuse. It has since been reclaimed by many LGBTQ+ people as a celebratory word, and as an umbrella term under which they can all sit. It can also mean anybody who has stepped outside what is culturally "normal." It's been added to other words, such as genderqueer, neuroqueer, and relationshipqueer. Queer is also a word that, over time, has become a verb as well as an adjective, so that people now can use it in sentences such as, "Karamo Brown and his buddies are queering our culture."

Because of the way language shifts and changes meaning, it's even more important to check in with people about the language they prefer. For example, being called queer may be retraumatizing for some people who were called that term as an insult during school bullying or family abuse. It may be affirming for others. Some may find it erasing of their more specific identity, as a lesbian or a bisexual person, for example. Others may regard it as a white western term, and prefer a more culturally specific term.

A lot of people who are attracted only to the same-gender use the word "gay," and most steer clear of the word "homosexual" these days with its background in medicalizing same-gender attraction as a disorder. However, again, some may prefer other terms because of the prevalence of "that's gay" as an insult, or because they like something more specific, like bear, stud, or dyke, or for other reasons.

Over the course of the book we'll explore more what language you might use for your own sexuality, how each term is actually a big umbrella for many different experiences and identities, and what applying a label to your sexuality might open up, and what it might close down. For now, let's just think about the words you already use.

Reflection point: The words you use

— Think about the words that you, and others, currently use to describe your sexuality. Maybe make a note of the ones you like, and those that feel uncomfortable to you.

— Are there any words around sexuality that you've heard used that you don't completely understand? Make a note of these too. It is hoped that we'll be coming back to most of them; but if not, feel free to have an online search if you have internet access.

The importance of language

Many philosophers, such as Ludwig Wittgenstein, have championed the importance of language in their writing. Language can shape our reality. For example, take a moment to imagine how you would describe a table if you had never come across the word "table" itself. Your description would probably depend on the object you're observing in the moment, such as a rectangular piece of wood supported by wooden legs. However, if you saw a triangular marble top supported by a square base, would you still recognize this as a table, if you didn't know this word and what it stands for?

Language helps us to know the world around us and ourselves. When it comes to sexuality, there are so many words to define. We cannot attempt to provide a complete glossary of all the words linked to sexuality here. However, we do want to take a moment to reflect on the importance of language in this area. Let's start from the word "sexuality" itself. What comes to mind for you when you see that word? How would you define sexuality? Has the meaning of this word changed over time for you? If so, how? If not, why not? Don't worry if you have no idea, as we'll define the word ourselves a little later in the chapter.

Because language shapes reality, the words for sexuality that we do or don't have access to, can offer a more expansive or a more restricted landscape. For example, the first time some people come across the word "asexual" can be a powerful moment to witness. Maybe someone has never previously been able to make sense of their own thoughts and feelings around their sexuality, or someone else's. Maybe they have been puzzled by their own lack of sexual interest, or even mocked by others because of it, and coming across the word "asexual" opens up a world of possibilities for them. What are the words related to sexuality that have opened up new possibilities for you over time? Maybe this is the first time you've come across the word "asexual" and, if so, what reactions are you noticing?

Language lets us know what's possible, what exists or what we can imagine individually and collectively. Personally, we've seen many words come into public awareness over our own lifetimes, in relation to sexuality. For example, controversial as it might be, the popularity of *Fifty Shades of Grey* introduced words such as "kink" and "BDSM" (bondage, discipline, dominance, and submission) to the general public, outside kink communities. People have also created words such as "heteroflexible," "skoliosexual," "stone butch" to be able to communicate their own sexuality to others. The internet has also had a major role in spreading words from community to community. In fact, sexuality also happens online and with the involvement of technology, giving rise to the word "digisexuality"—the integration of technology into our sexuality.

Language is a living, breathing, co-created phenomenon within history and culture. It can also have different meanings for different people across time and space. "Queer" is another good example of an Anglo word that has been adopted by other languages, where there might not be a direct translation for this word. As people connect across languages and cultures, they might find new possibilities for their own sexualities as they come across new words that maybe do not exist—or have been erased due to colonization—in their own language.

ACTIVITY: ALL OF THE WORDS

Here are all of the words that an article on the website Health-line was offering for different types of sexuality when we were writing this book. You might find it useful to circle any words that feel like a good fit for you (it is likely that there might be more than one of them), and also to reflect on any that other people might use that don't fit for you, as well as any that are unfamiliar to you. You could also notice whether any of the words you know, or like, are missing. For example, we notice "digisexual," "two spirit," "kinky," and "top/bottom" were missing.

Allosexual, androsexual, aromantic, asexual, autoro-mantic, autosexual, bicurious, bisexual, biromantic, closeted, cupiosexual, demiromatinc, demisexual, fluid, gray, grayromantic, graysexual, gynsexual, heterosexual, homosexual, lesbian, LGBTQIA+, libidoist asexual, monosexual, non-libidoist asexual, omnisexual, panromantic, pansexual, polysexual, pomosexual, queer, questioning, sapiosexual, sex-averse, sex-favorable, sex-indifferent, sex-repulsed, skoliosexual, spectrasexual, straight.

List of words from: www.healthline.com/health/different-types-of-sexuality#why-it-matters.

We won't provide definitions for every word that exists here, because language changes over time and new words will likely come into use between the time we're writing this book and the time you're reading it. However, we will introduce a range of terms and we'll try to provide succinct definitions when a new term is introduced. We invite you to also look up the meaning of the words we use to compare how they're used by others, given that language is a living, ever-evolving system.

In the next section, we'll address the difference between sex and sexuality. So, if you feel a little confused about which words are used in relation to sex, and which in relation to sexuality, or even if there is a difference between sex and sexuality, read on.

1.2 SEX AND SEXUALITY

Here we start by defining sex and sexuality, and then explore some other related terms, including "erotic," "romantic," and "asexual," and how they relate to sexuality.

Sex or sexuality?

Generally, the word "sexuality" is used to refer to the sexual attractions and desires that we have, whereas the word "sex" is used for the sexual practices we engage with. There's a sense that we *have* a sexuality, and that we *do* sex.

Also, confusingly, "sex" is often used interchangeably with "gender"—or to refer to certain aspects of gender. We've written a whole further book about that, *How to Understand Your Gender*, so check that out for more on sex/gender. In this book, we'll use "sex" in relation to sexual practices or activities.

In wider culture, both sex and sexuality are understood in pretty restrictive ways. Our sexuality is often seen as being just about the gender of the person we're attracted to: whether we're gay, straight, or bi, for example. It's also seen as a specific identity that remains fixed over time. Sex is seen as "the sex act" of penis-in-vagina (PIV) intercourse, or perhaps any form of penetration.

Actually, sexuality can be more helpfully understood as all of the sexual identities, attractions, and desires that feel relevant to us personally, which may—or may not—map onto each other and change over time. For example, sexuality might encompass the kinds of people we currently do and don't find attractive, the kinds of scenarios that excite us, the level of attraction and desire we have (from none to high levels), the roles we enjoy taking sexually (more active, passive, submissive, or dominant, for example), and much much more.

Sex is also a lot broader than just PIV. We'll say more about this through the book, but for now think about it for yourself.

ACTIVITY: WHAT IS SEX?

You already began to think about some of the diverse forms of sexuality in the last section, so now let's think about all the diverse forms of sex. Take a moment to make a list on a piece of paper, or in a notebook, of all of the activities you can think of that somebody, somewhere, would experience as sexual.

You might find it useful to put these on a scale from the ones that wider culture defines as "proper sex" to the ones that are often not seen in that way. We'll come back to this sense of cultural rules about what does and doesn't "count" as sex or sexuality—and the impact of that—throughout the book.

Erotic or sexual?

One of our favorite writers, Black feminist Audre Lorde, suggested that it's useful to question the distinction we often make between what is sexual and "the erotic." Reflecting on the activity you just did, you might notice that some of the activities in it would be sexual to some people but not to others. Some might be sensual, but are they sexual?

Lorde talks about the erotic as a kind of power or lifeforce which gets restricted by wider culture when it's limited to just things that are seen as "counting" as sex. There's a sense that anything that lights us up and makes us feel alive could be regarded as erotic. Lorde gives the examples of making love with a partner in a patch of sunlight, writing a poem, dancing, examining an idea, building a bookcase, and even having a conflict with both heat and respect.

We'll come back in the next chapter to all of the different practices we might find erotic, and how exploring those can help to expand our erotic menu or palette. For now, let's just touch on a few things that this idea of "the erotic" opens up.

First, we often think of sex as necessarily involving bodies. The idea of the erotic reminds us that this may not necessarily be the case. Some of the most exciting enlivening things can happen entirely in a person's mind, in the form of fantasy or imagination, for example. Others can happen in spoken or written communication between people, like messenger exchanges. Of course, we are embodied beings so our bodies are always involved in any experience. But the erotic reminds us that such experiences do not necessarily need to involve genitals or other body parts generally associated with sex.

Second, the erotic reminds us that encounters with

ourselves are just as real and relevant as encounters with others. Solo sex and self-touch are often regarded as less valid than interactions with partners, and are stigmatized as selfish, childish, embarrassing, or risky. Actually, erotic encounters of all kinds can be equally meaningful alone or with any number of others, whether that's appreciating a sunset or having an orgasm.

The erotic can also be a helpful concept for people on the ace spectrum—which we'll come to in a moment—because it challenges the idea that sexual experiences are any more valid than non-sexual ones.

Romantic or sexual?

In dominant discourse, such as Hollywood movies and popular songs, there's often little to no difference between romantic and sexual feelings. In fact, it's often assumed that the two are linked in some way and, if they're not, that's not morally acceptable. For example, people might be judgmental of someone who engages in sexual behaviors without any romantic feelings towards the other person. Of course, this also intersects heavily with gendered expectations, and sexual behaviors without romantic feelings are often viewed as more or less acceptable depending on the genders of the people involved.

If we separate the two, though, how do we know which is which? Romantic feelings are usually associated with love. Some definitions also view romance as particularly connected to idealistic or sentimental love. Here, we'll use a broader definition and just talk about romantic feelings as those connected to love towards someone who is not a family member. If you think this might include having romantic feelings towards friends, as well as partners, you are correct. We're using a broad definition of romance here, which means we can have romantic feelings towards a wide range of people, especially when we separate romantic from sexual feelings.

Romantic feelings might include wanting to spend time with a particular person or people, wanting to support them in their endeavors, expressing love through acts of service, words of affirmation, or gifts. Romantic feelings are often described as experiencing warmth and intimacy with someone. They might be accompanied by a desire for touch with the person(s) involved, such as wanting to hold hands, hug, cuddle, or kiss. But these don't necessarily lead to sexual feelings.

Sometimes romantic feelings are accompanied by sexual feelings. When this happens, usually the person wants more physical intimacy. For example, they might think of holding hands, cuddling, and kissing as a possible prelude to sex. They might also experience sexual attraction to the person they're romantically attracted to. This usually means that there's a component of sexual arousal when thinking about, or being in the presence of, the person(s) they are attracted to. Of course, being sexually attracted to someone doesn't mean that we inevitably want to act on it. We might experience romantic and sexual feelings towards someone and not act on either or one of them, for a wide range of reasons.

Romantic feelings can occur completely separately from sexual feelings, or around the same time, or one after the other. There's no "right" or "wrong" way to feel about someone. For example, we might be sexually attracted to someone and then develop romantic feelings, or the other way around. We might also feel romantic towards someone and never feel sexually attracted to them, or vice versa. One is not superior to the other, they are just different experiences. Growing up, it can be at times confusing to know whether we're experiencing romantic or sexual feelings. As we become more familiar with our own bodies, we usually become better able to distinguish if we are sexually aroused or not. We will discuss this next.

Sexual or asexual?

How do we know if we're having sexual feelings or not? We've just mentioned that some people don't experience sexual attraction towards others. However, this doesn't always mean that they don't experience sexual arousal.

Sexual arousal—or sexual excitement—means experiencing sexual desire when thinking about, or practicing, sex by ourselves or with others. Genital arousal is usually involved. This means that there are physiological changes such as increased blood flow to our genitals, lubrication in the genital area, increased heart rate, stiffening of nipples, heightened sensitivity to touch, and fluctuations of hormones, which are not things we usually perceive but which also occur during arousal.

Arousal is a response of our body that can happen regardless of how we feel towards someone. That means that, sometimes, we can become aroused even when somebody is non-consensual towards us sexually, or assaults us. This can be very confusing for many people who have experienced sexual violence, including childhood sexual abuse, or intimate partner violence. It's important to remember that our body responses are often independent from our brain's prefrontal cortex control—that is, our thoughts. If this is something that's happened to you, there's nothing to be ashamed about. If you've never talked about this with someone, we encourage you to talk with a sex therapist or a peer support group in order to challenge any residual shame you might experience. We'll return to the topic of power and abuse in Chapter 3, and support in Chapter 7.

Sexual arousal can also be experienced by people of any sexuality, including asexual people. Some asexual people engage in some sexual practices, such as solo or partnered sex, while others do not. Many of the sexuality terms we use, such as "asexuality," are umbrellas covering vast landscapes of identities, desires, and behaviors. This means that if someone shares their identity with us, we can't automatically assume whether they do or don't experience sexual feelings.

However, asexual people generally describe themselves as not being sexually *attracted* to others, or not being primarily driven by sexual attraction in their relationships. Once more, there's no right or wrong way to feel. People can have a range of relationships with others, which might or might not involve sexual desire or practices. So, how might you know if you're asexual? As you get to know yourself and explore possibilities, you'll start to get a clearer picture of your own desires. We hope this book might be a helpful starting point for such a journey.

So far we've discussed aspects of sexuality in a fairly polarized way: sex/sexuality; erotic/sexual; romantic/sexual; sexual/asexual. However, sexuality is not so easily captured in binaries: it's much more complex and multifaceted. This means that we can experience contradictory feelings, as well as different desires, across the lifespan. For example, we might go from being allosexual (that is, someone who experiences sexual attraction) to asexual or demisexual. It's okay for our sexuality to change over time and for us to have many desires at once. We'll come back to this in the following chapters, especially in Chapters 5 and 6, where we address identifying and living your sexuality, as well as sexuality in the context of relationships. For now, let's take a look at a range of experiences around eroticism, sex, and sexuality.

Multiple experiences: Eroticism, sex, and sexuality

"If somebody asked me my sexuality, I would say 'straight'; but now that I think about it, that would probably give people completely the wrong idea about the kinds of sex I have. Mostly, sex for me involves mutual masturbation with my partner, and I also really enjoy when she penetrates my arse."

"When I came across the term 'ecosexual,' something fell into place for me. I've always felt most alive in nature, on my own or with other people who feel similarly. I could sit in a woodland for hours. That, for me, is way more erotic than bumping my body against another person's! I have had orgasms out under the stars, but it's not necessarily about that: just feeling my body against the earth or under the sky, is amazing."

"I love celebrating special occasions with people close to me. I want to make sure they feel loved and celebrated if it's their birthday, or held and supported if they're going through a tough time, such as losing a loved one. Some people think it's strange that I show up for my friends in this way as they think that is 'partner behavior,' but this is how I show my love to those I feel closest to."

"I have a high libido, especially since transitioning and feeling more at home in my body. I love being in sexual spaces, such as sex parties, locking eyes with someone and negotiating touch in that moment. It's easy for me to feel attracted to someone if they're also present and available like that."

"I've never really understood what the fuss was about when it comes to sex. I haven't felt any desire to try it, although I did as a teenager because I thought I had to. Now I'm much more comfortable in my identity and I'm able to communicate to people that I'm ace and romantic. I'm up for relationships, but I don't really want to have sex."

In the next section we'll explore the biological, psychological, and social aspects of sexuality in more depth in order to give a more comprehensive sense of sexuality as a biopsychosocial phenomenon.

1.3 SEXUALITY IS BIOPSYCHOSOCIAL

A lot of media reporting—and scientific research—about sexuality is concerned with the question of whether it's biologically determined or not. Are we really "born this way," as Lady Gaga suggests? People who go to see a sex therapist often have similar concerns. There's a sense that, if their sexuality is in their nature, then it's somehow not "their fault," or is more real and legitimate.

We'll dig into the foundational elements of your own sexuality more in Chapter 3, but for now let's say something about this focus on finding biological causes, and offer an alternative perspective.

First of all, it's worth recognizing that very few of the studies or articles about the causes of sexuality focus on heterosexuality. Nobody asks whether people are "born straight," whether they might have chosen their heterosexuality, or whether they could—or should—have been otherwise. The concern is almost always with attempting to explain why some people are gay, bi, or otherwise outside heterosexuality. This is a heteronormative approach: a long word which means the assumption that it's normal to be heterosexual, and that anything else requires an explanation, and maybe even an attempt to change it.

Actually, when you look at studies of people's attraction, at least as many young people report that they're attracted to more than one gender, or to the same gender, as those who report they are "exclusively heterosexual." And some are also ace, as we've already mentioned. So heterosexuality is not really the norm when it comes to sexuality. There's no good reason that sexualities other than heterosexuality should require more explanation than heterosexuality does.

Some people argue that it would be useful to find a "gay gene," or to find evidence that bi people have a unique sexual arousal pattern, or to find that part of the brain is different for ace people, for example, because it would help legitimize these sexualities. This would prove that they are real, and that they should be given the same rights as everyone else.

However, researchers like Peter Hegarty and Felicia Pratto have demonstrated that believing in biological explanations of sexuality doesn't actually make people any less homophobic, biphobic, acephobic, and so on. Indeed, in the past, eugenics approaches have aimed to eradicate certain sexualities on the assumption that they were biologically caused.

Also, we need to question the underlying assumption that something being biological makes it somehow more real, or more valid, than something that we've learned through our lives, or something we've chosen to some extent. Our language is something that we've learned through our lives rather than something we're born with, and our political views are generally something we've chosen, albeit it with some external influences. We wouldn't say that either of those things about us aren't real because they are down to nurture or choice, or that it would be easy to change the language we speak or our political views.

It really shouldn't matter *why* our sexuality is the way it is. So long as we only act on it in ways which are consensual and ethical, it's just fine. Certainly, nobody should be trying to change our sexuality—as some conversion therapies try to do—regardless of how it was formed.

The final—vital—point here is that all of these arguments about nature versus nurture versus choice assume that it's easy to tease these things apart. Actually it isn't, because human sexuality, like most aspects of being human, is biopsychosocial.

The big word: "biopsychosocial"

Biopsychosocial means that the biological, psychological, and social influences on our lived experience are inseparable. Hence combining them into such a long word. We're not even biological-and-psychological-and-social beings; we're biopsychosocial beings.

Everything we experience is embodied: involving our bodies and brains. It is psychological: filtered through our unique experiences and patterns of how we make meaning of things. And it is social: embedded in the particular cultural context that we occupy. And all of those aspects (bio, psycho, and social) influence each other in all directions, in a complex set of feedback loops.

We could imagine that it might look something like Figure 1.1, except in practice it would probably never be possible to separate out the bio, psycho, and social bits this clearly in order to know all of the ways in which they impact each other.

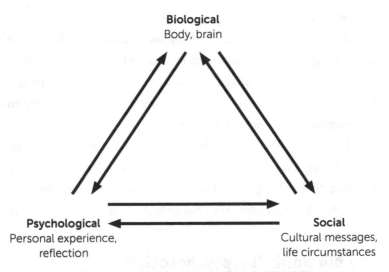

FIGURE 1.1: BIOPSYCHOSOCIAL MODEL OF SEXUALITY

Let's take a simple example before we move on to sexuality: making a cup of coffee. In order to learn how to make a cup of coffee, you have to live in a place where drinking coffee is a thing at all and where it's affordable (social). Then you have to be taught the different elements: how to grind the coffee, warm the cup, use the filter or stovetop, and so on (psychological). If you do this a few times, your neural connections will wire up in such a way that your body will remember what it needs to do and it will become your morning habit (biological).

That is how the social impacts the psychological, which impacts the biological, but it also works in the reverse order. In order to want to develop a coffee-drinking habit, you have to like the taste of coffee (biological), which will motivate you to learn how to make a good cup (psychological), which will impact how you experience the (social) world: your morning ritual, your time with friends, the way you break up your working day, and so on.

So what about sexuality? Working round the diagram from social to psychological to biological, let's think about sexual attractiveness. The world around us has very specific ideas about what makes a person attractive to others. This social world impacts our psychology, or lived experience. If we're seen as attractive in the particular culture we occupy, we'll have more potential partners and generally be treated far better than if we're not, perhaps escaping painful experiences of bullying, rejection, and discrimination. This will then impact our biology—or body and brain—because we're likely to develop more comfort in our body, and a more relaxed relationship to sex, than someone who is always painfully aware that they don't meet these arbitrary, and deeply problematic, standards of physical attractiveness. Clearly the bio, psycho, and social are intertwined when it comes to attraction.

Working round the diagram above, from biological to psychological to social, let's think about openness to experience. One way in which our genetics interacts with our environment is in how open we are. If our birthing parent is in a safe environment, and there is little history of intergenerational trauma in our family, gene regulation may mean that we are, from early childhood, more up for embracing new experiences, less fearful, and perhaps also more confident in expressing our needs and boundaries (bio). This is likely to impact our early sexual experiences in terms of both how free and experimental, and how safe and secure, these are (psycho). If we experience a more diverse range of sexual practices, we may become more open about sexuality in general, which has the potential—if we get together in solidarity with others—to change societal norms and values over time (social). Think about the impact of the gay rights movement or the #MeToo movement for example.

Biopsychosocial understandings also open up the potential for sexual fluidity—something that we'll come back to many times over the book. If our bodies and brains change over time, if we go through different positive and negative sexual experiences over the course of our lives, and if societal messages about sex keep changing—as they do—it's highly unlikely that our experiences of our sexuality, and how we express it, will remain static.

Reflection point: Your biopsychosocial sexuality

Pick one aspect of sexuality, perhaps something more personally relevant to you, and go around the diagram considering how each of these aspects might be involved—and relate to each other. Remember that it's something we can probably never really tease apart, but it's useful to remind ourselves that bio, psycho, and social are always involved, and that they interact in myriad complex ways.

Remember that just because an aspect of sexuality has psychological and/or social elements to it, that doesn't make it any less real, valid, or fixed over time than something that is purely biological, if such a thing is even possible.

ACTIVITY: BEING SEXUAL IN CULTURE

Throughout the rest of this book we'll emphasize the ways in which the culture in which we live and grow up has a massive impact on how we experience our sexuality both psychologically and physically. For example, solo sex has been seen, at different times in history, as an important outlet for our energies, as the cause of disease and death, as a morally suspect activity, and as only a kind of practice for the "real thing."

Imagine how you would relate to your own self-pleasure practices—if you have any—if each of these ideas was the prevailing view. Would you even engage in solo sex at all? If so, how would it differ in terms of what you did, how often, when and where, and how you felt about it before, during, and after?

Similar thought experiments are useful, for example, with having sex with somebody of the same gender in times and places where this was seen as a sin, a punishable crime, a medical disorder, something to "tolerate" but "don't ask, don't tell" about, or just one of many forms of embraced sexual diversity. What about the times and places where not being sexual was seen as sacred, as shirking a moral responsibility to procreate, as a psychological disorder to be treated, or as equally legitimate to being sexual?

In this section, we've referred to many different features

of a person's sexuality as being biopsychosocial: the kinds of people we're attracted to, the desires we have, the practices we engage with, and the ways we identify our sexuality. In the next section, we'll talk about these four different dimensions of sexuality and how they relate to each other.

1.4 MULTIPLE DIMENSIONS: ATTRACTIONS, DESIRES, PRACTICES, AND IDENTITIES

Given that we're still getting oriented to this vast landscape of sexuality, let's now define the multiple dimensions of sexuality: attractions, desires, practices, and identities. We'll talk in more depth about these in Chapters 2 and 5, as well as making reference to them throughout the book.

Sexual attractions

One of the ways we begin to connect with others sexually is recognizing who we are attracted to. What does sexual attraction mean though? First of all, people often conflate attraction with desire, using the two terms interchangeably. We'll define and discuss sexual desire next, but, for now, it's important to say that the two are different.

Sexual attraction is also not universal. This means that not everyone experiences it. Allosexual people are more likely to experience sexual attraction than asexual people, although people who are ace can also, at times, experience it.

Now that we've stated what sexual attraction isn't, let's talk about what it is. Attraction is generally about being drawn to someone. For example, we might be attracted to someone in a way that makes us feel we'd like to get to know them.

When the attraction is sexual, it means that we're attracted to someone in a way that makes us feel we'd like to know them sexually. This doesn't necessarily mean that we actually want to have sex with them, which is where the difference between attraction and desire comes in.

When we experience sexual attraction, we often notice how a person looks, smells, and moves and we feel interested in being in physical, sexual contact with them. In the case of demisexual people—that is, people who need emotional intimacy as a prelude to sexual intimacy—we might feel interested in getting closer to someone and getting to know them, and *then* we might experience sexual attraction, once we have established emotional closeness.

There are various theories about what drives sexual attraction, from whether our faces are symmetrical or not, if our pheromones smell "right," or what our visual diet is. Scholars are also beginning to understand that sexual attraction can happen quickly or slowly, or come and go over time, whereas in the past it was often believed that sexual attraction always happened quickly. Research on the impact of visual diet also shows us that sexual attraction is shaped by the media we consume. This impacts both whether we find ourselves and/ or others to be sexually attractive.

Despite being often thought of as based on physicality and chemistry, therefore, sexual attraction is not exempt from the influence of cultural, social, and historical contexts. Basically, if we experience sexual attraction, we're more likely to find people attractive whose bodies are frequently shown in the media, unless we're consuming non-mainstream media and making sure that our visual diet is different from the one we're fed by dominant discourse.

FIGURE 1.2: DIVERSE ATTRACTIONS

Sexual desires

If we summarize sexual attraction as being interested in someone sexually, then what is sexual desire? Sexual desire is the excitement some of us feel at the thought of being sexual by ourselves or with others. It is not the same as arousal, given that sexual desire often happens before arousal.

Sexual desire might be sparked by internal thoughts or fantasies, by reading something erotic, or by seeing someone we feel sexually attracted to. If sexual attraction is about interest, then desire is about wanting to act on that interest. As with all kinds of desires, just because we feel them, it doesn't mean we need to act on them, of course.

Our sexual desires are also shaped by our experiences

and can, sometimes, be confusing or upsetting, depending on whether they conform to cultural, social, and historical expectations or not. We'll talk more about this in Chapter 5.

Sexual desire is often talked about as "libido" by sex therapists and scholars—that is, the drive we may or may not feel to have sex with ourselves or others. When thought of as libido, sexual desire might be reduced to a physiological impulse. However, some have argued that desire can also be intentional and can be nurtured, if we so wish. For example, some people nurture solo sex practices as part of self-understanding or spiritual ritual, and some people in longer-term relationships intentionally find ways to connect erotically when the initial excitement has waned over time. Of course, it is also fine to only have solo sex if and when you feel the urge, or for long-term relationships to stop being sexual over time and for people to connect in other ways.

As with sexual attraction, sexual desire is not exempt from the influence of language, culture, society, and history. Who we feel "allowed" to desire and what kinds of sex we view as "legitimate" to have desire for vary across time and space. Some desires may have specific words to describe them in your language, and some may not, or the words might be scientific, or pathological, or only found in slang.

Once more, although sexual desire is most often studied as a physiological impulse, it's actually a much more complex and multifaceted phenomenon, which involves all aspects of our human experience, including interpersonal relationships, familial stories, cultural and social influences, as well as historical and political dimensions.

If you're still confused about the difference between attraction and desire, given that it is indeed subtle, here's an example that can help. Imagine that you pass by a bakery and smell all sorts of delicious baked goods. You might feel attracted by the smell but feel no desire to eat any of it (attraction), or you might feel attracted by the smell *and* have a desire to consume the breads and cakes producing such wonderful smells (attraction plus desire). Of course, you can then choose whether you want—or are even able—to consume such foods. The consumption would then be what you do, which leads us into the realm of sexual practice.

Sexual practices

Simply put, sexual practices are what we *do* sexually. This is, as you can imagine, a vast umbrella. Our sexual practices can encompass the way we masturbate, have sexual interactions online, have sex with others, and our sexual behaviors in community.

FIGURE 1.3: DIVERSE PRACTICES

As with attractions and desires, our sexual practices are influenced by the messages we received in our family of origin, including any religion or spiritual tradition we were brought up in, by the culture we grew up in and the one in which we live now, as well as by the social, historical, and political messages we receive across our lifespan.

For example, those of us who were brought up during the time in which same-gender sexual relationships were illegal might feel reluctant to engage in those practices or, when we do, we might feel secretive, ashamed, or fearful about them. Those of us who were brought up to see such relationships as part of human experience and presenting no risk are likely to feel very differently about engaging in the same sexual practices.

Our sexual practices are usually driven by our attractions and desires. We say "usually" because this is not always the case, of course. For example, some people might engage in sexual practices that they feel they "should want," rather than being consensual with themselves or, at times, even with others. Sexual practices are sometimes viewed as a "rite of passage" at a cultural level, as well as in some sub-communities such as fraternities, sororities, or gangs.

Some of our sexual practices might be part of our work, separate from our personal sexual attractions and desires. A sex worker, for example, might not be attracted to people of other genders but might engage in other-gender sex as part of their work.

It can be challenging, in the midst of all the cultural and social pressures, to even know which sexual practices we do or don't want to engage in. We'll return to this later in the book to support you in exploring what practices you may or may not be interested in. For now, let's move on to identities, given that our sexual practices are often also driven by how we identify ourselves, or how others identify us.

Sexual identities

So far, we've discussed who we might be attracted to, what kinds of desires we might experience, what we might do sexually, and how all of these categories are heavily influenced by language, culture, society, history, and politics. One of the categories we often hear discussed in dominant discourse— such as movies, media, and news—is sexual identities.

Sexual identities are also sometimes called "sexual orientations." The two terms do have differences though. Sexual orientation can literally be understood as who we are oriented towards—or are attracted to—sexually. However, some people, such as some ace and solosexual folks, are not necessarily oriented towards other people in their sexuality. For this reason, we use the term "sexual identity" to indicate all of the ways in which we can identify who we are sexually. Sexual identity is also more inclusive of sexualities which are more about engaging in specific practices, rather than the people we're attracted to.

Sexual identities don't need to be singular. For example, we might identify as straight and kinky—interested in practices that involve sensory experiences, power exchanges, and more.

In many ways, sexual identities are chosen and intentional. They are, after all, how we name ourselves and how we tell ourselves and the world who we are and what we want. However, as with all the other dimensions we've explored in this section, sexual identities are not exempt from the influence of all the messages we receive from family of origin, religion and spirituality, culture, and society. We've already touched on how language alone can shape our identities. If we don't have words for who we feel we are, it can be very challenging to name our sexual identities.

Sexual identities include words such as "straight," "bisexual," "lesbian," "kinky," "asexual," "allosexual," and so on. These are the words we choose to express who we believe we are when it comes to sexuality. Sometimes people impose their own sexual labels on us and it can be hard to reject them, especially if we have not shared some, or all, of our sexual identities with them. For example, people often assume everyone is straight unless they "come out" as having a sexual identity that differs from the dominant one. This is sometimes called compulsory heterosexuality.

We don't believe that you need to share all your sexual identities with the world, especially as we still live in a time where this is not safe for far too many people to do so. We also understand that an increasing number of people don't want to claim sexual identities for themselves, as they see that as linked to a sense of sexuality as fixed rather than more fluid and relational.

We do think that it can be powerful, for many people, to know what sexual identities are out there, as these labels often help us make sense of ourselves, our own attractions, desires, and practices. However, these dimensions do not necessarily align neatly. For example, over recent years there has been much media interest in men who identify as straight but engage in same-gender sexual practices. This is a phenomenon well known to HIV researchers, who coined the term "men who have sex with men" (MSM) to make sure they didn't miss those men who were not gay or bisexual but still engaged in same-gender sexual practices.

As we hope you can begin to understand, none of these dimensions of sexuality can be viewed outside the lenses of language, culture, society, history, and politics. Who we are sexually is shaped both internally, by our sense of who we are, what we want, and who we may be attracted to, and externally, by dominant discourses. In the next chapter, we'll turn to explore how the world views sexuality—and how that impacts us—in more depth. Before we do that, though, let's take a moment to identify where you're at, as well as to read some multiple experiences connected to attractions, desires, practices, and identities.

ACTIVITY: INITIAL THOUGHTS ON YOUR SEXUAL ATTRACTIONS, DESIRES, PRACTICES, AND IDENTITIES

Now that we've taken some time to define the different dimensions of sexuality, we invite you to jot down some words that describe what your attractions, desires, practices, and identities might be. Don't worry if you don't feel ready for this activity. This is just about your initial thoughts on all of this. You don't have to get it "right." We want to give you an opportunity to put your thoughts on paper now so that, if you want, you can revisit them after reading this book and doing more activities, and notice if they are still the same or if anything has changed.

Sexual attractions

. . . .

. . . .

. . . .

Sexual desires

. . . .

. . . .

. . . .

Sexual practices

. . . .

. . . .

. . . .

Sexual identities

. . . .

. . . .

. . . .

Multiple experiences: Attractions, desires, practices, identities

"My sexual identity, attractions, desires, and practices are pretty much in alignment I would say. I'm gay, I'm attracted to men, my fantasies are all about sex with men, and that's what I do in practice, meeting up with men I find hot on Grindr."

"For a long time, I felt I couldn't talk about my sexual desires. I felt so ashamed of wanting to be tied up, humiliated, and more. As a straight woman, I felt I was letting down feminists everywhere. It was only after finding a community that I started to feel a little more comfortable with myself. However, there are still desires that I would only share with people in kink communities and not elsewhere."

"My whole adult life I've been in the lesbian community. It's been politically hugely important to me, it's where my friends and sense of belonging is, and I don't plan on leaving it. However, when I think about sexual attraction, I'm not just attracted to women. I'm actually attracted to butchness, whether that's on a woman, a non-binary person, a trans guy, or a queer bear. And in terms of desires and practices, I'm a femme top, which means that I like to be the one in control."

"As a Black man, I struggled my whole life with my absence of sexual desire. It's just assumed that you'll be hypersexual and always up for it, but I was never interested. It was a big relief to find the ace community, and then my ace BIPOC [Black, Indigenous, and people of color] community within that, who really got it. They helped support me to bring my sexual practice in line with my actual desires, rather than feeling as if I had to be sexual or that there was something wrong with me."

"As a disabled person who is immersed in the disability justice community, I choose to only engage sexually with other disabled people. There are so many things I don't need to explain or justify when I have sex with other disabled people. We might not always immediately get each other, if our experiences have been different, but there's a way we can more easily connect and communicate about who we are and what we want that's just not there with abled people."

> **REMEMBER:** Sexuality is a vast and wonderful landscape. However, we're often not brought up to realize just how vast this landscape is, and how many possibilities there are. If someone's experiences are different from yours, and don't seem to make sense to you, take a moment to breathe. It's a lot to take all of this in. Don't worry if you feel a little overwhelmed; we'll return to many of the concepts introduced here throughout the book. This is just the beginning of our journey through this landscape and we have all the time we need to explore the map laid out here in more detail.

FURTHER RESOURCES

You can read more about all the words for sexuality in:

- Mardell, A. (2016). *The ABC's of LGBT+*. Miami, FL: Mango.

A great book on language, sex and sexuality is:

- Cameron, D. and Kulick, D. (2003). *Language and Sexuality*. Cambridge: Cambridge University Press.

There's more about the psychology (and biology and sociology) of sex and sexuality in Meg-John's books:

- Barker, M-J. (2018). *The Psychology of Sex*. London: Routledge.

- Barker, M-J. and Scheele, J. (2021). *Sexuality: A Graphic Guide*. London: Icon.

And also in:

- Denman, C. (2003). *Sexuality: A Biopsychosocial Approach*. Basingstoke: Palgrave Macmillan.

We'd like to invite you to take a moment, or two, or three even, and breathe... Then breathe again...

This can be a lot to take in, so let's take a little break before reading on.

As you breathe, take a moment to sense the support underneath you, whether that's the chair, couch, floor, or bed you're sitting or lying on.

Can you relax into that support, and into gravity, just a little bit more?

Can you let yourself feel held and supported in this moment?

Notice how this feels, with as much curiosity and non-judgment as you can manage right now.

If it feels good to relax into the support underneath you and gravity, let yourself savor that for as long as you can.

If not, it's okay to stop and do something else that helps you feel present and in the moment.

Then, when you're ready to pick this book up again, read on.

CHAPTER 2

HOW THE WORLD VIEWS SEXUALITY

Before we get into exploring your own relationship with sexuality, through the rest of the book, let's take a moment to think about how the wider world views sexuality. As we said in the last chapter, this is really important, because cultural norms and dominant discourses have a huge impact on how we experience our own sexuality. They influence how our attractions work, what we desire, and what sexual practices feel available to us, as well as whether we're free enough and safe enough to identify our sexuality in ways that are congruent and comfortable to us.

The first section of this chapter will look at sexuality across time and space. One reason that we know that there is no "right," "normal," or "proper" way of experiencing and expressing sexuality is that the way people do this has varied so much across history and between cultures. Things that are seen as highly erotic, or taboo, in one place and time are not in another.

After this, we'll focus on sexual attraction, sexual desire, and sexual practices. For each one, we'll consider how the dominant—white, western—culture has tended to understand these things: exploring how they are portrayed in the media, researched in science, and treated in medical and therapeutic contexts, for example. Then we'll look at some of the problems with the dominant understandings, and talk about alternative ways of understanding that come from research, and from sexual and asexual communities.

This will all be useful background information for considering, in the next couple of chapters, how your own sexual attractions, desires, and practices developed, and, in Chapter 5, how you might live them and identify them.

2.1 SEXUALITY ACROSS TIME AND SPACE

Before we consider sexuality from a historical and global perspective, let's take some time to address sexuality in dominant discourses in the societies where we, as authors, are currently located—that is, in the UK and the US.

Sexuality in dominant discourses

First let's define dominant discourse. We mentioned media, such as movies, TV shows, and popular songs in the previous chapter. These are all examples where we can find dominant discourses about sexuality. However, dominant discourses are much vaster than just media representation, as they shape our medical and legal systems, and more. They are about power and which narratives are given prominence and are perpetuated through almost every societal system you can think of.

For example, in *How to Understand Your Gender* we discussed how the gender binary—the division of people into "opposite" genders of man or woman—is a dominant discourse in both of our countries of residence. In their book *Gender Trauma*, Alex addresses in more depth how the binary is perpetuated systemically through all sorts of structures, such as education, politics, and architecture.

What are the dominant discourses when it comes to sexuality, and how are they perpetuated through a range of systems? One of the dominant discourses is directly connected to the pervasive belief in a gender binary. This means that often sexuality is viewed through the lens of gender and, as such, we frequently witness the media, as well as scholarly and clinical work, discussing "male and female sexualities," as if no other options are possible. Furthermore, male and female sexualities are viewed as inherently different because of some biological differences, with no room for biopsychosocial understandings.

For example, female sexuality is usually described as nurturing, with women being depicted as needing intimacy in order to feel sexual, and male sexuality is often described as assertive, with men feeling "always up for it" and being expected to be dominant in sexual contexts. This is a very binary view of sexuality and there is no room here for multiple femininities, masculinities, and gender expansiveness. Dominant discourses do not leave much room for multiplicity, and they tend to privilege and perpetuate one-dimensional notions of sexuality.

We'll cover many further examples of dominant discourses around sexuality throughout the book, and especially in this chapter.

Exploring the past

In *How to Understand Your Gender* we outlined how gender creativity, diversity, and expansiveness have always existed and how colonialism has often attempted to erase and control such a vast landscape. We can make a similar argument for sexuality. In fact, historically, many Indigenous populations and cultures have not conceived of gender and sexuality as two neatly separate categories in the way that Anglo-dominant discourses do.

Some of the examples given here are both past and present, given that Indigenous populations and cultures live on despite ongoing colonialism and Christianization. However, here we'll draw on more historical examples before considering some current ones.

The idea of monosexuality—that is, romantic or sexual attraction to just one gender, whether it's the same or another gender—is fairly modern. In recent times, we could consider pre-Nazi Berlin, in which sexual and gender fluidity were fairly visible and thriving. Going further back, in the Mediterranean areas, worshipping the Phrygian goddess Cybele was very popular and her followers were often fluid in both gender and sexuality.

Similarly, the worship of the Greek god Pan, mostly in rural areas initially, included ecstatic sexual rituals with people of all genders and seemed to be what we would now call fluid in terms of sexual practices. Pan's sexuality was different from what was considered acceptable in more urban-based dominant culture in ancient Greece, and seemed rather more aligned with a sexuality that predated the emergence of cities. Such division also points out how we can never fully separate sexuality from other social aspects, such as class or the urban and rural divide that emerged far earlier than the Industrial Revolution in many areas.

In China, sexuality was also linked to religious texts such as the *I Ching* (Book of Changes) in which sexual metaphors are used, and many other historical texts use examples of both same- and other-gender sex. Wherever we turn historically and globally, erotic and sexual practices seem broad, are rarely purely monosexual, and are often linked to religious and spiritual practices.

Even in more relatively modern times, such as the Renaissance, sex practices were not as puritanical as we might have been led to believe by mainstream history books. For example, across Europe, sex work was common and widespread, same-gender sex was practiced—at times openly so—and there were even what we would now call "sex clubs" in several places, such as Venice and England.

We can also find examples of polygyny—that is, one man having more than one wife—across history to the present day from Ancient Mesopotamia, to Egypt, to India, and even in the Bible. Polyandry—a woman having more than one husband—is less common but existed, and still does, throughout the Indian subcontinent, parts of Africa, China, and the Americas. And, as already mentioned, understandings of gender in some places mean that these gendered understandings of husband and wife don't always apply, and the concept of marriage has very different meanings in different places, not always connected to sex.

Exploring the present

Historical diversity demonstrates that there's no one right way of understanding or practicing sexuality. Now let's take a few moments to look at sexual expansiveness in the present and how, in many places, the identities and practices from the past have survived, albeit taking new shapes and forms.

Let's start from an example close to home for one of us—that is, the femminielli in Italy. "Femminielli" is a term mostly used in and around Naples to describe people assigned male at birth, who we might label as gay in an Anglo-dominant context. However, the femminielli are not just gay; they often dress in feminine clothing or use feminine accessories and defy the Anglo binary division of gay men and trans women. Interestingly, whereas in Naples the majority of the population might have negative attitudes towards a modern and Anglo-influenced idea of "gay and trans rights," the femminielli are considered lucky and have religious and popular rituals they partake in, including the Tammurriata and the Candelora in Avellino at the Madonna di Montevergine sanctuary. They are often asked to hold newborn babies and are respected as part of traditional cultural and religious practices. Femminielli are seen as expansive not just in relation to gender but also in sexuality.

Returning to non-monogamous relationships, globally today these are highly prevalent, if we combine Anglo-based relational configurations—such as open relationships, polyamory, and relationship—with those such as polygyny, polyandry, and walking marriages. The latter is a practice among the Mosuo people in China, where women can let a man know that they are open to him visiting at night. Any children born are taken care of on a familial level, rather than through a nuclear family unit. This means that in Mosuo culture there is no concept of husbands or wives. Intergenerational living is common, as it is in many parts of the world, and childrearing is shared among the family members of the birthing parent.

This point about the historical and cultural diversity of sexuality is especially important as same-gender sexual practices, kink, sexually explicit materials such as erotica and porn, and group sexual practices are often viewed as a by-product of Anglo-dominant cultures and even of the global connections enabled by the internet. We'd like to make clear that this is simply not true.

Humans have always sought out erotic connection with themselves, the land, and one another through a vast range of sexual practices. We have always had a broad range of sexual attractions and desires, which we have at times even formalized through religion and spiritual traditions. No matter where we come from, we can find examples of just how vast the landscape of human sexuality is and how pleasure—including sexual pleasure—is integral to our histories.

We could keep going with more examples, but there is so much more to cover in this chapter! Meg-John's *Sexuality: A Graphic Guide* includes more examples of how vast the landscape of sexuality is historically and cross-culturally, as do some of the books mentioned in the further resources at the end of this chapter.

Reflection point: Sexuality where you live

Take a moment now to reflect on what the dominant culture looks like where you currently live, when it comes to sexuality. Is it similar or different from what we've described? In what ways?

What have you learned in history about sexuality in your region of the world?

What are the current messages about sexuality in dominant discourse where you are?

If where you currently live is different from where you were born or brought up, you might want to consider those questions for all the different places you are connected to.

Decolonizing sexuality

Before we move on, we want to invite you to consider how your view of sexuality might have been impacted by colonialism. We want to acknowledge that the word "decolonizing" is being thrown about a lot, including by non-Indigenous people, so why title this sub-section "Decolonizing sexuality"?

First and foremost, we want to highlight the work of Indigenous activists and scholars. In our part of the world this includes Dr. Michael Yellow Bird, a Professor of Sociology and the Director of Tribal and Indigenous Peoples Studies at North Dakota State University, and enrolled member of the Mandan, Hidatsa, and Arikara tribes from North Dakota

(US), and Dr. Kim TallBear, an Associate Professor in the Faculty of Native Studies at the University of Alberta, and enrolled member of the Sisseton-Wahpeton Oyate in South Dakota (US).

Michael Yellow Bird uses the word "neurodecolonization" to capture how mind and brain functions are shaped by the stresses of colonialism and compromise the well-being of Indigenous people, which would include the imposition of coloniser understandings of sexuality. Kim TallBear applies Scott Morgensen's term "settler sexuality" to cover the ways in which the US and Canadian national states promoted certain sexual norms which were also bound up with ideals of marriage and private property as part of the project of taking native land and dividing it up into individual allotments. We'll come back to the shaping of minds and bodies in Chapter 5, and to Kim's work in Chapter 7.

If we truly understand that sexuality has been deeply impacted by colonial practices, then we can also ask ourselves, what does it mean to challenge colonial beliefs and practices when it comes to sexuality? What would it look like to question what we might have been brought up to believe about sexuality, including sexual identities, attractions, desires, and practices?

What are the history, the language, the religious and spiritual practices, the beliefs and traditions that have been impacted by colonialism and/or Christianization in your region of the world? What has been bypassed and hidden in major religious and spiritual traditions when it comes to sexuality, in order to establish different cultural and social practices?

We're not qualified to lead this work, but we do want

to make sure we signpost it so that you can look for more resources led by Indigenous people in your region of the world, and reconnect to traditional practices and knowledge that might have continued to exist where you live.

In the next sections, we continue to address what dominant discourses tell us about sexuality, focusing in on some of the aspects that we introduced in the previous chapter: attractions, desires, and practices.

2.2 SEXUAL ATTRACTION: FROM BINARIES TO MULTIPLE DIMENSIONS

So how does wider culture view sexual attraction? Generally speaking, the binary understanding of both gender and sexuality is still prevalent. This is the idea that people are either men or women in terms of their gender, and that people are either attracted to people of the "same gender" or the "opposite gender," which makes them either gay or straight in terms of their sexuality.

The heterosexual matrix and the sexual attraction binary

This approach—sometimes called the "heterosexual matrix"— is summarized in the diagram below.

		Attracted to	
		Man	Woman
Person is	Man	Gay	Straight
	Woman	Straight	Gay

Under this matrix there's a sense that our gender and sexuality are strongly linked: our sexual relationships are one of the main places in which we demonstrate our masculinity or femininity. There's also a sense that—in both gender and sexuality—there is a hierarchy, with men being seen as more "normal" and "superior" to women, and straight people being seen as more "normal" and "superior" to gay people. Even if we don't adhere to this matrix personally, it is one that has been in place for a long time, impacting laws, medical understandings, media depictions, and more. So it continues to have a strong impression on all of us, even if we resist it.

As you learned in the previous section, this matrix is not how people have understood sexuality in the past, or how they understand it everywhere around the world today. It's actually quite a recent western way of understanding sexuality, although sadly it is one that has been imposed across the world.

The idea that you could divide people into specific types of individual on the basis of their sexuality—homosexual and heterosexual—was actually invented in the late 19th and early 20th century. At that time, scientists were very engaged with trying to figure out what was "normal" humanity, and to categorize forms of "deviance" from this norm. This was very bound up with the projects of capitalism and colonialism, as the idea that the working classes were inferior to the middle classes, that "other" races and cultures were inferior to white western ones, and that women were inferior to men was used to justify unfair wages and division of labor, colonization, exploitation, and lack of civil rights.

Before this time, different kinds of sexual practice were categorized as morally inferior or superior, with "sodomy" having been a catch-all category for non-procreative forms of sex. But the kinds of sex you had weren't seen as making you a certain kind of person. After this time, having same-gender attraction was seen as making you a "homosexual," and it meant that you might be arrested and punished, and medically treated.

The famous inventor of psychotherapy, Sigmund Freud, actually did not believe in trying to "cure" homosexuality, as many of his followers did. However, his work did a lot to cement the heterosexual matrix in the public consciousness. His theories of the Oedipus complex suggested that children were born able to be attracted to any gender, but that they needed to deal with their attraction for their "opposite-gender" parent, and align with their "same-gender" parent, in order to reach a mature, binary gender and sexuality.

Freud and the early sexologists left us with a legacy of seeing gay men and women as an inferior kind of man and woman, which feeds into stereotypes that linger today of gay men as feminine, and lesbians as masculine. Of course, there are some gay men who celebrate femininity, campness, or drag, and some lesbians who embrace butchness in many forms. But there are men and women of all sexualities—not to mention non-binary people—who do the same. Also, there are many gay men who embody more conventional masculinity and lesbians who embody more conventional femininity.

What about the bis?

One of the major problems which you've probably already spotted with the heterosexual matrix is that there's no space for anybody who falls beyond the binary—that is, for bi people, who are attracted to more than one gender, and non-binary people, who are not men or women. We care so much about this—as bi non-binary people ourselves—that we wrote a whole book about what everyone might lean from binary-busters: *Life Isn't Binary*.

Focusing on sexuality, the sexual attraction binary leads to a problem which has been called "bi invisibility" or "bi erasure." The heterosexual matrix means that people have been assumed to be straight or gay, and anybody who is bi has been denied legitimacy. We see this in TV shows and movies where, up until recently, anybody who experienced attraction to more than one gender was depicted as moving from straight to gay, or vice versa. We see it in the re-closeting of bi people: a common experience where bi people who have come out to friends and family are still assumed to be gay or straight on the basis of their current partner. We see it in scientific research which has attempted to claim that bi people are really "straight, gay, or lying," and in stereotypes of bisexuality as "just a phase" or "not real," and bi people as "confused," "greedy," "promiscuous," "duplicitous," and needing to "pick a side."

There is now a wealth of research on bi people which demonstrates that they quite clearly *do* exist, and that their sexuality is just as legitimate as anybody else's. Bi people are no more likely to be promiscuous, confused, or "going through a phase" than anybody else, and there is also nothing wrong with any of those things. In fact, given the complexity and fluidity of sexuality, it's likely we'll all have some confusion around it, and go through a series of phases with it—we know that we do!

Binary or spectrum?

So we can replace the binary with three sexual attractions then—gay, straight, and bi—right? Well, as with everything we'll cover in this book, it's a bit more complex than that.

First, not all people whose sexual attraction falls outside the straight/gay binary identify as bi. Although some bi people would say they are "attracted to more than one gender" and some would say they are "attracted to people regardless of gender," in recent years many people have started to use the words "pan," or "pansexual" for the latter experience. Also, many folks use "queer" as a label for non-binary attraction. Some have delineated "bisexual" and "pansexual" from "biromantic" and "panromantic" in order to distinguish sexual and romantic attractions more clearly. Some academics have begun to use "plurisexual" as an umbrella term for all of these non-binary attractions.

Second, many researchers over time have suggested that, instead of having three categories of sexual attraction, it might be smarter to view attraction on a spectrum. This was the basis of the famous "Kinsey scale" by awesome bi researcher Alfred Kinsey in the 1940s. He measured sexual attraction on a seven-point scale from "exclusively heterosexual" (0) to "exclusively homosexual" (6), with an X for ace folk. Really ahead of his time!

Sadly, many researchers following Kinsey went back to the heterosexual matrix, and sexual attraction was often recorded as only "gay" or "straight," because people assumed that's all there really was. This meant that plurisexual experiences got erased. However, there's been a recent return to measuring sexual attraction on a spectrum in some studies. For example, the surveying company YouGov found that 88.7 percent of adults *identified* as heterosexual, 5.5 percent as gay, and 2.1 percent as bisexual. However, when asked to place themselves on the Kinsey scale, 72 percent of all adults—and 46 percent of young adults—put themselves at the "exclusively heterosexual" end, and 4 percent of all adults—and 6 percent of young adults—put themselves at the "exclusively homosexual end." This means that around a quarter of all adults, and a half of young adults, view themselves as somewhere between the extremes.

One spectrum or many?

Despite its plus points, the Kinsey scale is still a pretty imperfect measure of sexual attraction. You might have already noticed a few problems with it. One is that it assumes that the more you are attracted to the "opposite gender," the less you are attracted to the "same gender," and vice versa. It would be a bit like having a spectrum that went from "exclusively liking coffee" to "exclusively liking tea," leaving no room for those who love both coffee and tea, no room for those who dislike both, and none for those who prefer a cup of hot chocolate (hot chocolate in this case being non-binary people, to stretch the analogy slightly!). The other problem with the spectrum is that it assumes there are only two genders and, as you'll know if you've read our other book in this series, this is very much not the case.

Also, tastes may change over time. People might change whether they like coffee, tea, or hot chocolate best over their lifetime (okay, enough with the hot drinks!). Some researchers, like another awesome bi scholar, Fritz Klein, tried to build on Kinsey's spectrum to capture change over time, and to enable people to map different aspects of their attractions on multiple spectrums.

On his Klein grid, Fritz asked people to rate themselves on different features of attraction such as who they were attracted to, who they fantasized about, who they formed strong emotional bonds with, who they felt politically affiliated to, and more. He also asked people to rate themselves (from exclusively straight to exclusively gay) on all of these spectrums for ten years ago, five years ago, the present, and where they imagined they'd be in the future. As with Kinsey, though, there's no space for being attracted to people outside the man/woman binary on these measures.

More recently, researchers like Lisa Diamond have found that, indeed, many people's sexual attractions—in terms of the gender they are attracted to—change over time, based on things like the gender of their current partner, and the communities they're embedded in.

However, all of this still assumes that the most important aspect of sexual attraction is the gender of the people we're attracted to. Agh! There is so much more to sexual attraction than this. Diamond's research certainly found that people's attractions were often much more about the specific person they found attractive, or were in a relationship with.

Reflection point: Attraction beyond gender

Think about somebody who you are attracted to—sexually if you experience sexual attraction, or romantically, emotionally, or otherwise. This may be a partner or celebrity for example. Consider all the things about them that you find attractive. How many of these things are closely tied to gender?

Spectrums or dimensions?

Queer theorist Eve Kosofsky Sedgwick has a great quote criticizing this narrow focus on gender. She says:

> It is a rather amazing fact that, of the very many dimensions along which the genital activity of one person can be differentiated from that of another (dimensions that include preferences for certain acts, certain zones or sensations, certain physical types, a certain frequency, certain symbolic investments, certain relations of age or power, a certain species, a certain number of participants, and so on) precisely one, the gender of the object choice, emerged from the turn of the century, and has remained, as the dimension denoted by the now ubiquitous category of "sexual orientation". (p.8)

One alternative approach that we'll come back to a few times over this book—because we like it so much—is the "sexual configurations theory" of feminist scientist Dr. Sari Van Anders. She points out that, even with gender of attraction, we need to tease it out on more than one dimension. For example, we might be attracted to men, women, or non-binary people, or some combination of the three, but when it comes to how people express their gender we might be attracted to masculinity, femininity, or androgyny, or some combination of those three. You may remember in the last chapter, for example, the multiple experience involving someone who was attracted to masculinity, whatever the gender of the person.

Like Klein, Van Anders highlights that we can have different attractions—or the same—when it comes to who we fantasize about, read about, or watch during solo sex, and who we want to engage with in partnered sex, if anyone. We can also have different attractions—or the same—in terms of sexual attraction and romantic, or nurturing, attraction.

Van Anders particularly considers one further form of sexual attraction, along with gender, although she opens up the space for many more, and that is number of partners. People can be attracted to being alone, being with one other person, being with two people, up to being in a massive group. And that, like gender of attraction, may vary between solo sex (e.g. what they fantasize about) and partnered sex (what they enjoy with other people), and between sexual and nurturing kinds of attraction. For example, you might like watching orgies when you masturbate but prefer sex with just one other person. You might live in a triad with two other romantic partners, but only have sex one-on-one.

We'll get more into all of the different dimensions that sexuality can operate on in the next section, because many of them are more about desires than they are about the kinds of people we're attracted to, or not. Before we do that, have a go at the following activity to start to explore the multiple dimensions of attraction.

ACTIVITY: DIMENSIONS OF ATTRACTION

Taking sexual attraction—if you experience this—or another form of attraction if you don't, think about what you find attractive in other people, if anything, under the following dimensions. Feel free to add further dimensions, change these if they don't work for you, or just notice if this activity doesn't apply to your experience at all. That's all fine.

Personality/character. . . . .

Age . . . .

Gender . . . .

Sexuality. . . . .

Other intersections (e.g. race, disability, class). . . . .

Background . . . .

Physical appearance. . . . .

Number of people . . . .

Let's take another moment to breathe...

That was a lot of history and science and we have
some more to go before the end of this chapter.

So let's take a little break.

First of all, notice how you're feeling right now.

If you want to, look around and
name, preferably out loud:

Five colors

Four shapes

Three textures

Two things you can hear

One thing you can taste or smell.

You can adapt this exercise to whichever senses are available to you.

The goal is to orient yourself to the environment around you.

Now, notice how you feel again.

Do you feel the same as or different from how you felt before you did the exercise?

There is no right or wrong, just notice what helps you become more present.

When you're ready, feel free to read on.

2.3 SEXUAL DESIRES: FROM VANILLA TO ALL OF THE FLAVORS

As we said in the last chapter, sexual desire is a lot broader than sexual attraction. It *can* encompass what we find sexually attractive in others, but it also includes all of the things that excite us erotically. This might include, for example, certain roles, sensations, experiences, dynamics, scenarios, body parts and forms of bodily contact, emotional states, and more. We may or may not act on these desires in terms of having fantasies about them, engaging in sexual media or porn related to them, or having sex based on them alone or with others.

The next section, on sexual practices, will consider the desires that people *do* act on. In this section, we'll think more about the range of sexual desires that people can have—and not have—whether acted on or remaining in the realm of inner experience.

It's important to consider both desires and practices because, in order to have enjoyable sex, or to feel okay about *not* having sex, we need to be able to tune into what we do and don't desire, *and* to decide whether and how to act on this.

Being normal

Probably the biggest restriction we have in tuning into our erotic desires is the limited dominant cultural ideal of what it means to be sexually normal. We're bombarded with this over and over again in pop songs, Hollywood movies, magazines, dating apps, and more. It is also replicated in laws, medical texts, sex education, and so on.

One major component of normal desire is heterosexuality, as we explored in the previous section. It's seen as more normal to desire men if we're a woman, or women if we're a man, than it is to desire people of the same gender, or to desire non-binary people (or to be a non-binary person with desires!).

However, there's much more to what's considered normal desire than this.

> **Reflection point: Other elements of normal desire**
>
> What other elements of sexual desire can you think of that we see depicted most often, that sex education covers, or that our doctor or friend will likely assume we have unless we tell them otherwise? You might think of the last time you saw a sex scene on TV. What kind of people were involved? What did it seem was turning them on? What did they end up doing?

Back in the 1980s, in her "charmed circle" theory, sociologist Gayle Rubin suggested that there were multiple elements to what culture regards as normal sexual desires. Basically, the more that your desires fall inside the middle of these two circles, the more normal they are regarded as being. The more they fall into the outer circle, the more abnormal or suspect they are seen as.

The charmed circle:
Good, Normal, Natural,
Blessed Sexuality
Heterosexual
Married
Monogamous
Procreative
Non-commercial
In pairs
In a relationship
Same generation
In private
No pornography
Bodies only
Vanilla

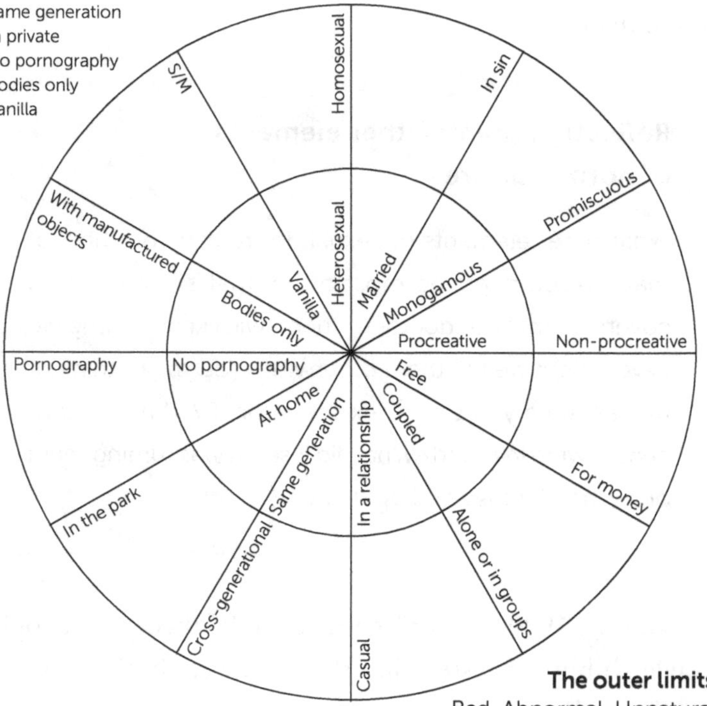

The outer limits:
Bad, Abnormal, Unnatural,
Damned Sexuality
Homosexual
Unmarried
Promiscuous
Commercial
Alone or in groups
Casual
Cross-generational
In public
Pornography
With manufactured objects
Sadomasochistic

FIGURE 2.1: THE CHARMED CIRCLE

Things may have shifted a little in the last few decades, but many of Rubin's suggestions still stand. Our desires are viewed as being more normal if they are for coupled sex with somebody of the "opposite gender," with whom we're in a romantic relationship and who is around the same age and level of cultural attractiveness as ourselves. They are viewed as being more normal if what we want to do with that person is to have foreplay followed by penis-in-vagina (PIV) penetration, in bed in our home.

Our desires are viewed as being less normal if they are for sex with ourselves or with more than one other person, if they are outside the context of a romantic relationship, and if any others involved are of the same gender as us, or are quite different to us in terms of age, "attractiveness," disability, race, or some other aspect. Desires are viewed as less normal if they are for other kinds of contact than kissing, oral sex, and PIV; if they involve toys, power-exchange, diverse sensations, or role play; if they involve being in public, watching or being watched; or if financial exchange is involved, as in sex work.

There is also what Charles Moser calls the "Goldilocks" amount of desire that's considered to be normal: not too much and not too little. It's seen as a problem if we want a lot of sex, or diverse forms of sex, but also a problem if we don't want sex at all, or aren't up for some experimentation.

As with the idea of normal sexual attraction, the idea of normal desires became enshrined in sexological texts in the late 19th and early 20th century. Some medics wrote huge tomes categorizing all the forms of "sexual perversion" they had come across in their work, detailing case studies of how they had tried to return these people to normal sexual desire. Some of these were only published in Latin because there was such fear about the impact they might have if everyday people got hold of them!

We see the legacy of these texts in the current psychiatric and medical manuals which set out "paraphilic disorders": the kinds of sexual desire that are regarded as abnormal or disordered. At the time of writing, the most recent version of the American Psychiatric Association's *Diagnostic and Statistical Manual of Mental Disorders*, (5th edition, *DSM-5*) categorized the paraphilic disorders as strong and consistent desire for sexual interactions that don't include, or lead to, intercourse with a "normal" consenting adult partner.

This means that only desire for genital sex counts as normal, and that it has to be with a partner who is also "normal" in terms of their observable physical characteristics. So desires for solitary forms of sex, mutual masturbation, or touching other body parts aren't regarded as normal here, and neither is sex with—presumably—intersex people, trans people, and possibly disabled people or people with larger or smaller body sizes than the norm (depending on the meaning of "phenotypically normal").

The *DSM* goes on to list paraphilic disorders which involve, for example, desire to watch others being sexual, or to be watched yourself; being humiliated, tied up, and/or receiving painful stimulation, or doing that to someone else; or being excited by objects or materials, by wearing clothes associated with the "opposite gender", or by rubbing up against people.

Problems with the normal/abnormal hierarchy

We only have to look back to the history of how "homosexuality" has been treated, in wider culture, and in medical manuals, to see one of the big problems here. Same-gender desire was included in the *DSM* until the 1970s and in the World Health Organization medical manual, the *International Statistical Classification of Diseases and Related Health Problems* (*ICD*), until the 1990s. Now, of course, it's not in there, and there are even psychiatric statements making it clear that no psychiatrist or therapist should ever try to "treat" same-gender desire, as they once did. If the way same-gender desire is viewed can change so radically in 50 years or so, then what about these other forms of "paraphilic" desire?

The *DSM* does now say that the "paraphilic" desires it lists only count as "disorders" if they are acted on non-consensually, or if they cause distress. However, the fact of having these listed—as opposed to other forms of sexual desire—contributes to a wider cultural view that they are somehow inferior or suspect, which has a negative impact on people who have these desires. Also, we might argue that culturally "normal" sexual desires can also be acted on non-consensually, and in fact they very often are, as highlighted by the #MeToo movement. And culturally "normal" sexual desires can cause huge distress: think about the pain of unrequited love, sexual obsession, or break-up, for example.

Actually, many of the things listed in the *DSM* are very common indeed. You only have to consider the huge popularity of the *Fifty Shades of Grey* novels and movies to realize that vast numbers of people have kinky desires. Studies back this up, suggesting that from a half to two-thirds of people have desires involving tying up, and spanking.

Watching and being watched are also highly common features of sexual desire. And we might ask where we would draw the line between the majority of people who find it satisfying to be regarded as desirable and attractive by others when walking into a room or down the street, and what might be defined as "exhibitionism." There are similar questions to be raised about the line between enjoying wearing sexy lingerie, for example, and having a "fetish."

Of course, the issue of consent is extremely important, and we should ensure that people do not have sex with anybody who can't consent, and that they don't engage in non-consensual behaviors, such as watching people or rubbing against people, without their knowledge. However, critics have questioned whether it's appropriate to categorize non-consensual forms of sex as "mental disorders," or whether this is more appropriately dealt with in the arena of justice, rather than psychiatry.

Our feeling is that any sense of a hierarchy between normal and abnormal desires is bad for everybody: both for those whose desires do roughly fit into what's viewed as culturally normal, and for those who do not. Those outside the cultural norm, we know, face stigma and abuse, and this often takes a toll on their mental health. Those inside the cultural norm are often extremely scared of making a mistake and slipping outside it, which also takes a toll on them. A recent UK National Survey of Sexual Attitudes and Lifestyles found that over half of the people asked said they thought they had some kind of sexual problem.

When you look at books of sexual fantasies, such as those collected by Nancy Friday over the years, you find that the majority of fantasies contain some aspect that would be seen as culturally "abnormal" or taboo. It's actually incredibly common to fantasize about sex with more than one person, public sex, sex involving power play or pain, even sex involving significant age differences and animals.

This is not to say, at all, that it's fine to act on any sexual desire we might have. Certainly that is not the case with non-consensual desires. We'll come back to ensuring consensual practices in Chapters 5 and 6. But policing people's desires, and making us feel bad for having these extremely common desires, is a real problem. At its worst, it contributes to significant levels of anxiety and shame, and makes it harder—rather than easier—for people to think clearly and ethically about which of their desires they do want to put into practice, and which they do not.

Diverse levels and types of desire

Instead of a binary normal/abnormal model of desire, we could turn to a model of diversity. Most aspects of human experience are, of course, on one or more spectrums rather than a binary. Think about physical attributes like height, weight, and body shape, or different kinds of intelligence, for example.

So instead of assuming that there is a normal level of sexual desire—for sex twice a week, for example—we could assume that there will be massive diversity between people on the level of desire that they have: from no desire to high levels of desire. For some, this may remain fixed, whereas for others it will change over their lifetime, depending on all kinds of factors.

Acknowledging this could save ace folks from a lot of the grief they currently experience from friends and others who try to pressure them into being sexual. It could also reduce the stigma of "sex addiction" for people with high levels of sexual desire.

This could also remove a lot of shame from people in long-term relationships. As therapist and writer Esther Perel puts it, it is incredibly hard—if not impossible—to retain "heat" and passion in a relationship, as well as the "warmth" and companionship which develops over time. However, we are sold a story that continuing to have "great sex" throughout a relationship is some kind of moral obligation, and that if we can't do that we have somehow failed.

Similarly, types of desire could be seen as diverse, rather than defining a norm and viewing everything else as abnormal. Some in the kink community use ice-cream flavors as a nice analogy for this. Vanilla ice-cream may be delicious to many of us, but that doesn't mean we can't also enjoy chocolate, raspberry ripple, and rocky road. It's also fine not to like ice-cream at all, or to prefer sorbet!

We'll come back to helping you explore the range of erotic, sexual, or sensual desires that you might have over the course of the next few chapters. For now, you might just want to think about which flavors of ice-cream or sorbet appeal to you. Remember that we're expanding out the concept of desire here to include all kinds of:

— roles you might take

— sensations you might like

— experiences you might enjoy

— dynamics between you and others

— scenarios you might play out

— body parts and forms of bodily contact you might like

— emotional states that might excite you, and more.

Here are a few examples of the diversity of desires that people experience to illustrate some of these.

Multiple experiences: Diversity of desires

"For me it's all about role. Whether in fantasy or reality, I only find it hot if I can get into this confident, cocky side of my character, pretty different to my everyday self. If I'm there, then I'm all about it; if not, forget it. Sometimes I take chems to get there, at parties and stuff. But with a few of my regular fuckbuddies they know what to do to bring that side of me out. It honestly doesn't matter what kind of sex we have, or even if we have sex at all, it's all about being that guy for a while."

"Sensation is the one that stands out for me. I'm ace and aro, so I don't do sexual or romantic relationships. But I do love certain sensations. I'm really into fabrics like wool and tweed: the way they feel against my skin. I make my own clothes using those. I also love a kind of cosy sensation: snuggling up under the duvet, cuddling my cat, going outside in a warm winter coat. That's a big thing for me."

"My partner and I found it really helpful to think about our different desires. For me sex is all about intimacy. I want to gaze into each other's eyes, take our time, build to this shared experience together, even saying each other's name or telling each other how much we love each other as we come. For her, we realized, sex is about going into this altered state. She wants to spin off into a black hole where she's at one with the universe or something. I don't quite understand it, but recognizing this difference has helped a lot to make sense of how we were missing each other in sex."

"I'm all about the feelings when it comes to desire. Most of my sex life is reading slash fic and fantasizing. I'm totally into the hurt/comfort genre. I love reading about the characters from my favorite TV shows being put in super emo situations, till they cry and release all that feeling, and then they get looked after and loved. It's the best."

"It might sound basic, but I'm into boobs. I can't get enough of them. When I look at porn—ethical of course—I'm searching for women with large breasts. Most of my partners have fit that description. I love nuzzling up to breasts, rubbing against them. That's my thing."

"The dynamic is what gets me off. I'm a submissive guy and I just want to be dominated: told what to do, made to follow the rules, maybe rewarded when I do it well. People think of BDSM as being all about pain, and for some people it is, but for me I'm just as happy serving my dom for hours as I am when they spank me, or have sex with me."

In the next section, we explore sexual practices: the kinds of things people do to act on their desires, or to conform to an ideal of normal sexuality.

2.4 SEXUAL PRACTICES: FROM PIV TO THE EROTIC

We've talked about attractions and desires, so let's turn to how the world views sexual practices, before getting more personal in the next chapter. Take a moment to think about what sexual practices you see represented in movies, popular songs, in the news and in sex education, if you received any, growing up.

Where we grew up, as well as where we live now, the main sexual practices in dominant discourses seem to be centered around PIV (penis-in-vagina) sex. Other practices, such as kissing, petting, fondling, and so on, all seem to be viewed as foreplay for the "real" thing, PIV.

However, dominant discourses are not just about the kind of sex we have, but also who we have it with, how often, why, and what it leads to. PIV sex is usually seen as most legitimate in those discourses when it is between a cisgender woman (someone who was assigned female at birth and identifies as such) and a cisgender man (someone who was assigned male at birth and identifies as such).

As we mentioned earlier, the motivations for PIV sex are regarded as different between men and women in dominant discourses. Women are viewed as having sex to seek and maintain intimacy, whereas men do so because of their higher sex drive. When this sexual script is challenged, there's usually some level of uproar and pushback. For example, shortly before we started writing this book, Cardi B and Megan Thee Stallion released a new music video, *WAP*, which is highly sexual in a way that flips the normative sexual script by including representation of women as active sexual beings, leading to a high volume of social media and media responses.

Of course, *WAP* is not just about women's sexuality but specifically Black women's sexuality. Dominant discourses about sexual practices intersect with those about how bodies are racialized, as well as gendered and sexualized. This means that sexual practices, in dominant discourses, are viewed differently for Black women than white women, and so on. Generally, Indigenous, Black and Brown feminine bodies are hypersexualized in the cultural contexts we both live in and, as such, are objectified in ways that are different from the way in which white feminine bodies are objectified. We'll explore more about how various intersections of identities shape our sexuality in the next chapter.

The main point we want to make here is that, as well as inferring what is considered normal and abnormal in relation to sexual desires, dominant discourses also dictate what is considered acceptable when it comes to sexual practices, and this is heavily dependent on how bodies are racialized, and categorized in relation to class, disability, religion, citizenship, and other aspects of our identities and experiences.

The medicalization of sexual practices

One way in which dominant discourses legitimize their sense of what is acceptable—or not—is to use systems that reproduce knowledge and regulate bodies. Medicine, sexology (the scientific study of human sexuality), and sex therapy are disciplines that people often turn to for better understanding of their own and other people's sexualities. However, as we saw with the example of "homosexuality" earlier, much of what these disciplines have had to say about sexuality over time has been shaped by dominant discourses, rather than being some kind of objective "fact" about human experience, despite being put across in this way.

In the second half of the 1900s, the branch of sexual medicine emerged, reinforcing the ideas that had emerged with Freud and his followers that there was a "proper" way to have sex, and that was PIV sex between a cisgender man and woman. Sexual medicine did not stop there. The ways in which sexual organs worked began to also be categorized as functional or dysfunctional, levels of sexual desire began to be quantified and measured, and some sexual practices were labeled as abnormal or dysfunctional.

Reflection point: How you view sexual practices

Take a moment to think about your view of sexual practices. Are there things you consider functional or dysfunctional? What kinds of sexual practices seem acceptable to you or not? Where did you learn which practices were acceptable or not? Are there sexual practices you would hesitate sharing with a doctor? If so, why? If not, why not? Which sexual practices would you seek advice from a medical professional for, if any?

What is considered functional for cisgender men, for example, is to have a penis that is capable of becoming erect on command and that is able to ejaculate. If this does not happen, someone might be labeled as having erectile dysfunction. Cisgender women are expected to have genitals that can accommodate PIV sex without pain, and to produce an appropriate amount of lubrication—unless going through menopause—to enable said penetration. If they do not, they might be diagnosed with a sexual pain disorder, such as vulvodynia, or if lubrication is not at an "appropriate" level, vaginal dryness.

Both cisgender men and women are expected to be able to orgasm and, if they do not, they might be labeled with an orgasmic disorder, such as anorgasmia. Sexual disorders are often neatly categorized as "male and female sexual disorders." Intersex, trans and/or non-binary people do not have specific categories as, in some ways, we are still viewed as inherently disordered, although this is very slowly changing.

Sexual medicine also distinguishes between masturbation and partnered sex. When taking a sexual history, for example, a provider might ask whether the inability to orgasm happens both when masturbating and having sex with a partner, or only in one situation or the other. The underlying expectation often is that our bodies should work at all times, in all situations and, if they do not, something has gone wrong, either physiologically or psychologically, or both.

Other information usually gathered when taking a sexual history is the gender(s) of the people we have sex with, the frequency at which we have sex, how often we masturbate, how long it takes us to orgasm by ourselves or with others, and whether we use sexually explicit materials or not, such as erotica or porn, and how often. Some in sexual medicine still regard certain frequencies or types of sex as signs of sex addiction, whereas others have moved to a model of diversity, focusing on whether it feels pleasurable and self-consensual to the person involved. There is more on this in Chapter 5.

Regardless of the frameworks used, sexual medicine has historically determined which sexual practices are healthy, and therefore functional, and which are not. This has led to the medicalization of practices that, previous to the establishment of this field, were not necessarily labeled as functional or dysfunctional and might have been negotiated with partners, religious or spiritual leaders, or through community support, such as advice from elders.

Please note that we're not saying that sexual medicine is always problematic—after all, we're both sex therapists! Rather, we need to be aware of how the ways in which we view and understand sexual practices have been heavily influenced by the emergence of this field over the past five decades. We also need to understand that this field is still relatively new and evolving, and that it has been historically dominated by cisgender white men, which has also shaped what has been studied, and how sexual practices and functioning have been categorized.

More than PIV: Broadening sexual practices

Some people in the field of sex therapy and sexual medicine have shifted their focus from the goal of sex to the process. Rather than aiming for PIV sex resulting in orgasm as the goal and golden standard of "functional sex," they have suggested that we should support people in understanding that sex is a very large umbrella, and that sexual intimacy can be nurtured through many practices other than PIV sex.

For example, Professor Peggy Kleinplatz, a Canadian clinical psychologist and sexologist and colleague of ours, pointed out that the field has historically been overly focused on what doesn't work in the form of "dysfunctions." She suggested instead asking what leads to pleasure. This is, after all, one of the main reasons why people might engage in sexual practices. Before reading on, you might like to make a note of how you'd answer the question she asked in her research: "What things do you think contribute to 'great sex'?"

Professor Kleinplatz and her colleagues found that the following components were mentioned by research participants in answer to this question:

— being present, focused and embodied

— connection, alignment, being in synch, a sense of merging with the other

— deep sexual and erotic intimacy

— extraordinary communication

— heightened empathy

— authenticity and transparency

— feeling uninhibited

— transcendence, bliss, peace

— transformation and healing

— exploration and relational risk-taking

— fun

— vulnerability and surrender.

Some participants did mention desire, chemistry, and

attraction, as well as intense sensations and orgasm, but those were considered minor components, unlike the others listed above, given that they were mentioned by fewer people and with less emphasis.

This research illustrates that the process of sex is, for most people, much more important than the goal. After all, unless we are trying to procreate, many of us have sex because we're seeking pleasure and/or connection. PIV sex is only one way towards this, and it only works for certain bodies and people. In fact, even people who could technically have PIV sex often prefer other forms of sexual practices, such as oral sex, anal sex, mutual masturbation, or touching body parts other than the genitals, because they are more pleasurable for them.

Opening up and exploring our erotic potential

If we shift our focus from goal to process, when it comes to sexual practices, we can also open up to the vast landscape of eroticism that is our capacity for sensual pleasure. When we stop seeking the "right way to have sex," which many of us are brought up to believe exists, what becomes possible?

We would say that the potential for what becomes possible is only limited by our imagination and the fact that we're embodied beings and, as such, limited by physicality in what our bodies can do! Our erotic potential is about exploring how our senses connect us to ourselves and the world around us.

For example, what kind of self-touch do you find pleasurable, not just when masturbating, but also when showering, or simply exploring your body? What kind of sounds are most pleasing and produce certain states emotionally? Which food experiences are the most pleasurable? What are the smells that bring you delight? What do you find enticing to look at? What can you imagine that provokes a sense of pleasurable well-being throughout your body? You can use any of the senses available to you to explore what brings your embodied being pleasure—including sexual and sensual pleasure—either by yourself or with others.

In fact, it is often when we take time to find what is pleasurable for us that we can then better connect and communicate with others, if indeed we choose to engage erotically with other people. We'll return to how to do these things in Chapters 5 and 6.

We don't need to engage with other people to explore our own erotic potential but we can do so, if we want to. Many people also find that connecting with nature is when they feel most in touch with their own erotic potential, as well as with a larger sense of the erotic as a life force that pulsates through everything, such as flowers, rivers, rocks, trees, and the air we exchange with the green bloods, that is plant life, around us in every moment.

ACTIVITY: WHAT MAKES US FEEL MOST ALIVE?

Make sure you reserve plenty of time for this activity. Take time to find a spot where you feel comfortable and undisturbed. Choose which sense you'd like to explore this time. Please note that you can do this exercise with any senses you want to, however many times you want to. You might choose smell, taste, hearing, sight, touch, or imagination. If you're so inclined, you might also include your spiritual senses, whatever these might be according to your belief and practice systems.

Once you have chosen which sense you want to explore

this time, find ways to connect with this sense to find out what helps you feel most alive when you focus on this channel. For example, if you chose to focus on taste, which flavors make you feel most alive? You might also want to expand this to which flavors you experience as most sensual or pleasurable. Please note that you might find multiple flavors and types of aliveness and sensual pleasure!

Take all the time you need to notice your body sensations when you find something that helps you feel most alive and brings you pleasure. As well as body sensations, notice what images, memories, and emotions come up. What does your body want to do when you feel alive? What becomes possible?

Take time to savor the experience fully. Whenever you're ready to be done, you might also want to record the experience by journaling, dictating a voice memo for yourself, or making art, such as painting, a collage, making music, and so on. Know that you can come back to this activity whenever you want to.

In this section, we've discussed how dominant discourses are rather limited when it comes to sexual practices. We've also considered how the emergence of sexual medicine has not only reinforced dominant discourses but also categorized sexual practices and what our bodies can or cannot do as functional and dysfunctional. Fortunately, all fields change over time and some researchers and practitioners have shifted their focus from PIV sex and orgasm as goals, to sexual practices as processes connected to pleasure. Finally, we've invited you to consider opening up to your erotic potential. Before we end this chapter and invite you to explore your sexuality background, we'd like to share a few points of view about sexual practices for different people.

Multiple experiences: Many paths to pleasure

"Growing up, I felt that sexual intercourse was this slightly frightening, slightly mysterious, thing looming over me. I was supposed to keep myself safe from all those boys who 'wanted only one thing' but I wasn't even clear what this thing was. When I finally had sex for the first time in my twenties, it was painful and disappointing but also a relief. I didn't know enough, which it's why it was painful and not pleasurable. But also, it was over. It wasn't a mystery anymore."

"Getting older has been such a gift for my sex life! Finally I could let go of all those expectations. I actually had sex with someone of the same gender for the first time and it was a revelation. The pressure was off and I could just focus on what felt good."

"When all the boys started whipping out their penises and comparing sizes or seeing who could pee further, I felt like an alien. I didn't want to do that. I didn't even want to touch it. When I had my first partner, she made me feel as if there was something wrong with me for not wanting to put my penis in her. The doctor agreed. Nobody ever asked me what I wanted to do sexually, or how I felt about my genitals."

"I feel most excited and alive when I swim. I don't care much for touching myself and I don't want to have sex with other people, but swimming in a lake, river, or better still the ocean, is when I feel I can let go. I feel one with the water, and the world disappears. It is bliss."

"Genital sex was always a bit 'meh' for me. It was brilliant to discover BDSM and to realize that it was okay to play with bondage, sensations, role play, and things like that instead. Genital sex is just one, pretty minor, kind of sex—there are so many other kinds out there."

REMEMBER: Sexuality has a rich history and it's a vast landscape of possibilities, especially when we unlock the even larger landscape of eroticism, of which sexuality is only a part. It can be a lot to consider that what you have learned about sexuality may or may not match up with what we've shared in this chapter. You might also feel a little overwhelmed by considering how dominant discourses have shaped the ways in which we experience certain attractions, desires, and practices as acceptable or not. Take as long as you need to digest this information. In the following chapters, we start to get a little more personal and invite you to explore your own background, as well as your current experiences, identities, and relationships.

FURTHER RESOURCES

You can read more about the history of sexuality in:

- McCann, C. (2018). *All You Need to Know... Sexuality*. London: Connell Publishing.
- Lister, K. (2019). *A Curious History of Sex*. London: Unbound.

You can read about Michael Yellow Bird's work here:

- www.indigenousmindfulness.com

And Kim TallBear's work here:

- https://kimtallbear.com
- www.criticalpolyamorist.com

You can read more of our views on non-binary sexualities in:

- Barker, M-J. and Iantaffi, A. (2019). *Life Isn't Binary*. London: Jessica Kingsley.

Find out more about Eve Kosofsky Sedgwick's work in:

- Sedgwick, E.K. (1991). *Epistemology of the Closet*. Berkeley, CA: University of California Press.

Gayle Rubin's paper, which the charmed circle comes from is:

- Rubin, G. (1984). "Thinking Sex: Notes for a Radical Theory of the Politics of Sexuality." In G. Rubin (2012). *Deviations: A Gayle Rubin Reader*. Durham, NC: Duke University Press.

If you're interested in reading the original article with the components of "great sex" that we mentioned in this chapter:

- Kleinplatz, P.J., Ménard, A.D., Paquet, M.P., Paradis, N., *et al.* (2009). "The components of optimal sexuality: A portrait of 'great sex'." *Canadian Journal of Human Sexuality*, *18*(1–2), 1–13.

If you're interested in increasing your sensory awareness, this can be a helpful book:

- Brooks, C.V. and Selver, C. (2007). *Reclaiming Vitality and Presence: Sensory Awareness as a Practice for Life*. Berkeley, CA: North Atlantic Books.

CHAPTER 3

YOUR SEXUALITY BACKGROUND

We mentioned earlier that we were going to get more personal in the following chapters, and here we are. It's time to consider how all the aspects of sexuality introduced in Chapter 1, and the historical, societal, and cultural dominant discourse discussed in Chapter 2, impacted your own sexuality growing up.

In this chapter, we invite you to explore your personal background in relationship to sexuality. This is something you may have already done, of course. If so, we encourage you to consider whether there's a new point of view from which to gaze at the landscape of your own sexuality history. Don't worry if this all seems too historical—we'll turn to your current sexuality in Chapter 4.

We're going to take a trip back in time, starting from your birth. What were the expectations that preceded your birth? How did all these dominant discourses show up in your own family when you came to be in the world? We'll then proceed to explore the intersections of class, culture, community, race, ethnicity, faith, generation, geographical location, language, citizenship, disability status, and so on, with your experiences of sexuality while growing up. After that, we invite you to reflect on how your sexuality was shaped by what you experienced, especially in your childhood and teenage years. Finally, we'll close the chapter by addressing issues of power, trauma, and abuse. Unfortunately, most of us do not live in healthy cultures when it comes to sexuality. This means that many of us, growing up, experience unhealthy power dynamics and, far too often, abuse and trauma around sexuality.

You may want to have some paper and pens in different colors, and your journal or notebook with you for this chapter, given that getting personal means plenty of activities! If activities are not your thing, or seem overwhelming, take a breath and give yourself permission to just read through the chapter. There is no right or wrong way to use this book. It is your book and, more importantly, your life we're inviting you to explore. You can do so at whatever pace feels most comfortable for you at this moment. Please remember that each activity is an invitation, and you can accept it, refuse it, come back to it, or modify it to fit your needs. We really want you to be as consensual as you can be with yourself throughout this book, and this includes the way in which you choose to engage in activities or not.

Content note: There are mentions of sexual violence, abuse, and assault in a couple of places in this chapter—in the intersectional experiences that we both share in section 3.2, and in the whole of section 3.4, which focuses on these themes. Please check in with yourself before reading on about whether you're in a good place to read about those topics. If not, you may want to leave them for now, or perhaps avoid reading the reflections on our drawings in 3.2, and the multiple experiences at the end of the chapter, which contain more descriptive material about sexual violence and its impact.

3.1 BORN THIS WAY? ON NATURE, NURTURE, AND BEYOND

Let's think about the body, situation, and world that you were born into. All of these things will have shaped the understandings of sexuality that were available to you, the desires and attractions you developed, the pressures that you felt under to express—or not to express—your sexuality in particular ways, and more.

Here we'll revisit the idea of sexuality as biopsychosocial from Chapter 1, as well as the wider cultural understandings that we covered in Chapter 2: which of those were present in the time and place you grew up, and were they accepted—or resisted—in your particular upbringing?

Your embodied sexuality

Remember the diagram below from Chapter 1? It helps us to remember that our sexuality, like most aspects of our experience, is always deeply social, it is always impacted by our unique life experiences and ways of making sense of the world, and it is always embodied. That's why we can never tease apart aspects of our sexuality that are down to "nature" or "nurture," however much some scientists and journalists may want us to!

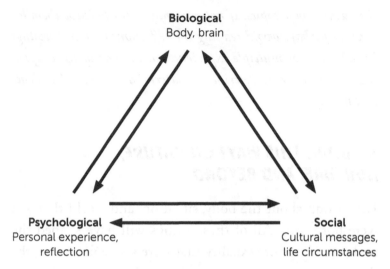

FIGURE 3.1: BIOPSYCHOSOCIAL MODEL OF SEXUALITY

What embodiment means is that our sexuality becomes engraved onto our bodies and brains as we learn about sex, form sexual memories, and experience pleasurable or tough things sexually. Our sexuality also plays out through our bodies and brains as we imagine erotic scenarios, become aroused or not, engage sexually with ourselves and others or not, or try to avoid certain sexual thoughts or experiences.

So the wider world, and our life experiences, impact our bodies and brains, and our bodies and brains impact our life experiences, and our wider world, when it comes to sexuality.

For example, if we're born into a time and place when being same-gender attracted is heavily policed, this may mean that safe same-gender experiences are very difficult to come by, and that we try to police our same-gender desires, become very tense in our bodies, and perhaps contract sexually trans-mitted infections (STIs) because it's hard to find safe enough ways to have sex (social-psycho-bio).

If, on the other hand, as we grow up, we find that we don't experience sexual attraction in the way some of our friends do, and we're living in a culture where asexuality is understood as part of the diversity of human sexuality, this might mean that we focus our life experience on things other than sexual relationships, and that we join ace communities and that becomes an important feature of our wider world (bio-psycho-social).

Reflection point: Your embodiment and sexuality

Think about the body that you were born into, and the ways it developed over your childhood and adolescence. How did this positively and/or negatively impact your experience of your sexuality? Go gently with this reflection because it can be painful and traumatic to revisit difficult experiences from childhood, and many of us—sadly—do struggle with our bodies growing up in a world which has such rigid and shaming ideals about how bodies should look and function.

You might want to consider the following features of your bodymind, and any more you can think of:

— your body shape and size

— how quickly or slowly you developed in relation to those around you

— whether you were disabled in any ways growing up

— neurodiversity (this includes experiences that may

be labeled as autism, attentiony deficit hyperactivity disorder (ADHD), dyslexia, and dyspraxia, for example)

— your mental health (for example, whether when growing up you experienced things that may be labeled as anxiety, depression, disordered eating, or addictions)

— whether you were gender expansive as a kid or not

— whether you got sick often, or not, as a kid

— what your genitals—and other parts of the body that are often connected with sexuality—were like, and how that impacted your relationship with them

— bodily experiences like menstruation, sweating, erections, wet dreams, hair growth/removal, and how you related to those.

Of course, all of these things are biopsychosocial rather than only a matter of bodies. That's why we used the term "bodymind" here (see further resources). For example, being neurodiverse in a culture where that is understood, and within a family that is open to multiple kinds of experience, is going to make navigating neurodiversity and sexuality very different from those experiences within a culture and family that have very rigid ideas about the necessity of being normal or successful in particular ways. If you live in a culture and community with very narrow beauty ideals rather than in one where beauty is understood and represented in more expansive ways, your body shape and size will likely have a negative impact on your sexual experience.

We'll come back to disability as an important aspect of our lives which *intersects* with sexuality in the next section.

Intergenerational understandings

In the last chapter, we covered many of the dominant ways in which the wider world views sexuality. These are often passed down to us *intergenerationally*. This means that our parents take on the sexual attitudes of their parents, and they of their parents, and so on. One of us—Alex—has written a whole book (*Gender Trauma*) on how dominant, binary, understandings of gender can be seen as a form of intergenerational trauma. We could say the same about restrictive ideas around sexuality.

Here are a few of the dominant ways of understanding sexuality that are, sadly, often passed on through families. You might want to consider whether these were present within your own family growing up, either explicitly or implicitly. How did this impact your relationship with sex and sexuality?

- *Compulsory sexuality:* This is the expectation that people will be sexual, rather than asexual. It can be communicated, for example, in teasing teens about when they are going to "lose their virginity," ideas about the "right" age to do so, and expectations that they will be interested in sex, dating, and so on. Compulsory sexuality is also present in the way asexual people have to "come out," while allosexual people do not.

— *Compulsory heterosexuality:* This is the expectation that people will be heterosexual. It can be communicated through asking whether a boy/girl has a girl/boyfriend yet, making gendered assumptions about which celebrities they would fancy, and assuming that their future lives will take a heteronormative course. Compulsory heterosexuality is also present in the way gay and bi people have to "come out," while straight people do not, and the sense that it is legitimate for families to have reactions like disappointment and anger if this happens.

— *The coital imperative:* This is the idea that sex equals penis-in-vagina (PIV) penetration. It can be communicated through "the talk" in families, if the focus of that is on avoiding pregnancy and STIs, rather than there being a sense of the diversity of sexual practices people might engage with, and how they can do so consensually and safely.

— *Mononormativity:* This is the sense that the only place for sex to happen is with the monogamous couple. It can be communicated through expectations that people will be looking for "The One," should only date one person at a time, should only have sex with people they're "serious" about, and so on.

— *Rape myths:* These are the prevalent ideas about what it means to have survived sexual assault, harassment, or oppression. They include denial (it didn't really count), minimization (it wasn't that bad), victim blame (it must somehow have been the fault of the survivor), and defensiveness (it was nothing to do with me, the survivor shouldn't have responded in the way they did). We'll come back to sexual assault and its impact in the last section of the chapter, but it's important to state here that these responses are forms of cultural gaslighting, which make it very hard for survivors to name their experiences—even to themselves—and to get the support that they need.

If it is safe enough for you to do so, you might find it helpful to chat with any family members of previous generations who are still around about the attitudes towards sex and sexuality that were prevalent when they were growing up, to get a sense of how these are passed down through the generations, sometimes staying the same, and sometimes shifting radically. For example, there were significant generational shifts around sex in the 1960s, when birth control became available and the free love movement took hold, and for millennials in the 2000s when life became lived far more online and there was an explosion of sexual communities available there.

Multiple levels of influence

Our own embodiment and the intergenerational patterns in our families are two levels of experience which shape our sexuality. Let's now widen out to explore all of the nested circles of influence that shaped your understanding and experience of sexuality growing up.

You can see the widest level of influence as the culture you grow up in, in your particular geographical location and generation. You may have quite a singular experience of dominant culture, or you might experience two or more very different dominant cultures; for example, if you emigrated or moved around during childhood, or if your family includes people of different culture, class, or faith backgrounds. Your parents may be very stuck in the culture of the generation they grew up in, or they may be moving forward with you into the current cultural moment. There may be tensions around sexuality between different cultures and generations which impact you profoundly.

The next level is the communities and institutions you're part of. This may include, for example, faith communities, schools you attend, the neighborhood you grow up in, and leisure communities you engage with. All of these have the capacity to accept the prevailing understandings around sexuality in the dominant culture and pass this on to you, or to resist those prevailing understandings and to pass on understandings which are either more or less restrictive. For example, attending Catholic school might mean sex education involving anti-abortion and anti-contraception messaging, within a dominant culture which encourages choice in these matters. Being part of a naturist community might mean growing up with a very different relationship with naked bodies than that of kids who are not part of this community.

The next level is relationships, which includes family but also relationships with peers, educators, and relationships in which you might have early sexual and/or romantic experiences. Again, the people you're close to can either reproduce wider cultural attitudes around sexuality unquestioned, or they can resist those attitudes in ways that are more or less restrictive. For example, you might have influential friends growing up who are queer, or have queer parents, or ones who use slut-shaming as part of bullying behavior.

The innermost level is you, yourself, and the ways in which you take on board all of these levels of influence that you're surrounded by. Again, you may have accepted most of what you learned, because it was so unquestioned in the world around you, or you may have found yourself resisting some of it, either because it didn't fit the experiences you were having, and/or because you heard about people who were doing things differently.

ACTIVITY: YOUR LEVELS OF INFLUENCE GROWING UP

We'll come back to exploring the influences and experiences that shaped your own sexuality in more depth in section 3.3. For now, using the diagram below, sketch out some of the main messages you remember receiving about sexuality on the following levels: culture, institutions and communities, and relationships. You might want to think particularly about whether each level accepted or resisted wider culture, and put in the middle the beliefs and understandings that you remember holding personally. You can fill this out for the periods when you were growing up in general, or focus on a particular age, or do it more than once for multiple ages.

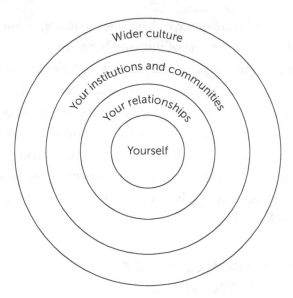

FIGURE 3.2: MULTIPLE LEVELS OF INFLUENCE

We'll come back to these levels of influence as they surround you in your life now in the next chapter.

Now let's go into more depth about how all the different intersections in our lives impact our sexuality, before exploring your own developing sexuality in greater detail in section 3.3.

3.2 INTERSECTIONS

We've already mentioned how our sexuality cannot be neatly separated from the ways in which our bodies are gendered, racialized, classed, and so on. Our sexuality is shaped by the culture and societal structures we were born into and social-ized in, by our sex assigned at birth and our gender identity, by language, by the historical moment and geographical locations we were born into, and more.

In this section, we invite you to think of as many aspects

of your identity and experience as you can. This is to better understand how your sexuality, including aspects of identity, attractions, desires, and practices have been shaped by your own personal history. For the moment, our focus will be on the intersections you were born into up to childhood and the teenage years. We'll address your current intersections in the following chapter, as some of our identities and experiences change over time.

FIGURE 3.3: INTERSECTIONS

We believe that understanding where we come from, when it comes to sexuality, or any other aspects of our identities and experiences, helps us to better understand who we are now, especially in relationship to aspects such as power, oppression, and privilege.

Power, oppression, and privilege

These are words that can feel loaded. They're used in a range of ways, especially on social media, which can be confusing and even upsetting. You might be noticing a reaction within yourself right now while reading those words. What are you noticing in this moment? How is your breathing? What thoughts are going through your mind? What emotions are rising? Notice all this with as much compassion and non-judgment as you can. We'll take a moment to define these words before considering how they have manifested in our own experiences of sexuality growing up.

We've already introduced the idea of dominant discourses. Those are discourses that are pervasive and have power because of how widespread and accepted they are. In fact, many of us might not even notice dominant discourses because it seems to be just "what's normal," "what everybody knows," or "the way things are for most people." Power is not always necessarily visible but it is influential, whether we know that we're being shaped by it or not. For example, the ways in which we're educated, the legal system, even the ways public buildings are designed, all have some power over the way we think individually and collectively.

Sometimes this power is invisible and other times it's not. If we're really comfortable with the way things are, it might be because we hold identities and experiences that have power in dominant discourse. This is what's meant by the idea of privilege. Privilege is something we've done nothing to earn. It's just a given, often something we're born with. For example, in both countries where we live, being born with white skin has privilege. It means that we don't need to be hypervigilant around the police, at least as long as other aspects of our identities, such as being trans—or in Alex's case "foreign"—are not visible. This also demonstrates how privilege is not one-dimensional.

We can have power and privilege in one area but not in another. For example, Alex currently benefits from white privilege living in the US and is not a citizen. However, not being a citizen while living in white skin means that they are less likely to be targeted on sight by Immigration and Customs Enforcement (ICE) when raids sweep their neighborhood. This leads us on to oppression.

When people don't have power and privilege in a particular area, they experience oppression on a cultural and societal, as well as often historical, level. Most of us are likely to experience power and privilege in some areas and oppression in others. However, it is a little more complicated than that. For example, cis white women in both the UK and the US experience misogyny—that is, structural prejudice against feminine identities and expressions—but their experiences differ from those of cis Black women, and from those of trans women. Trans women's experiences also differ from one another depending on how their bodies are racialized.

This is where the concept of intersectionality comes in handy. We don't experience an additive model of power, privilege, and oppression—that is, we cannot just add the identities where we have power and subtract those where we experience oppression, and have a perfect formula that gives us our place in society. We're complex and multifaceted beings and our experiences and identities are more than the sum of our parts.

Intersectionality is a theory that enables us to look at

this complexity. This term was first introduced, in the late 1980s, by Kimberlé Crenshaw, a Black legal scholar in the US, to describe the experiences of Black women in the criminal system, and how they differed from those of white women, and Black men. We're strongly influenced by intersectionality in our thinking and writing. However, it's important to remember and highlight that this theory was born within Black feminism and scholarship, due to the marginalization of Black voices within a largely white, Anglo-American feminist movement. We encourage you to go to the source and read Black scholars if you want to find out more about intersectionality. We list a couple of resources for further reading on this at the end of the chapter.

Power, privilege, oppression, and sexuality: Our intersections growing up

Now it's time to apply these ideas of power, privilege, and oppression to sexuality, and particularly to our own, personal stories. We'll each share some of our own reflections on our experiences with sexuality growing up. We'll then ask you to reflect on your own. We hope these examples give you an idea of what we're asking you to do in this section.

Meg-John drew this picture reflecting on their intersections.

FIGURE 3.4: MEG-JOHN'S INTERSECTIONS

MEG-JOHN REFLECTS:

For me, the intersections that come to mind, which heavily influenced my sexuality, are sex assigned at birth, gender, body-mind, location, and generation. Growing up in the north of England in the 1970s, I remember reading teen girls' magazines in order to try to fit in at a school where there were very rigid ideas about how femininity should be performed on a body like mine. There was very little mixing between the 50 percent boys and 50 percent girls, or between the 50 percent white British and 50 percent South Asian British kids at that school, which meant no other real options than striving to fit into your gender/race group if you wanted to avoid bullying. The magazines focused on relationships and "looks" as the most important things for white girls to focus on in order to get love, which was definitely something that I was desperate for.

At the same time, I was convinced that I was abnormal as I had what I think would now be diagnosed as a microperforate corona (a small opening in the part of the body that was previously called the hymen). This meant I could not use tampons and was therefore sure I would never be able to have the kind of sex that was supposed to be the passport to love (PIV was the only sex we were aware of at all). The huge taboo around menstruation talk in my family, and the impossibility of using toilets at school due to the bullying that occurred there, meant that my shame and secrecy around my "abnormal" genitals continued throughout my teens.

I also grew up only a few blocks away from Peter Sutcliffe, the serial murderer known as the "Yorkshire Ripper." The news was full of his crimes, and there was a high degree of victim blame around his sex-worker victims, and a disbelief that any "respectable lasses" could really have been his targets, which was a key factor in why he wasn't stopped far earlier. Football fans even had celebratory chants about their local sex killer. The graphic novelist Una has written a stunning graphic memoir, *Becoming Unbecoming*, about the impact on her sexuality of growing up in the time and place of these murders, much of which I relate to. The high degree of whorephobia and rape mythology sunk in deep: you had to have sex in order to get love, but you mustn't have too much of it, or really want it. Sex was dangerous, it could come with violence or death; and if that happened, it was probably your fault.

It's quite hard to think of an intersection growing up that influenced my sexuality in a positive way. Perhaps I would go for where I am on the aphantasia to hyperphantasia spectrum of neurodiversity. This relates to the capacity for visual image-ry. I have always been able to fantasize vividly and this was a vital escape and survival strategy for me as a kid (more on this in the next section). There was one place—my mind—where my sexuality could be explored more safely and pleasurably, away from the pressures and dangers of sex with other people, or the assumption that sex equaled PIV.

Alex drew this picture when thinking of their intersections growing up.

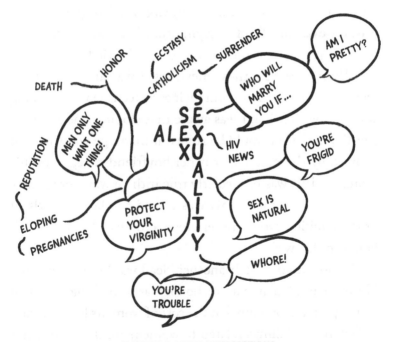

FIGURE 3.5: ALEX'S INTERSECTIONS

ALEX REFLECTS:

Growing up, a major influence on my understanding of sex and sexuality was my maternal grandmother and her sisters. They were Sicilian and I spent most of my time during school closures in Sicily with my great-aunts. I also started living with my grandmother when I attended middle school and high school. The messages I got from them were focused on protecting my virginity as the most precious thing I "owned," and that men were predators who only wanted one thing and, if they got it, I would be ruined. The one thing was, of course, my virginity. This was not just place- and time-specific but also related to class. As a person assigned female at birth without substantial familial financial means, my worth was attached to my appearance and my virginity. My grandmother was, for example, fond of saying that I should never cry in front of "prospective husbands" because I "cried ugly."

While receiving these messages, I was also witnessing many of my peers in Sicily, in their early teenage years, eloping and getting married. I was aware that eloping was a risk, as a girl's reputation would be ruined if marriage was then not allowed by the parents, or if her boyfriend reneged on his promises. This was particularly true if there was a pregnancy involved. Once more, this was linked to class, as girls of "good families" would never elope and tarnish the family's honor in this way.

Honor was definitely another idea I was brought up with. However, in Sicilian culture, honor was something that men had to protect, sometimes at the cost of women's lives. In Italy, in fact, honor killings related to women's infidelity were not uncommon, and were only scrapped by law in 1981. At that time, I was ten years old and had already absorbed the idea that men could literally kill you if you made them look bad, whether you actually cheated or not.

Men might be the ultimate arbiters of honor when it came to sex and sexuality, but women, especially mothers and grandmothers, were also supposed to police my honor. For example, I will never forget when my grandmother called me a whore, because, as a young teenager, I had dinner with a man in his early twenties who lived alone. He was one of the church youth leaders, but this didn't matter because what was important were the gendered appearances and class implications of my behavior.

If cultural, class, geographical, socioeconomic, and gender intersections weren't confusing enough for me, history added another layer when HIV became world news. I was coming of age and exploring my sexuality at a time when the news and public health posters warned me that sex could literally kill me. Of course, I had got that message already, but now dominant discourse seemed to say that, no matter how trustworthy my sexual partners might be, a silent virus could be lurking in their bodies. Early HIV messaging in Italy seemed definitely focused on highlighting the fear factor, and reinforcing cultural messages about the importance of virginity.

These cultural messages were closely linked to the dominance of Catholic religion in my country. Interestingly enough, though, I was also a devout Catholic and really loved reading mystical texts written by saints. It's through their words that I first learned about surrender and ecstasy, which are concepts that can also be applied to sex and sexuality. In fact, much of the imagery used by several saints who experienced ecstasy is pretty sexual, highlighting merging with spirit and experiencing a loss of boundaries as an individual: a component of great sex, as we mentioned in the last chapter! Needless to say, my ideas of sex and sexuality were mired in confusion and mixed messages, and it would take time to consider these intersections from a critical viewpoint. In fact, I'm still unpacking some of them.

This is only the beginning...

These pictures are, of course, just snapshots of our memories at this point in time. If we revisited this exercise, after writing this book, they might look slightly different. There are things that are missing, and things that we might not want to share with the wider world right now. Our stories are not fixed in time. We come to new understanding and insights as we grow and change.

This means that although our experiences stay the same, our stories about our experiences shift and change with us. We're not asking you to draw the ultimate and definitive picture of your sexuality growing up, but rather to take a snapshot, like we did. We invite you to do so at this stage so that you can then look back and revisit it whenever you want to, including after finishing the book.

ACTIVITY: YOUR INTERSECTIONS GROWING UP

Now that you've read our reflections and seen our diagrams, it's time to create your own. Take a few moments to reflect on which aspects of your identities and background shaped your sexuality growing up. Then notice how these aspects might have intersected and interacted with one another.

You can draw, make a mind map, or whatever makes sense to you. You can dance your intersections out, compose a song, or make a collage. Use whatever method best suits the way you think, explore, and create. Notice how both of us did this activity quite differently. As we'll keep saying, there's no right or wrong way of doing this. Just have a go, if you want to.

Reflection point: Your own and other people's sexualities

By now you should feel a little more familiar with your own sexuality growing up: how it was shaped by familial, cultural, and societal expectations, and how it was influenced by your own intersections of identities and experiences. Notice if there were sexualities, including identities, attractions, desires, and practices, that you had no idea existed growing up. Which were the sexual identities, attractions, desires, and practices that you were aware of, and how were they labeled by adults around you? Which were seen as acceptable, and even celebrated through rituals such as marriage, and which were not? Which sexual identities, attractions, desires, and practices did you have little or no contact with because of your own intersections of identities and experiences, and those of the adults around you? How did this influence the way you viewed other people's sexualities, when you first came across them, if they were not familiar to you when growing up?

3.3 GROWING UP SEXUAL: THE SHAPING OF OUR SEXUALITY OVER TIME

Now that we're focusing in on your sexuality background, let's think some more about how your sexuality developed over time, particularly during your childhood and teenage years.

In Chapter 1, we touched on the important research finding that our sexualities are not fixed. Every aspect of us—biopsychosocially—changes over time, and this means that our sexuality will change too. Biologically our bodies and brains change as we grow, learn, and age. Psychologically we develop different understandings over time, we strengthen or weaken our habits, and we have life experiences that alter the direction of our lives in big and small ways. Socially we're exposed to different ideas, people, and relationships in a culture that's also constantly changing.

Fixity and fluidity

The concept of sexual fluidity is easy to grasp when you think about age. For most of us who experience sexual and/or romantic attraction, the age of the people we're attracted to changes as we age. This is certainly impacted by the dominant cultural view that youth is more attractive than age—particularly for women—but there's at least some change in the age of attraction for most people over time.

You might also consider the erotic fantasies that you've had over time, or the sexual media that you've enjoyed most, if any. You could note down the fantasies or media that you remember being your "go to" at different times in your life, and you'll likely see some shifts in themes, bodies present, types of interaction involved, and other features.

Sex drive—or extent of desire—is another thing that goes up and down a lot for many people. It can be heavily influenced, in either direction, by things like sickness, loss, and stress. It's also often relationship dependent. People in long-term relationships frequently find that their desire for each other—and perhaps more generally—diminishes over time after an initial burst. For some it also goes up again, perhaps at retirement, when kids leave home, or when a new sexual possibility is explored together.

Lisa Diamond, and other researchers, have also found that gender of attraction is fluid for many, with people shifting in how they identify and experience their sexuality in terms of being gay, bi, straight, pan, queer, and so on.

However, vitally, not every feature of everyone's sexuality changes over time. Many people experience some—or all— aspects of their sexuality as being fixed. For example, for many, the gender or physical appearance of those they find attractive does remain relatively stable, while the kinds of things they want to do sexually with those people changes a lot. For many ace folk, there's not much change in how much attraction they feel, or whether it's tied to emotional connection, as it is for many demisexual people. However, there might be changes in other features, such as whether they enjoy any form of self-pleasure and how they do that.

Importantly, just because an aspect of sexuality is fluid, this doesn't mean that the person could easily choose for it to be otherwise. It's often felt very much as a direction we need to take, and being denied that direction, or pressured to take another one, would feel very painful and restrictive.

Whether fixed or fluid, people cannot simply choose for their sexuality—or their sexual journey—to be other than what it is.

Influences on our developing sexuality

So what things influence our developing sexuality? There are many, some of which are obviously linked to sex, and some of which are not.

In terms of ones that are clearly linked to sex, you might consider things like the way your family did or didn't talk about sex, the sex education you received at school or youth groups, any books, magazines, or websites you read about the "facts of life" or relationships, early experiences you had of self-touch or solo sex, the first time you saw porn or other forms of sexual media, early crushes, first sexual experiences with another person if you had those, and any experiences of sexual assault, abuse, or bullying, which we'll return to in the next section.

However, for many of us, our erotic landscape is equally—if not more—shaped by the things that happen to us outside sex. The author of *The Erotic Mind*, Jack Morin, explains that many of us use sexual fantasy—or eroticization—as a way of surviving the difficult or traumatic things that happen to us. This perhaps explains why collections of sexual fantasies frequently include so many that relate to power and control, assault, humiliation, and exposure, and the like. We tend to enjoy imagining, viewing, or reading about experiences that were similar to our tough ones, but where it was somehow hot or arousing, romantic or nurturing, or had a different, perhaps happier, ending.

The particular tough thing that happens to us doesn't

necessarily define how it will shape our erotic landscape, however. This is different for different people. Consider somebody who is bullied at school, for example. They may develop fantasies where they experience similar bullying, but in a context where they then get rescued or looked after. They may imagine being a bully and getting their own back. They may eroticize rescuing other people from a similar fate. There are many other possibilities, or it may be that, for this person, the bullying doesn't impact their erotic landscape, and it is more influenced by other aspects of their experience. Whatever the case, this kind of experience may shape the fantasies we have, the sexual media we watch, the desires that excite us, the kinds of people we're erotically drawn to, and the practices that we want to engage with.

Linked to this is the influence of non-sexual media. When you ask people where their desires came from, it often isn't specifically porn or sexual stories that they talk about. More often they refer to themes they found exciting in children's books, or characters or scenarios they were drawn to in TV shows and movies. There are vast communities of fanfiction writers and readers who enjoy explicitly slashing and shipping such characters, or celebrities; but beyond that, many of us have key aspects of our sexual attractions and desires shaped by our first celebrity crush, or a scene in a book or show which we found inexplicably arousing, for example.

It may well be that the reason we find this so appealing is because it links to difficult or traumatic experiences. For example, we find this comedian hot because he acts in the kind of outrageous ways that wouldn't have been possible for us to do as a kid without getting rejected or told off. Or we eroticize a scene in a children's book where somebody gets trapped in a trunk, because we imagine that being a warm, safe place away from the world.

Multiple experiences: Key moments that shaped our sexualities

"For me, it was watching *Dr Who* as a kid. I had such a massive squish on my Doctor (Matt Smith). I used to imagine him turning up in the Tardis and taking me off time-traveling. I love that kind of dynamic in platonic relationships now: someone who leads me into crazy adventures."

"Jennifer Carpenter. Her name still makes me flush. She sat in front of me all year in math class and I fell hard. I used to doodle the back of her head in my notebook. I never once spoke to her, but she's who made me realize I was into girls. I still often fancy women who look like her: tall, dark, and fierce."

"I was sick quite a bit as a kid and often had to go for various medical examinations and surgeries. That left me with quite a thing for medical scenes, although always with a super-kind 'doctor' nurturing me through it. I was glad to find the kink community and realize there were people I could act out my fantasies with."

"I stayed over at my friend's house and they let the kids stay up and watch *Sex and the City* with them. I didn't even know masturbation was a thing until then. I couldn't wait to go home and try it out."

"My mate showed me this porn video on his phone. It was about bodily functions—meant to gross you out—but I found myself getting aroused. I was so scared by my reaction, and also couldn't seem to stop myself going online and looking for more. It took me years to open up to a therapist about it and he helped me realize that it's okay to be into that stuff, as long as you only act on it consensually."

Now that we've touched on some of the key things that shape our developing sexualities, we invite you to do an activity to consider some of your own. Instead of exploring our inter-sections—as we did in the last activity—here we want you to think about key moments that influenced you.

ACTIVITY: RIVER OF EXPERIENCE

Imagine your developing sexuality as a river. You can use the image here in the book—if it's your book!—or draw your own. Each bend in the river is a significant moment that led you to your experience of your sexuality today: a person, event, book, movie, song, encounter, object, fantasy, tough or pleasurable experience—anything really.

You can start at any point in your life, but we suggest start-ing from birth or early memories. Annotate each bend with a few keywords or images, to remind you what each bend represents. Please remember to be gentle with yourself as you go through this activity, and take your time to breathe and take breaks as needed.

Some people prefer to use a different metaphor for this activity. For example, you might think of chapters in the book of your life. Or levels in the computer game of your life.

Of course, you can draw as many rivers as you like. For example, you could do different ones for sexual identities, attractions, desires, and practices; for solo and partnered sex, or different erotic and romantic rivers. You could do one for the tough and traumatic things that shaped your sexuality, and one for the pleasurable and joyful things. We certainly find that our responses to this activity change every time we do it for ourselves.

You may want to share your river with close people in your life, perhaps people you're sexual with, a therapist or other practitioner, or friends who are also doing this activity. It's also absolutely fine to keep it private if this doesn't feel comfortable.

FIGURE 3.6: YOUR RIVER OF EXPERIENCE

In the next section, we'll explore in more detail the impact of the abusive, non-consensual, and traumatic experiences in our lives on our developing sexuality.

3.4 POWER, ABUSE, AND TRAUMA

We've dedicated a whole section to power, abuse, and trauma here, and in the next chapter, because, even though we include these themes throughout the book, we want to clearly spell out how much these experiences often shape our sexualities, especially growing up.

Given that dominant discourses around power, abuse, and trauma in our culture are so confusing, limiting, and damaging, we want to make sure we don't perpetuate the collective gaslighting that happens around sexual trauma by hiding these themes away. This means the ways in which survivors are encouraged to doubt the seriousness of the impact of their experiences—or even whether they really happened—and to blame themselves rather than the perpetrator and the wider systems that enable assault and abuse to occur.

Cultural influences

Let's start exploring these themes from the cultural level of influence and then move inwards towards our personal experiences. As you might have noticed when reading our own reflections on our experiences, the cultural level of influence can carry some truly abusive messages about sexuality, especially for people with marginalized identities and experiences. For example, the idea of honor killings is deeply steeped in power structures that view women and girls as property of husbands, fathers, and brothers. This is abuse at its extreme: murder, justified—and at times even made legal—through societal structures and cultural discourses.

The cultural messages about sexuality, about whose bodies can express and explore freely, and about which bodies are policed, punished, and viewed as disposable, also influence the ways in which communities and families act around those issues. For example, intimate partner violence is incredibly common globally, and it's often protected by the binary separation of private and public spaces. If what happens in our intimate relationships is private, then the community cannot, and will not, generally intervene in those "private affairs." In fact, the relatively modern and western-dominant model of the nuclear family can become the perfect petri dish in which intimate partner violence and childhood sexual abuse can thrive, if we do not challenge some of the dominant discourses that enable it.

One of those dominant discourses that enable intimate partner violence and childhood sexual abuse to thrive is the myth that sexual violence is perpetrated by "outsiders," when, in fact, data tells us that partners, family members, and religious or spiritual leaders are the most likely actors in abuse. Indeed, one of the reasons that Peter Sutcliffe, who Meg-John mentioned before, was not caught sooner was that he was "somebody's husband and somebody's son" and not the monster "maniac" that everyone assumed he'd be.

The "stranger danger" messages often conveyed to women and children (and yes, let's notice the conflation that indeed happens in society of women and children as "vulnerable victims") combined with the widespread cultural messages of husbands and fathers as "protectors," create the perfect distraction away from the reality of sexual violence and abuse. If the danger is the "unknown other," then we don't need to notice how toxic cisgenderism and masculinity, compulsory heterosexuality, and the coital imperative manifest in our interpersonal and often familial relationships. As long as the danger is "out there," then abuse can continue undisturbed and the status quo is maintained.

Increasing awareness

This is one of the most challenging things, in many ways, when addressing sexual violence, especially in the context of growing up, as it troubles societal and cultural ideas of who is a "good man" or a "good parent," and what and where is safe. The #MeToo movement has definitely brought to the spotlight many of these conversations. The hashtag was created in 2006 by Black activist Tarana Burke and was then picked up a decade later by several people, including white celebrities, to illustrate just how widespread sexual violence against women and femmes is. Through more public conversations—although these can be often triggering and challenging for many reasons—people have also begun to realize that many sexual behaviors that are often viewed as "acceptable" are, in fact, abusive and traumatizing.

Despite the rise of public awareness around sexual harassment and violence in the workplace, intimate partner violence remains taboo, and childhood sexual abuse even more so. Yet those experiences are often formative when it comes to sexuality. For example, how can we know what healthy sexuality is if we have witnessed coercive and violent behaviors growing up in a home where there was domestic violence? How do we even begin to talk about childhood sexual abuse when this means challenging cultural scripts of family as a safe haven from the "dangers of the world"?

Abuse and trauma have many shapes

Abuses of power in relation to sexuality are not limited to direct sexual violence. Growing up in homes and religion or spiritual traditions where slut-shaming and/or queerphobic and transphobic remarks are common is also traumatizing. These messages can take deep roots into our bodymind and make it near to impossible for us to have a healthy relationship with ourselves and others.

When the boundaries of sexuality are rigidly and diligently policed by those closest to us, we learn that straying from what is considered "legitimate" around sexual identities, attractions, desires, and practices can be severely punished. At the same time, we might experience conflicting situations in which our own boundaries, including our sexual boundaries, are persistently and inappropriately crossed by people who are supposed to be "safe," such as parents, family friends, or priests. This cognitive dissonance can lead to severe mental health issues, including self-harm and lifelong suicidality for many people, as our bodymind, especially when we're a child, cannot make sense of it and, therefore, easily internalizes stories in which there must be "something wrong with me."

No matter what abuse we may or may not have experienced growing up, most of us have received troubling, and at times traumatic, messages about sexuality at a cultural and social level. The level of abuse is not necessarily what dictates the degree to which our sexuality might be affected.

For example, two people can experience the same childhood sexual abuse, but one might not be as deeply impacted by it as the other. There are so many factors for this, including whether it's okay to talk about what happened within the family, or whether the denial becomes gaslighting, making it impossible for someone to make sense of their own experience, let alone be held, heard, and supported in their healing.

There's much more to discuss around these topics and we're aware that we can't comprehensively cover all of it here. We've included further resources at the end of this chapter, which are more exclusively focused on these topics. For now, we just want to remind you that, if some of the experiences we mentioned happened to you, you're not alone. Sadly, sexual violence, including childhood sexual abuse, is far more common and closer to home than dominant discourses would have us believe. This is why we want to conclude this section with some multiple experiences. Knowing that other people have gone through situations similar to ours can challenge isolation, and even help us to begin to talk about our own stories of sexual abuse and trauma, if we have kept those to ourselves until now.

Multiple experiences: The impact of sexual trauma

"I have been paraded in front of doctors for as long as I can remember. This is common for a lot of disabled children. The first time a doctor sexually assaulted me, I wasn't even sure it happened. Was it me? Did I imagine her penetrating me during the exam in a way that was sexual and not medical? Who would believe me? Now, I always take someone with me to the doctor, but during the Covid-19 pandemic this has become almost impossible, so I've just stopped going to doctors, unless it's absolutely necessary."

"I struggled to name what happened to me as abuse until I read about controlling relationships, because it didn't happen with a partner and because it was emotional rather than sexual. My best friend throughout my teens was a guy who constantly belittled me and made me feel stupid. His way was always the right one and I had to go along with him or he'd punish me in all kinds of subtle ways. I learned what I needed to do to keep him happy, and I dreaded his temper when I didn't manage it. I was constantly worrying about getting it wrong. It was such a relief to drift apart when we both left home, but it eroded my confidence and took a big toll on my later sexual and romantic relationships. I'm always second guessing myself and fearing that partners will lash out at me if I make a mistake."

"Everyone talks about how excited they are to be going home for the winter holidays. I never know what to say. I don't want to go home. I don't want to sit at the same table as my uncle. He raped me when I came out as a lesbian. I told my parents but they didn't do anything. They didn't tell me it was my fault... but they kind of implied it. I don't know how to explain to people around me why I choose to stay in an empty dorm during the holidays."

"I miss religious services. I miss my community, my family, and making special food, and things making sense. After having sex with my partner for the first time, I started having flashbacks and eventually pieced together that I had been sexually abused as a child by our rabbi. It took a lot of therapy. I still haven't told my family. I don't know how to talk about this. Sometimes I still don't believe it happened. I'm just glad he's dead so I don't have to feel guilty that he might do this to someone else."

"I don't think my mom understands that what she did was abuse. It took me a long time to understand this too. After all who has ever heard of a mom being sexually abusive, right? Well, apparently it happens, or so my therapist tells me. She crossed my boundaries a lot, touched me more than she needed to, when washing me, especially when I was old enough to wash myself, walked into the bathroom and my bedroom when I was naked, and so many more little things that now I'm starting to think might not have been so little. I think she was lonely and 'skin hungry.' I have learned that word in a peer support group. I think she met her sexual needs by being physically close to me, whether I wanted closeness or not. I think that's one reason why I freeze when people get too close to me or touch me, even if it's an innocent hug from a good friend."

"I was doing fine till I left home. I went to college, joined a bunch of societies, and started writing for the campus paper. The guy who edited it asked me out and I was thrilled. On our third date, he raped me. There was nothing I could do. Nobody would ever have believed me. I didn't even believe it myself at first because he acted like nothing had happened. I just kind of retreated into my studies and sleep-walked through the next three years. Five minutes it took for him to force himself on me, and I'm still living with the consequences."

Reflection point: Sexual boundaries growing up

Take a few moments to reflect on what boundaries you were aware of growing up, especially in relation to your body and sexuality. If you want to, you can even go one step further back and reflect on how and what you learned about boundaries and consent growing up. Which boundaries did you have? Were they respected or not? Did you feel you could communicate these boundaries clearly or not? For example, did you have to kiss and hug relatives, or could you say no? Did you know the difference between privacy and secrecy? Did any adults ask you to keep an important secret when you were a child (not a surprise, like a gift, but rather a family secret, or a behavior)? Are there behaviors that seemed okay at the time, and that now you see as inappropriately sexual, upsetting, or abusive?

Take your time when doing this. It can be upsetting and even triggering to think about our experiences growing up, especially when we might be just beginning to realize how certain things may not have been okay, or even abusive. If strong feelings or new information come up for you when reading this section or reflecting on these issues, please seek support from a therapist or a support group specializing in mental health and/or sexual violence. It can be really hard to realize how our boundaries might have been crossed by those close to us growing up. You might even notice a little defensiveness. It's natural to feel protective of our caregivers, families, and communities. Breathe, take care of yourself, and then return to this book when you're ready.

REMEMBER: Exploring our past can be extremely helpful in understanding how and why our sexuality is the way it is in the present. Recognizing the myriad internal and external influences on us can help to lift the shame around aspects of our sexuality we might find difficult, as well as helping us to own those aspects we might want to celebrate.

However, journeying back into our past can also be a hard process, particularly when it involves recognizing some of the traumatic things that happened to us when young and how we might have downplayed these over the years. Please go gently on yourself around these processes and remember that you can take your time and get support from others.

When our past does include non-consensual experiences, and gaslighting around these issues, this can make it hard to trust ourselves and to tune into our bodies to know what we want and need, and where our boundaries and limits are. For this reason, we end the chapter with a slow-down page, which is good practice in learning self-consent. We'll keep returning to consent throughout the book, and will come back to how to find your yes, no, and maybe, in more depth in Chapter 5.

And let's breathe…

We've been getting real personal in this chapter.

Take a moment to notice, with as much curiosity
and non-judgment as you can manage in this
moment, how you're doing right now:

What's happening in your bodymind?
What sensations are present?
What thoughts and emotions?

Then take some time to ask yourself:
"What do I need right now to feel supported?"

This could be simple, like a snack, or complex,
such as more trustworthy people in your life.

Whether your need can be met or not,
can you let yourself know what you need
and hold this with tenderness?

Is there something you can do right now to
consensually meet your bodymind where you're at?

Try to keep it as simple as you can right now.

Maybe you just need to take a break from
reading, have a nap or call a friend.

Take time to ask your bodymind:
"What do you need and want?"
As if they were the precious friend they are.

FURTHER RESOURCES

You can read more about the concept of bodymind, which we referred to here in:

- Schalk, S. (2018). *Bodyminds Reimagined: (Dis)ability, Race, and Gender in Black Women's Speculative Fiction.* Durham, NC: Duke University Press.

A great basic introduction to intersectionality is:

- Hill Collins, P. and Bilge, S. (2020). *Intersectionality.* Cambridge: Polity.

And a collection of Crenshaw's writing on intersectionality can be found at:

- Crenshaw, K.W. (2017). *On Intersectionality: Essential Writings.* New York, NY: The New Press.

The graphic memoir about growing up in the time of the Yorkshire Ripper, which Meg-John mentioned is:

- Una (2015). *Becoming Unbecoming.* London: Myriad.

Jack Morin's book on how tough and traumatic experiences influence our sexual fantasies and desires is:

- Morin, J. (1995). *The Erotic Mind.* New York, NY: Harper Perennial.

If you are interested in the intersection of gender, sexuality, and trauma, you can find more in:

- Iantaffi, A. (2021). *Gender Trauma. Healing Cultural, Social and Historical Gendered Trauma.* London: Jessica Kingsley Publishers.

A useful book on healing from sexual trauma:

- Haines, S. (2007). *Healing Sex: A Mind-Body Approach to Healing Sexual Trauma.* Minneapolis, MN: Cleis Press.

A project collecting stories and responses to childhood sexual abuse:

- livingbridgesproject.com

A project focused on healing personally and collectively to end childhood sexual abuse:

- https://heal2end.org

Here is a good selection of books and web-based resources for young people about sex and sexuality, which can be great whether you are a young person, or you want to give yourself some better sex education than you received back when you were young:

- Silverberg, C. and Smyth, F. (2015). *Sex is a Funny Word.* New York, NY: Seven Stories Press.

- Moen, E. and Nolan, M. (2019). *Let's Talk About It.* London: Penguin Random House.

- Corinna, H. (2007). *S.E.X.* Emeryville, CA: Avalon Publishing Group.

- Bish: www.bishuk.com

- Scarleteen: www.scarleteen.com

CHAPTER 4

YOUR CURRENT EXPERIENCE OF SEXUALITY

This chapter turns from the influences that shaped your sexuality growing up, to the influences on your current understanding—and experience—of sexuality. The first two sections of the chapter return to the multiple levels of influence that you experience, and your intersections, but this time exploring how those impact you currently, rather than in the past. Then we come back to the theme of trauma, and the ways in which this impacts our bodymind and sexuality, even if the trauma was in the past, in previous generations, or in the wider history of our families and communities.

We'll end this chapter by starting to map out your current experiences of your sexuality on a number of spectrums. Some people find that locating themselves on scales or spectrums is a helpful way to get concrete information about their lived experiences. If this isn't for you, don't worry, we'll explore your sexuality in more depth in other ways in the next chapter.

Content note: As in the last chapter, there's some mention of sexual trauma and assault in Meg-John's example in section 4.1 of this chapter, and in section 4.3, which deals with trauma specifically. You may want to avoid reading that example (after the picture Meg-John drew), or the multiple experiences in 4.3 if you want to avoid brief descriptions of traumatic experiences. If you want to leave out section 4.3 altogether, because this is too live for you right now, feel free.

As always, please go gently with yourself, particularly around the theme of trauma. Most trauma-informed practitioners agree that trauma work must be done slowly. It's generally not a good idea to push into traumatic materials or memories. It's awesome if you find yourself honoring feelings like "I'm not ready for this," "I need to slow down," "I'd rather come back to this later," or "I'd like a friend to read this first and tell me if it'll be okay for me."

4.1 SEXUALITY IN YOUR WIDER WORLD, COMMUNITIES, RELATIONSHIPS, AND SELF

In the last chapter, we encouraged you to reflect on how different levels of influence impacted your developing sexuality. Let's start your reflections on your current sexuality by exploring how those multiple, embedded levels of influence impact your experience now.

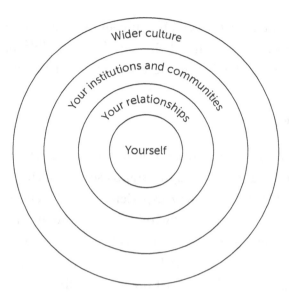

FIGURE 4.1: MULTIPLE LEVELS OF INFLUENCE

As we go through this section, you can keep coming back to this diagram and writing or drawing on any thoughts you have about the sexual messages you receive at each level of your experience, and how you relate to them, with the ones that you've internalized—or signed up to—yourself in the centre. You could draw a copy of the diagram in your journal and do it there, or just reflect on it. You might want to read through the rest of this section first to get a sense of it—and to see Meg-John's own example—before coming back to complete the diagram.

You could fill out this diagram for your sexuality now, as a whole, or it's also a great template for exploring specific aspects of sexuality. For example, you could reflect on each level in relation to the sexual identities or practices that are available to you and how those are portrayed. You could reflect on the messages and models around consent which are present at each level. Or you could pick a certain aspect of your sexuality, such as being ace, heteroflexible, or kinky, and complete the different levels just for that aspect.

Wider culture

We've already spent some time in Chapter 2 talking about how dominant culture understands sexuality, and how the options for understanding, experiencing, and identifying our sexualities shift over time within that culture. An important further point about wider culture is that the current economic and social system in which the two of us live, "neoliberal capitalism," has a big impact on our sexualities.

Key features of neoliberal capitalism are the idea that capital—or wealth—is valued over humans, and that the graph always needs to be going up in terms of how much capital an organization or country has. Injustice is built into this system because it can only work by paying people less and less for the products they produce, in order that others can consume them. So some people, lives, and labor are valued far more than others. It is also inherently non-consensual because it relies on people continuing to produce and consume more and more—whether they want to or not—beyond the limits of what's good for individual mental or physical health, or the health of the planet.

How does this relate to sexuality? You may have heard the phrase "sex sells." One main way in which people are pressured to consume more and more is to encourage them to feel flawed or lacking in relation to their sexuality and attractiveness. Advertisers and industries then sell them products of all kinds which offer to enhance their appearance, get them sexual partners, and improve their sex lives. Such messages are perpetuated through the fashion industry and sex advice industry, in mainstream media which portrays certain kinds of appearance, relationships, and sex in idealized ways, and across social media and dating apps, to name just a few.

Neoliberal capitalism also works by individualizing problems which are actually structural, in order to focus people's attention inwards on self-improvement rather than outwards on this problematic system. This is exemplified in common approaches towards sexual assault, which focus on what people can do to avoid getting assaulted, rather than on addressing cultures which enable assault. Neoliberal capitalism encourages the sense that we are in competition for scarce resources, which underpins problematic sexual behaviors like that of some "incel" communities who believe that women owe them sex. Finally, it encourages us to monitor ourselves, compare ourselves against others, and shame others to make ourselves feel better, which lies behind a lot of the "us and them" approaches we see, where people of some sexualities attack those of others as inferior or threatening.

Neoliberal capitalism comes into sex in multiple ways; for example, in the pressure to conform to "normal" sex, and taking a goal-focused approach to "getting laid" and "reaching orgasm." People are encouraged to be sexual entrepreneurs, working hard at sex—on top of everything else—and they're told that they should find this pleasurable and fun, and are flawed if they don't.

ACTIVITY: CULTURAL MESSAGES

On Figure 4.1 you might like to jot down a few notes about

the particular messages you receive about sexualities in your wider culture. Maybe think specifically about the media that you consume: the shows you watch, magazines you read, music you listen to, social media you engage with, sexual media you enjoy, and so on. In what ways do those close down or open up your options when it comes to sex and sexuality?

Then think about how your experience of your sexuality fits within the options that are available. Which wider cultural messages about sexuality do you accept and which do you resist?

Your institutions and communities

At the next level in, from our wider culture, come the institutions and communities that we're part of. Institutions include organizations that we work for, educational settings, prisons if we're incarcerated, and care homes, hospitals, or clinics if we spend a lot of time in these. Communities include groups and networks such as faith or spiritual communities, communities based on shared interests or leisure pursuits, the neighborhood we live in, and specifically sexual communities like the queer community, ace community, sex worker community, and so on. You might find it useful to reflect for a moment on the institutions and communities that you're embedded in.

All institutions and communities have their own micro-cultures, and these will also have their own ways of viewing sexuality. It may be that they follow wider society in their understandings and assumptions about sexuality, or that they say very little about it, or that they have alternative ideas about sexuality to those in the dominant culture.

ACTIVITY: COMMUNITY MESSAGES

On Figure 4.1 you might like to jot down a few notes about the messages you receive about sexuality in your various institutions and communities. In what ways do those close down or open up your options when it comes to sexuality?

Then, again, think about how your experience of your sexuality does or doesn't fit within those options that are available. Which institutional and community messages about sexuality do you accept and which do you resist?

Your relationships

This next level in is about the most significant relationships in your life at the moment, which we'll reflect on more in Chapter 6. These could include the people you're closest to and/or spend the most time with; for example, your friendship group, any sexual or romantic partners or hook-ups you have, family, work colleagues, and people you meet regularly online via social media or gaming.

We give and receive a lot of messages about sexuality in the everyday babble of chat, gossip, support, and discussion that we have with our close people. These messages might reproduce the assumptions about sexuality that are there in wider culture, or our surrounding institutions and communities, or they might offer alternatives to these, or a bit of both.

ACTIVITY: RELATIONSHIP MESSAGES

On Figure 4.1 you might like to jot down a few notes about the messages you receive about sexuality in your various significant relationships. In what ways do those close down or open up your sexuality options?

Then, again, think about how your experience of your sexuality does or doesn't fit within those options that are available. Which relationship messages about sexuality do you accept and which do you resist?

Yourself

Finally, we come back to you. There you are at the centre of the diagram, within those nested circles of wider culture, institutions and communities, and personal relationships. All of the ideas, messages, and understandings about sexuality that we receive from those outer levels are filtered through our own bodyminds, and then echo back up those levels as we co-create meanings with our friends, colleagues, and so on.

You can think of it as an internal conversation. The babble of thoughts that are constantly passing through our minds— and feelings that pass through our bodies—are the way that we internalize all of these sexuality messages. They are how we do that self-monitoring, comparing, and self-criticism that neoliberal capitalism sadly encourages.

ACTIVITY: INTERNAL MESSAGES

On Figure 4.1 you might like to jot down a few notes about the ideas that you find yourself having about sexuality. What are the thoughts and feelings about your sexuality that flit through your mind as you go about your day. You could use meditation, or regularly record your thoughts, in order to slow down and notice them. In what ways do your internal conversations with yourself about sexuality close down or open up your options when it comes to sexuality?

Think about how you'd like to relate to your internal thoughts and feelings about sexuality. Which of the messages that you give yourself about your sexuality do you accept and which do you resist?

Meg-John's levels of sexuality

Here's an example of one of us—Meg-John—thinking through their own experiences at each level of sexuality. They've just given a few thoughts at each level, but there are plenty more they could have mentioned.

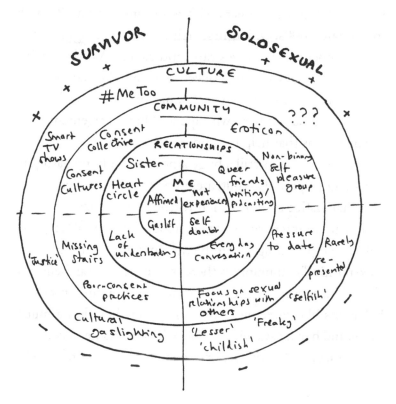

FIGURE 4.2: MEG-JOHN'S REFLECTION

MEG-JOHN REFLECTS:

I've chosen two aspects of my sexuality to reflect on in the diagram: one more challenging and one more celebratory. These are being a survivor and being currently solosexual (only having sex with myself). For both I've put the more positive aspects at each level of influence in the top half of the diagram and the more negative ones in the bottom half.

SURVIVOR

At the cultural level, the #MeToo movement, media coverage of this, and television like *The Morning Show* and *I May Destroy You* are certainly helpful in raising awareness about how common sexual violence is. However, for me, it was the Consent Culture movement within the kink community, back in the late 2000s, which first helped me to recognize that what happened to me was rape and assault. Working with the organization Consent Collective has also helped to affirm my experience and its impact, as has my sister Bee's brave speaking out about her own rape and her engagement with organizations that help to support other survivors.

However, there's still a huge amount of cultural gaslighting around rape and assault, including terrible practices in the criminal justice system which further traumatize survivors and focus on interrogating them about their sexual "respectability," perpetuating victim blame. In many alternative and "sex-positive" communities there is a veneer that all behavior should be consensual, but a normalizing of non-consensual behaviors like agreeing to one thing but then doing much more, and having sex with people who are unable to consent. There are often "missing stairs": people who are known to be non-consensual but whose behavior is ignored by the group until someone who is unaware is treated non-consensually and "trips on the missing stair."

In some of the longer-term relationships in my life, with people from previous generations, there's still a sense that sexual assault isn't something you talk about, isn't that bad, or is somehow the survivor's fault. Even with everything I know—and have written—on this subject, I still find myself self-gaslighting at times, and that's when my close friendships and consent/survivor networks are really important.

SOLOSEXUAL

As I mentioned in the last chapter, fantasy and solo sex have been a key part of my sex life for as long as I can remember, often more satisfying—and safer—than the sex I've had with other people. However, great solo sex and sexual relationships with yourself are barely represented at all in wider culture. Solo sex is always depicted as lesser than "the real thing," and people who enjoy it are seen as questionable, childish, selfish, or abnormal. I'm fortunate to have great communities which support forms of solo sex, such as the Eroticon conference for erotic writers and readers, which I attend most years, and the non-binary self-pleasure groups I've been part of where we've met to discuss and practice solo sex together. I've included a reference where I wrote about that in the further resources at the end of this chapter.

However, even in queer and sex-critical communities, I have received kindly advice from friends about engaging in dating or hook-ups, have had people look sorry for me when I said I was having solo rather than partnered sex during lockdown, and have felt left out of chats about group sex experiences people had lately... Until I was brave enough to offer a recent orgy in my head as a legitimate addition to this conversation! It certainly helps a lot to have friends who treat all sexual experiences as equally valid, and to write books and make podcasts on these themes. This helps me to tell myself—and others—that solo sex is a great way to practice both sex and self-love. I'm not without self-doubts about my solosexuality, but mostly it is a place of great pleasure and learning for me.

You might now like to return to the concentric circles diagram in Figure 4.1 and write a bit more on it, having read this example. You might find it helpful to write—or share with a friend—some reflections on it as Meg-John has here.

In the next section, we explore how your current sexuality intersects with all the other aspects of your identities and experiences in your life right now.

4.2 SEXUALITY IN YOUR CURRENT INTERSECTIONS

In Chapter 3, we invited you to consider how various identities and experiences intersected for you historically; that is, at birth and through your childhood, teenage years and young or even middle adulthood, depending on how old you are now. We also introduced the concept of intersectionality. In this section, we revisit all of that but we do so in your current intersections, wherever you might be in your life course.

ACTIVITY: YOUR INTERSECTIONS NOW

Let's go back to the activity you did in section 3.2 and revisit your drawing, diagram, mindmap, dance, or whatever you created, to explore your intersections growing up. If you haven't done the activity, you may want to go back and do it now. Or you can, of course, just keep on reading.

As you revisit what you created before, what similarities and differences do you notice between then and now? What has changed and what has stayed the same? What has stayed the same, but you experience it differently because your insight and understanding might have changed? Just notice with as much curiosity and non-judgment as you can manage in this moment. This is information and not a moral judgment on who you were or who you are. Take some time to jot down, in whichever way feels comfortable to you, whatever you notice when comparing your sexuality-related intersections then and now.

Your current intersectional experiences of sexuality

We hope that you can hold the information from the activity above with open hands. As you consider your current sexual identities and experiences, we want to remind you that intersectionality is the multifaceted web of our identities and experiences, and that the whole is greater than the sum of its parts. This activity is not about comparing how privileged and oppressed you were in the past versus now, or even versus other people. This is not the oppression Olympics of sexuality! Rather, we want to support you in understanding your own position right now—your own complex web of intersecting identities and experiences in the realm of sexuality.

Here are some questions that you might find helpful to consider as you explore where you are right now:

- Do you live in the same place where you were born, or have you moved? Is your main language(s) the dominant one where you live?

- Is it easy for you to access information from popular media around you, or are most sources of information freely available to others not as accessible for you?

- Are your skin color and tone the ones you see reflected back in popular media images, such as movies, TV, magazines, and so on?

- Did you learn the history of your people in school growing up and, if so, from which perspective?

- Is your culture the same as the dominant culture around you, or does it differ?

- Is your body considered normative where you live, or does it differ from the images reflected back in popular media because of its size, appearance, disabilities, and so on?

- Is your appearance considered normative or viewed as "exotic" and othered where you live by being non-consensually commented on and pointed out by people around you, including strangers?

— Are you considered attractive by the beauty standards dominant where you live?

— If you are part of any religious or spiritual traditions, are they the same ones that other people around you belong to? For example, do the religious holidays you celebrate coincide with the closure of schools and workplaces?

— Is your economic access similar to or different from that of people portrayed in advertisements and popular media?

— Is your class status similar to or different from that of people portrayed in advertisements and popular media?

— Is your education level similar to or different from that of people portrayed in advertisements and popular media?

— Are you allowed to vote, if you are of an age where a person can vote where you live? Are your legal rights the same as those of any other citizen where you live?

— Is it safe for you to express your sexuality openly, in public, or do you have to worry about people judging or harassing you, being discriminated against, encountering violence, and being arrested?

— Do you see your own sexual attractions, desires, and practices portrayed in popular media? If so, are they portrayed as acceptable or not?

— Did you learn about your own sexual identities,

attractions, and desires if you received sex education during your schooling?

— If you want to, is it easy for you to find suitable sexual partners where you live?

— If you so desire, can you access toys and any other devices you might want or need to use to engage in whichever sexual practices you might be interested in, including solo sex?

— Does your family know and/or understand and accept your sexual identities, attractions, desires, and practices?

To give you an example of what we mean to address here, let's revisit Alex's own reflections from the previous chapter.

REVISITING ALEX'S EXAMPLE AND REFLECTION:

When I read what I wrote in the previous chapter, I noticed several differences to where I'm at now. First of all, I'm no longer a virgin (not a secret, given that I'm a parent, and talk about that publicly), which means I no longer need to worry about protecting my virginity! I have openly embraced several sexual identities, attractions, desires, and practices that were not acceptable and that I wasn't even aware of growing up. Interestingly enough, I seem to have fulfilled expectations around marriage, given that I did legally bind myself to my co-parent and life partner and, at the time of writing this, I have been with him for the past 20 years. I'm quite sure though that our polyamorous marriage, my partnerships, and my practicing relationship anarchy are not quite what my family of origin had in mind.

Even though I am partnered, I still have lots of doubts about my sexual attractiveness. Some of this comes from those early criticisms, some from relational and sexual trauma, and some from living in a cultural context where the images considered attractive in popular media are very different from my own body. I have also come out as trans and non-binary, and made some body modifications that are not viewed as normative. As I age, I'm also beginning to struggle with internalized ageism and worry about "losing my looks," as I have been trained to do by dominant discourse. One of my disabilities also means that my body is not living up to ableist expectations in dominant discourse, which impact my own perception of what erotic capital I may or may not have.

I don't worry about HIV in the same way I did when I was in my teens. I am more informed, due to my own research and training, and I have people close to me who live with HIV. I'm much more worried about the rise of fascism or capitalism killing me, and wish there had been public service announcements about this growing up! I have also come to understand honor killings as a facet of a cisgenderist patriarchy, and have dedicated so much of my life to dismantling this system!

I am no longer a practicing Catholic and I am openly Pagan, which, for me, includes reclaiming ancestral practices such as learning to play and dance the tarantella, which is also linked to sexual healing and freedom. I am still attracted to ecstatic spiritual practices though, and I see my love of saints and mystical experiences as the root for this, and as an early expression of my own sexuality.

Finally, I no longer live where I was brought up. This has in some ways afforded me expansiveness and freedom but it has also come with an expensive price tag. As I have grown older, I have come to understand the geographical distance between where I was born and where I live as a displacement partly due to my economic background but, even more so, to my own gender and sexuality—that is, to my transness and queerness.

Here are a few more experiences from a broader range of people to capture some of the diversity of how our intersections can impact our understandings and experiences of sexuality.

Multiple experiences: Sexuality at the intersections

"It took me a long time to get here, but I'm comfortable now being really open about being a professional domme. I make more money than anyone in my family ever has, I set my own hours, and I feel in control of my own sexuality. I don't have to depend on a man to support me. I also love having this job after being told that nobody would ever find me attractive because I'm fat. Every time I get paid, it's like a giant 'f*&^ you' to all the bullies growing up."

"I'm married, have two kids and have good maintenance sex with my spouse. I know my life might seem boring, especially after being brought up in a queer, polyamorous commune, but this is who I am. I grew up knowing I had lots of options, and realized pretty early on that I was straight, vanilla, and monogamous. I converted to Judaism when I got married. Feeling that I belonged to the same faith community as my spouse was important to me."

"I keep my sexuality pretty quiet. Being who I am where I live is not legal, so I have to be careful. There is a pretty good, underground community of queer people and that helps. A lot of people have emigrated over the years. I thought about it, but I want to take care of my parents since I'm an only child."

"I didn't have any sex education growing up because Deaf people are often infantilized and not given proper access to information. I became HIV positive at 19 years old because I didn't know how to have safe sex. Now my work is focused on sex education with Deaf youth. I'm happy to be me, including being positive, and I want more for young people in my community."

"My parents were truly flower children of the sexual revolution. Coming out as ace wasn't easy, because they just didn't get it. It got so bad I had to limit contact with them. They kept asking me if something had happened to me, or if I thought I couldn't have sex because I use a wheelchair. They sent me all sorts of sex-positive books and websites. I wish they could understand this is who I am, and my partner and I are happy as we are."

"My queer family is so important to me and it's where I learned what healthy relationships can look like. I was brought up in a really uptight, upper-middle class, white suburban household. When I came out as bisexual—and a few years later as trans—I wasn't rejected, everyone just kind of ignored it. I have had to learn how to do emotions, communicate, have conflict, and be vulnerable and accountable over the past ten years. It was worth it because I get to have this amazing, intergenerational, multi-racial queer family to support my partners and I as we parent our kids."

Reflection point: Our changing sexuality

Returning to the idea of fluidity that we covered in the previous chapter, you might like to reflect now on how your sexual identities, attractions, desires, and practices have—and have not—shifted and changed over time. Some might have changed more than others, some not at all. Are there aspects of your sexuality that feel foundational to you, like a rock that supports you, no matter what? Are there aspects that feel particularly fluid, maybe regularly in flux? How comfortable are you with shifts and changes in your own and other people's sexualities? Take a few moments to reflect and, if you want, to jot those thoughts down in a notebook or record them in whichever way feels most accessible to you.

4.3 THE IMPACT OF TRAUMA ON YOUR SEXUALITY

When considering our intersections of identities and experiences, we're also getting in touch with how systemic power has shaped our stories. This means looking at historical, cultural, and social trauma and how this has impacted our sexuality, in all its aspects. What do we mean by this? Remember section 3.4 on power, abuse, and trauma? We're going to return to those ideas now but, this time, we're looking at how they might be impacting your current sexuality.

Historical, intergenerational, cultural, and social trauma

When we talk about historical, cultural, and social trauma, we're addressing what could be called the atmosphere of collective trauma that all of us are born into, and that—depending on our intersections—we might be more or less aware of and impacted by. The term "historical trauma" was first introduced in the literature by Hunkpapa/Oglala Lakota scholar Dr. Maria Yellow Horse Brave Heart who compared the impact of the Holocaust on survivors with that of events like the Wounded Knee massacre on the Lakota people.

In her scholarship, Dr. Yellow Horse Brave Heart noted how disparate historical actions and events can have similar impacts on different populations and be grouped under the umbrella term of historical trauma. When a population is impacted by historical trauma, they often experience higher rates of depression, anxiety, substance use, alcoholism, suicide, intimate partner violence, and abuse. If this picture feels familiar, it's because almost all marginalized populations experience those issues. As discussed in Chapter 3, some of those issues are directly relevant to shaping our sexuality as they include sexual violence, encompassing intimate partner violence and childhood sexual abuse.

Historical trauma is usually passed on intergenerationally (potentially genetically, but the science on this one is still evolving). This happens both vertically, from one generation to the next, and/or horizontally, between people of the same generation such as peers. Intergenerational trauma is different from historical trauma though. While historical trauma is always intergenerational, the reverse is not true. Some intergenerational trauma is more about what happened in our own family line. For example, if a parent, or grandparent is abused by their parents, that trauma is passed on intergenerationally, but it's familial, as in specific to that family, and not necessarily also historical.

Historical trauma is closely entwined with cultural and social trauma. In fact, some people even wonder whether we need different terms, or whether the historical umbrella could cover all of it. We use cultural and social trauma to highlight how issues such as the ways that bodies are racialized, gendered, classed, and so on are not just in the past, but rather are manifested in our everyday culture and societal structures. These forces shape us and our personal stories. We may or may not be aware of this, depending on a number of factors, including our own position within dominant culture and society.

We might also experience the impact of this atmosphere of trauma without realizing it. In fact, we might think that what we're struggling with—around mental health issues or substance use—is completely personal. If our childhood seems alright to us, we might even blame ourselves, or think there's something wrong with us, when we could be wrestling with much larger systemic issues that can be hard—if not impossible—to untangle individually. Let's turn to how all of this might shape our current sexuality.

Trauma in the body

Many trauma experts have highlighted the ways in which our traumatic experiences live on in the body. As humans, we need belonging, connection, and safety for our systems to work in an optimal way. When this has been taken away from us, in whatever way, our nervous system starts to function in survival mode, which puts a strain on all parts of our bodymind. If you're interested in learning more about this, we have listed some further resources at the end of this chapter. For the purposes of this book, we'll keep it fairly brief and describe some of the main trauma-related patterns and responses that you might notice within yourself and others around you, and which may show up around sex and sexuality.

Hypervigilance

When we're constantly in survival mode, we often become hypervigilant rather than spending most of our time feeling relaxed yet aware. When we're hypervigilant, our nervous system is constantly scanning for potential danger. While this can be incredibly useful in crisis situations—for example, in helping us see whether there is a bear approaching in the woods—it's not sustainable in the long term, as it can lead us to believe that all the trees are bears. This means not only that we can't distinguish what is truly dangerous and what's not, but also that nobody and nowhere ever feels safe. If nowhere and nobody is safe, then we also cannot truly relax or rest, which puts our bodymind under strain and hinders connection with others, including erotic connection.

Shutdown

Instead of, or as well as, hypervigilance, we might experience intense dorsal vagal shutdown—an intense freeze response (more about this later in this section). When we're in dorsal vagal shutdown, we cannot connect, and can find it impossible to distinguish what and who are safe from what and who are not. Sometimes we experience this alongside hypervigilance. This might feel something like pushing hard on the brakes in a car while revving up the engine at the same time. The system is on high alert but going nowhere. This too puts incredible wear and tear on our bodymind, and makes any kind of connection with ourselves and others difficult.

All-or-nothing thinking

Another common pattern we might notice, when we have experienced historical, cultural, social, or developmental trauma (trauma that happens while we're still growing up), is that of all-or-nothing thinking. All-or-nothing thinking is very polarized and binary. It's helpful when we need to survive in a crisis: do I run, or drop down and play dead? However, it's not so helpful in our everyday lives and gets in the way of connecting with ourselves and others. There can be no nuance with this type of thinking. For example, in relationships, we might feel that either our needs can be met, or those of the other person, but not both. This can lead to a scarcity and competitive mentality that does not foster intimacy or collaboration. We've written a whole chapter on how non-binary thinking can be helpful to loosen all-or-nothing thinking patterns in one of our other books, *Life Isn't Binary*.

Flashbacks

If we've experienced emotional, physical, sexual, or other forms of abuse or neglect—especially but not exclusively at an early age—we might experience something called emotional or sensory flashbacks. These flashbacks can be confusing if we don't know what we're experiencing. For example, we might feel an intense wave of emotions that does not seem to be connected to what's happening in the present moment. Fear and shame are frequent emotions that show up as emotional flashbacks, but any emotions can present in this way. Or we might suddenly experience a sensation such as pain, nausea, tightness, or tingling, seemingly "out of nowhere." These might be flashbacks that are happening on the emotional or sensory levels, often without explicit images or memories. We mention these as they're not uncommon experiences during sex, or even when we're around other people. They can be confusing and scary, and we might end up trying to make sense of them by thinking there is something wrong with what's happening in the present, even when what is happening is not the source of our experiences. Of course, sometimes what's happening in the present is not okay, and that is why we're having those experiences. Trauma and memory are tricky things to untangle, and it's helpful to have trusted support when trying to do so.

The four Fs for survival

The freeze response that we mentioned above is one of the four F responses that we experience when in survival mode, which, for some of us, might be our daily state. The responses are: *fight*, *flight*, *freeze*, and *fawn*. Our particular combination of these responses impacts how we are in relation to sex and relationships, both with others and with ourselves.

Fight takes place when our sympathetic nervous system is fully engaged, and we're ready to face whatever danger—actual or perceived—is in front of us. This might not necessarily mean a physical fight, of course; it just means that we're in a high arousal state. Our hearts beat faster, our breathing is likely to be shallow, our muscles tense up, and we may find ourselves speaking loudly, being more forceful and emphatic, and so on. When in fight mode, we might come across as aggressive, recognizing that this is a very culturally dependent perception of course. In sexual situations, for example, we might become dysregulated if we're feeling abandoned, which can be a very core wound for many of us (more on this in Chapter 6), and we might come across as demanding, controlling, or pushy. This can impact the capacity to consent in others, especially if they're prone to freeze or fawn. We might also be flooded by shame after experiencing a fight reaction, especially if we were physically abused and we have a challenging relationship with anger because of it. This is particularly true if we dissociate while having a fight response. Dissociation is when we feel disconnected and detached from what's going on, feel unreal, or even struggle to form memories and recall what happened. When we're dissociated, we're not in the here-and-now, and the past can bleed into the present.

Flight is also about being in a high arousal state, but instead of being ready to engage and fight, our body wants to run, or disappear, or be anywhere but here. A flight response can also tip into dissociation, when getting away from some-thing or someone is not possible and there is a combined freeze and flight reaction. Suicidal ideation can be viewed as an extreme flight response—that is, a desire to no longer exist and have to engage with what's happening, because it's intolerable. A flight reaction can be triggered when someone gets too close emotionally or physically, especially if we have experienced closeness as dangerous growing up and fear our boundaries are being crossed. This can impact our sexuality in a range of ways, from our relationships to sexual encounters.

For example, we might feel like running away, and may do so, if someone communicates their interest in us, even if we're interested in them as well. Or we might become dissociative during sex because it feels intolerable to be present.

Freeze takes place when the parasympathetic nervous system decides that the safest thing to do is to just shut down. When in freeze mode we might feel paralyzed, unable to say what we really want to, unable to move, and even trapped. Physically we might experience coldness, numbness, or stiffness, feel a sense of dread, and we might find we're holding our breath. A freeze response can also tip into dissociation. When we experience freeze, we are usually not able to say things like "no," or "stop," which is very relevant to our capacity to consent to sexual activities. Our freeze mode may or may not be obvious to others around us. Some of us might be in an almost constant state of functional freeze. This means that we might seem fine and even extremely competent on the surface but, inside ourselves, we're not able to easily get in touch with our emotions, our own sense of yes, no, or maybe, and we feel completely unable to communicate this.

Fawn is a more recent addition to the Fs of survival responses and, as far as we're aware, it was first coined by Pete Walker in his book *Complex PTSD: From Surviving to Thriving*. This is also known as the appease response, or people-pleasing for survival. When we're fawning, we might or might not be aware that our main goal is to avoid conflict, danger, or simply displeasing those around us. This means that we may say or do anything that we think will appease the other person, whether that person is actually a threat to us or not. Fawning means that it can be hard for us to say no, and that we might even say yes to things we don't want to do.

This is, once more, very relevant when it comes to our sexuality. For example, we might identify with cultural and social expectations of sexuality because of our fawn response, and not wanting to upset people around us, especially our family. We might also feel unable to express our authentic attractions and desires, or what we want to do sexually, because we're not sure of how these will be received. Fawning can get in the way of authentic consent with ourselves and others. If we're trying to please and appease, how can we know what we really want to say yes, no, or maybe to? Fawning, combined with all-or-nothing thinking, can lead us to always "choose" others at the expense of ourselves, instead of entering the complex dance of relationships to figure out how all of us can have needs and desires, whether they're met or not.

Please bear in mind that these four F responses happen when we're in actual danger, as well as when present situations which aren't dangerous trigger memories of past danger, or of being abandoned in emotional states that were beyond our capacity to process. It's a little tricky when we've experienced trauma as we might not always be able to assess what's happening accurately or to trust ourselves with ease. When healing from trauma, the goal is not to "get rid" of these responses, but rather to become able to differentiate past from present, so that our survival responses can do their job more accurately and keep us safe.

ACTIVITY: GETTING TO KNOW OUR OWN SURVIVAL RESPONSES

Let's take some time to apply these ideas to your own experiences. You might want to use a blank piece of paper for this activity, or a notebook. As ever, you can record your thoughts in whichever way works for you, or skip the activity altogether. If you experience quite a bit of dissociation, or are easily triggered by thinking about these things at the moment, we suggest leaving this activity, or doing it with your therapist, support group, or a trusted person, if you think it might be helpful.

If you're using a blank piece of paper, you might want to divide it into four quadrants, one for each response: fight, flight, freeze, and fawn. Like this:

Fight	Flight
Freeze	Fawn

In each quadrant—or as a list in your notebook—take a moment to think of times when you might have experienced each response. Think of times when you have experienced those reactions, but please don't pick your most traumatic experiences. What do you notice in your own bodymind when you're in fight, flight, freeze, or fawn? What sensations do you observe— what thoughts, emotions, images? What does your body want to do in those moments? We all have these survival responses, even though we might favor one or two over the others. If it's difficult to identify what happens in your body, it's okay just to leave this activity for another time.

If you have the capacity to identify what happens in your

bodymind for each survival response, you might want to expand the activity to think about times when those responses were triggered during sexual encounters. Again, if you can, try not to pick the most traumatic examples in your life. What did you notice in those moments? Try to notice all of this with as much curiosity and non-judgment as you're able. This is information to increase self-awareness and, ultimately, to be able to engage with your sexuality in a more intentional and present way.

To better illustrate how all of this might impact your sexuality, let's take a moment to consider some multiple experiences before moving on to the next section.

Multiple experiences: The impact of past trauma on our current sexuality

"When trying to have sex it's really hard for me to let go. If I start to relax, my body goes on high alert... My heart starts pounding, I tune into every little noise around me, and I just can't enjoy whatever is happening. I have this sense of dread come over me and I feel as if something bad is going to happen. I just don't feel safe, no matter how many doors are locked or how much I trust the person I'm with."

"I love jerking off. It's my go-to soothing activity. But when I'm a bit low there's always this danger point right after I come. Sometimes it feels okay, but sometimes I go into this big shame spiral about what a loser I am for masturbating, and how I can't keep a partner, and what a terrible person I must be. Most of the time I'm so fine with my sexuality, and it feels rotten the way those messages sneak in right when I've done something that's meant to be kind to myself."

"I'm ace and I would really rather never have sex. It does nothing for me. But because I'm a 'fawn' I've really struggled to keep that boundary in relationships where the other person wants it. They say they get it at first, but fairly soon they're asking whether I'm sure I'm ace, or I can just feel them wanting more when we cuddle. I tell myself it's no big deal if it gives them pleasure, but once I've done it I start to feel this scary feeling, like I've lost myself. That's when I have to walk away. It feels so sad because I have to lose everything I've built with that person, and they often blame me because they don't understand."

"I got off with a friend at a sex-positive con. We wound up back in her room and it was all going great. Then I noticed she'd gone pretty still and wasn't really responding to what I was doing. I stopped and asked how she was. She didn't say much and looked pretty tired so I helped her get into bed and went back to my room. The next day she thanked me. She said I was the first guy who hadn't just kept going when that happened to her. I found that really shocking and made sure I read up a lot about trauma after that."

"After I play, I just need to get out of there, or, if I'm at my house, I want the other person to leave. I go really cold and distant if they don't. If they want to cuddle, or talk, or express affection in any way, I feel trapped. I start to think about all the things they might need from me and I feel as if there's no space for my own needs and feelings. I just want to run away from the entire mess."

"I seem to have fights with my partner whenever we get too

close. We've been together long enough now to know the dance: we get really close, I start to relax in the relationship, then they miss something (leave the dishes, or forget to check in about an important project at work that they knew I was worried about) and I feel so incredibly angry. I tell them to leave if they don't care, and that I know they don't love me."

"When I have sex, no matter how casual, I really need the other person to be present and connected. I want to feel wanted. I want to make sure they want to be there with me. If I can't see their eyes, or if they seem distracted, or bored, it's really hard for me to keep going. Afterwards, I like to cuddle for a little while and even say really intense things, like 'Don't leave me' or 'I never want this to end.' I know that's a lot for some people, especially if it's a hook-up. I just feel so vulnerable and small after sharing my body with another person. It's hard to explain."

Reflection point: Past or present

Once more, feel free to ignore this reflection point if this section is just a little too much for you right now. We always want you to respect your self-consent first and foremost!

If you have the capacity, take a few moments to reflect on when the past might have bled into the present for you, especially around sexual situations. Have there been times when you haven't been sure whether you were reacting to what was happening in that moment, or to something from the past? Have there been times when your own emotions and responses to a situation have felt confusing, or out of control? Have you experienced being really turned on, and wanting to engage with someone sexually, and then feeling suddenly shutdown, angry, or scared, even though there did not seem to be an immediate reason for it? It can be challenging to consider those questions, so please take the time you need, be gentle with yourself, and do this with a trusted person or people, if that feels more supportive, or even leave this reflection point and read on instead.

We'll come back to learning how to treat yourself consensually in the next chapter, and how to ensure consensual sex and relationships—including in relation to trauma—in Chapter 6. For now, here's a slow-down page describing a bodily technique which can be helpful for this.

Let's breathe, for as long as you need...

Really, take your time, there is no
need to rush through.

Then, think about an activity that you usually
find particularly nourishing and supportive,
which you could do right now.

Then be as still as you're able for a
few moments and ask yourself:
"Do I want to do this activity right now?"

Keep listening until you get an
answer: yes, no, or maybe.
(Try to not overthink it, if you can!)

What sensations, thoughts, emotions,
images, reactions, or stories have emerged
within yourself that let you know whether
your answer is yes, no, or maybe?

Pay attention to how you know the answer, and even jot down what you notice, if you want to.

If the answer was no or maybe, you can try to consider a different nourishing or supporting activity until you feel a full yes. (Pay attention to how you know it's a yes!)

You can do this exercise with as many activities as you like until you have a clear, embodied sense of your yes, no, and maybe.

You can also use food, or colors, or smells if some activities don't work so well for you. Just use something that gives you a range of responses!

4.4 LOCATING YOURSELF IN THE LANDSCAPE OF SEXUALITY

Now that we've explored the influences on your current sexuality in more depth, let's consider where you might locate yourself in the vast landscape of sexuality. After this, Chapter 5 will go into more depth about how you might relate to the various aspects of this.

In Chapter 2, we briefly introduced the sexual configurations theory of feminist scientist Sari Van Anders. In this section, we'll draw on her ideas, and others, to consider some of the main areas of the sexuality landscape and to help you map where you would locate yourself in these, if anywhere. If you want to learn more about Van Anders' theory, and how you might apply it to yourself, we wrote a whole zine about it with her, beautifully illustrated by Jules Scheele (who also draws the covers for these books). We've included that in the further resources at the end of this chapter.

Four zones of the sexuality landscape

As we mentioned before, Van Anders suggests that we can divide sexuality into four zones, like this:

	Erotic	Nurturant
Solo	Solo erotic	Solo nurturant
Partnered	Partnered erotic	Partnered nurturant

— *Solo erotic* includes the things we find attractive and desirable erotically with ourselves, or to fantasize, read about, watch, and so on. For example, this might include enjoying imagining group sex in a sauna, lying naked in a patch of sunlight, or using a vibrator on your genitals while looking at pictures of a particular celebrity. Remember that "erotic" can encompass experiences beyond what we usually define as sexual.

— *Partnered erotic* includes the things we find attractive and desirable erotically with others. For example, this might include enjoying slow PIV sex with lots of eye contact, having kinky threesomes with strangers, or getting a sensual massage.

— *Solo nurturant* is one people don't often think about. It includes the things we find nurturing, caring, loving, or romantic with ourselves. For example, this might include making yourself a delicious meal, stroking or cuddling yourself, or talking gently to yourself when you're having a hard time. The concept of being plural rather than singular can help with this, which we'll introduce at the end of the next chapter.

— *Partnered nurturant* includes the things we find nurturing, intimate, close, or romantic with others. For example, this might include snuggling up with the folks you live with to watch your favorite TV show, taking someone on a date, or having a deep conversation.

All of the spectrums of sexuality that we'll consider in the rest of this section can apply to each of these zones. For example, the ace spectrum applies to them all, as it's possible to be asexual, aromantic, both, or neither. Asexual people may not relate to the erotic zones and aromantic people may not relate to the nurturant zones. Some people who are asexual are solo-sexual but not sexual with partners; some who are aromantic are romantic in relation with themselves but not with others; and some ace and aro people are not sexual or romantic with themselves either.

Similarly, people can define as bisexual, or biromantic, or both, if they experience erotic and/or nurturant attraction with people of more than one gender. In each case, this could differ in relation to solo and partnered interest, or not. For example, a person might be attracted to people of more than one gender, but only fantasize about people of a specific gender.

There may be nuances within each zone, as well, of course. For example, we might have different erotic attractions in terms of the kind of people we like to flirt with, hook up with, or form longer-term sexual relationships with, and what we like to do in those contexts. We might look to different people for different forms of nurturance (e.g. listening, hugging, advice giving, or practical support).

Questions to ask of each spectrum

Before we go on to the spectrums themselves, there are some useful questions you can ask about each one, which we'll repeat under each set of spectrums we give you.

First you can ask whether this spectrum is relevant to you at all. If it's not, feel free to leave it out. For example, if gender of real/imagined partners is irrelevant to you, you may want to leave out the spectrums relating to gender entirely.

Next, it may be that you're in a very specific place on this spectrum, or it may be that you encompass the whole thing, or somewhere in between. For example, some people like all kinds of sex from "vanilla" through to full-on kink, while others are all about one end of this spectrum, or a specific place in the middle. For a broad range, you could put Xs all the way along the spectrum; for specific, just one X.

Next, these three questions can help you dig into each spectrum in even more depth:

— How fixed or fluid are you on this one? Remember that some people experience their sexuality as more stable, others as more changing over time, and this can differ for different aspects.

— How close or far are you from the cultural norms on this one? It's always useful to locate yourself in relation to the assumed cultural norms, to recognize whether you experience marginalization and/or oppression in relation to this aspect of your sexuality.

— Does your current status match your place on this spectrum? It can be helpful to consider whether your life right now enables you to experience your sexuality in the way it's represented here, or not. For example, if you'd like multiple partners but you're currently single, monogamous, or with just one polyamorous partner.

Multiple spectrums

Enough preamble, let's get to some spectrums! If you experience sexual attraction and/or desire, we'd suggest doing this for the partnered erotic zone initially—so consider each spectrum in relation to the people you find sexually attractive and your desires in relation to partnered forms of sex.

You could then go through the list again, perhaps with a different color pen, for the solo erotic, partnered nurturant, and solo nurturant zones, to see whether your answers for those align or differ. Remember that for the solo ones it would be about both what you enjoy doing with yourself, and in your imagination, or in any sexual media you engage with (so the spectrums about other people may still be relevant).

ACTIVITY: YOUR SPECTRUMS

Put a cross—or multiple crosses—on the following spectrums for where you feel right now in relation to your sexuality, reflect on the questions, and make any notes.

Of course, as we saw in Chapter 2, spectrums are never a perfect way of capturing these things because there are often more possibilities than the two ends of these spectrums. Feel free to put question marks rather than crosses for any you're uncertain about, to scribble out our suggestions and replace them with ones that are more relevant to you, and to add your own further dimensions to fit your experiences better. We're just doing the best we can here, given the restrictions of a two-dimensional page, but really we'd need to work in a multi-dimensional space to fully map the complexity of the sexuality landscape!

How much attraction/desire do you experience?

None ——————————————————————— High

— How fixed or fluid is this?

— How close or far does this put you from cultural norms?

— Does your current status match your place on this spectrum?

— Any further notes?

What number of partners would you prefer?

None ———————————————————————— Many

— If more than one, would this be at the same time, or separately?

— How fixed or fluid is this?

— How close or far does this put you from cultural norms?

— Does your current status match your place on this spectrum?

— Any further notes?

What's your gender preference?

Women ———————————————————— Men

Gender normative ———————————— Gender expansive

Feminine ——————————————————— Masculine

Trans ———————————————————————— Cis

— How fixed or fluid are these?

— How close or far do they put you from cultural norms?

— Does your current status match your place on these spectrums?

— Any further notes?

What roles do you like to take?

Passive ———————————————————— Active
Receptive ———————————————————— Penetrating
One who follows ———————————— One who initiates
Submissive ———————————————————— Dominant

- — How fixed or fluid are these?

- — How close or far do they put you from cultural norms?

- — Does your current status match your place on these spectrums?

- — Any further notes?

How often, and for how long, do you want to engage?

Never ———————————————— Several times a day
Quickies ———————————————————— Long sessions

- — How fixed or fluid is this?

- — How close or far does this put you from cultural norms?

- — Does your current status match your place on this spectrum?

- — Any further notes?

What kind of desires do you have?

Vanilla ———————————————————— Kinky
Enjoy watching ———————————— Enjoy being watched
Light sensations ———————————— Intense sensations
Gentle contact ———————————— Rough contact
. . . . ———————————— . . . .

— How fixed or fluid are these?

— How close or far do they put you from cultural norms?

— Does your current status match your place on these spectrums?

— Any further notes?

What kind of dynamics do you like?

Kind/loving ————————————————— Aggressive/harsh

Casual ————————————————— Serious relationship

I'm more experienced ————— They're more experienced

We're very similar ————————— We're very different

· · · · · · · · · · · · · · ————————————— · · · · · · · · · · · · · ·

— How fixed or fluid are these?

— How close or far do they put you from cultural norms?

— Does your current status match your place on these spectrums?

— Any further notes?

Add your own spectrums here, for others that are important to you, such as other aspects of appearance, character, relationship, and activity.

· · · · · · · · · · · · · · ————————————— · · · · · · · · · · · · · ·

· · · · · · · · · · · · · · ————————————— · · · · · · · · · · · · · ·

· · · · · · · · · · · · · · ————————————— · · · · · · · · · · · · · ·

· · · · · · · · · · · · · · ————————————— · · · · · · · · · · · · · ·

— How fixed or fluid are these?

— How close or far do they put you from cultural norms?

— Does your current status match your place on these spectrums?

— Any further notes?

Reflection point: The relationship between the spectrums

Reflect on the relationship between where you are on these different spectrums. Do they seem to come together in alignment to form quite a coherent map, or are they quite contradictory and diverse? As with all aspects of sexuality, neither of these is better or worse than the other. You might also like to reflect on whether, and how, they relate to any of the other intersecting aspects of your experience we introduced in section 4.2, such as your age, race, class, or disability.

Don't worry if you weren't sure about your place on all of these spectrums yet! In the next chapter, you'll have the opportunity to dig much deeper into your body and relationship with other bodies, your desires, your practices, and your identities.

REMEMBER: Our sexual landscape is constantly unfolding in front of us as we continue to explore it. It's a work in progress rather than something we could ever map out entirely. It will continue to shift and change as long as our bodies grow and age, we learn and have new experiences, and the world around us alters.

It's fine to have areas that you haven't mapped out yet, or that you're not ready to map out yet. Go slowly and gently with this stuff. Trust your sense of "not this" or "not ready," if you feel it. You can always return to something later, and you don't have to go anywhere you don't want to.

FURTHER RESOURCES

You can read Meg-John's chapter on self-pleasure groups, mentioned here, in:

- Barker, M-J. (2019). "What Could Non-Binary Love Look Like?" In F. Benson (ed.) *Trans Love* (pp.102–120). London: Jessica Kingsley.

The great consent organizations which Meg-John also mentioned are:

- Consent Culture: https://consentculture.com, https://consentculture.co.uk

- The Consent Collective: www.consentcollective.com

Here are a couple of resources on sexuality from an intersectional perspective:

- Taylor, Y., Hines, S. and Casey, M. (eds) (2010). *Theorizing Intersectionality and Sexuality*. Basingstoke: Palgrave Macmillan.

- Jónasdóttir, A.G. (ed.) (2012). *Sexuality, Gender and Power: Intersectional and Transnational Perspectives*. London: Routledge.

In addition to the trauma resources we included at the end of the previous chapter, you might find the following useful:

- Haines, S. and Poo, A-J. (2019). *The Politics of Trauma: Somatics, Healing, and Social Justice.* Berkeley, CA: North Atlantic Books.
- Kain, K.L. and Terrell, S.J. (2018). *Nurturing Resilience: Helping Clients Move Forward from Developmental Trauma.* Berkeley, CA: North Atlantic Books.
- Walker, P. (2013). *Complex PTSD: From Surviving to Thriving.* CreateSpace Independent Publishing Platform.

You can listen to Alex talking about complex PTSD on their podcast, Gender Stories:

- https://genderstories.buzzsprout.com/156032/1326742-complex-ptsd

And Meg-John has written a number of blog posts about trauma at:

- https://rewriting-the-rules.com/?s=trauma

We love Love Uncommon's approach to learning self-consent on their website, and they also have lots of great material about trauma, boundaries, and feelings:

- https://loveuncommon.com/2017/09/28/self-consent

The zine that we wrote about Sari Van Anders' theory is here:

- Iantaffi, A., Barker, M-J., van Anders, S. and Scheele, J. (2018). Mapping your sexuality: From sexual orientation to sexual configurations theory. Available at https://rewriting-the-rules.com/wp-content/uploads/2018/08/MappingYourSexuality.pdf

CHAPTER 5

LIVING YOUR SEXUALITY

In this chapter, we'll go more in depth about the different features of your sexuality. We'll start with sexual bodies, which encompasses your sense of your own sexual attractiveness, who you're attracted to, and what you're aroused by. We unpack how this is impacted by the kinds of trauma patterns and cultural norms that we've mentioned previously.

After that, we'll spend some time exploring how you can tune into your sexual desires—if you have them—and what you might want to think about if you're considering acting on those desires in practice.

Finally, we'll return to the question of sexual identities. What does it open up, and close down, to identify aspects of our sexual attractions, desires, and practices with the kinds of words we introduced back in Chapter 1? How might we capture the multiplicity and complexity of our sexuality in words, if we want to?

5.1 SEXUAL BODIES

In Chapter 3, we started using the term "bodymind," from the field of disability studies, to challenge the separation between mind and body, which is so embedded in Anglo and western-dominant cultures (something we explore in our other books *How to Understand Your Gender* and *Life Isn't Binary*).

Here, we focus on the bodymind in relation to sexuality. We begin from the foundational understanding that our mind and body are not separate, and are in a relational dynamic with one another. After all, our brain is made of physical matter, as is our whole nervous system! They're located within our body and are part of the complex communication systems that govern our voluntary and involuntary physical responses, hence the more accurate term "bodymind."

Understanding our bodymind

The separation between mind and body, however, is part of dominant discourses in both the UK and the US, where we live. A big part of the reason for this is that we live under neo-liberal capitalism regimes, which profit from this separation. What do we mean by this? If the body and mind are viewed as separate, and the mind is viewed as inherently superior to the body, then it's easier to promote the ideas that:

— our minds can override our bodies

— our bodies are commodities we "own" and "use."

Let's unpack this a little bit more before moving on. Think for a moment about the advertisements you might have seen on TV selling medication to get rid of a cold, or even a flu, as quickly as possible so that you can return to being "productive." Anglo-dominant discourses usually highlight productivity. The ability to work as much as possible becomes a moral value, which is very consistent with Protestant ethics.

The common English expression "mind over matter" also highlights how we're expected to understand the mind as superior to the body. The implication is that, if we're strong and trained well enough, we should be able to govern our bodies through our minds. This is simply not true. However, if we believe it to be true, then our bodies can be viewed as just "instruments" that do the bidding of the superior mind. This means that we can override our capacity in service to capitalist productivity, as well as being likely to buy more products to enhance our physical capacity, whether that's caffeinated drinks, gym memberships, self-improvement books, classes, or Viagra.

You might notice that you have a reaction to reading this. If you do, that's okay. The belief that our minds are superior to our bodies is strongly embedded in many western cultures. We think it's a harmful belief, especially given all that we know from interpersonal neurobiology, as well as from much older Indigenous and global wisdom—especially from Asian traditions, such as Buddhism, that have long promoted non-dualism—which doesn't separate mind and body.

Let's go back to the four Fs of survival described in section 4.3. Those responses cannot be overridden by logical thinking when we're already experiencing them. This would not be efficient for our survival! We can, of course, challenge the beliefs that come from our trauma brain, or we can steer away from them if we see them coming, when there is no actual danger present. If we're in danger—real or perceived—the limbic system, responsible for fight, flight, or freeze (fawn works a little differently), kicks into action to keep us safe, and there's no amount of thinking, or level of skills, that can override it.

The limbic system not only governs three of the four Fs, it's also responsible for emotional responses, long-term memory, hormonal regulation, the sleep/wake cycle (circadian rhythms), and sexual arousal responses. This means that our responses to sexual stimuli are not under the control of our prefrontal cortex—or logical thought. This is why we might experience arousal even when what's happening is not what we want, as we mentioned in Chapter 1.

We feel it's important to name this again here because many survivors feel a great deal of shame if they have experienced any arousal when being abused or raped, or later when remembering those experiences or imagining similar ones. These responses are not under our logical, rational control. However, because we're continuously told that we *are* in control of our bodies, when we experience something out of our control, such as arousal or trauma responses, we can blame ourselves for it, instead of understanding that this is part of involuntary physiological responses, just like breathing and our hearts beating.

The bodymind and sexual responses

In both of the places where we live—the US and the UK—dominant discourses actively encourage constant monitoring and control of our bodies, on both individual and systemic levels. We'll start with the individual and then move on to the systemic, although it's important to remember that these can never be truly separated (another important element of non-dualism).

Even though sexual arousal is governed by areas in the temporal lobe, including the hypothalamus, which are not under the governance of the frontal lobe, dominant discourses would have us believe that we should be in perfect control of our bodies, including arousal. People often experience shame about non-sexual involuntary responses too, such as how frequently they need to urinate or defecate, their hunger, stomach noises, and so on. Given that sexuality isn't part of everyday conversations in many households, and the poor sex education that most of us experience, it's not surprising that many of us experience shame when dealing with sexual responses in our bodyminds.

Sexual stimuli might come from a range of sources. We may become aroused when in nature—swimming or watching the sunrise—when near someone who smells "just right," when looking at ourselves in the mirror, when listening to music that moves us, when watching a certain dynamic play out on a TV show, or when experiencing the pleasurable sensation of our clothes against our body. What we consider attractive or pleasurable can vary greatly, and this includes the realm of sexuality.

We might feel confused, upset, or even ashamed if what we find pleasurable or attractive doesn't fall within dominant cultural and societal expectations, because we've been told that our bodies are under the control of our minds. However, because humans are biopsychosocial, the body and the mind are actually in constant conversation, in an ongoing relationship that is complex and interdependent. This is where things get tricky.

As we've mentioned before, some research has found that our visual diet—that is the media that we engage with—can have a great influence on what we find attractive within ourselves and others. Does this mean that the mind is in control of the body then? Not really. It means that there's an active relationship between what we're told to find attractive and what we find attractive, or not. However, this is only a part of it.

We're far more complicated than one single research study can account for, and, no matter how hard the dominant neoliberal and capitalist discourses try to influence us, we respond to whichever stimuli we find arousing, whether they're considered socially acceptable or not! If this sounds paradoxical, it's because a biopsychosocial model doesn't fit well with either/or dualistic thinking.

It is not that either the body *or* mind is responsible for our sexual responses, including attraction and arousal, it's that the body *and* mind, together, are responsible, in relationship. Erotic pleasure is a whole bodymind experience. Experiencing arousal or pleasure does not mean that we necessarily want—or need—to engage with it, either by ourselves, or with other people. Our sensory, emotional, physiological experiences and responses are separate from our behaviors.

Multiple experiences: Our sexual bodymind

"I've always loved being naked. When I was little, I would loudly announce 'naked time' before bath! Nothing much has changed. I've been a nudist since I found out that was an option. After I was raped, on the way back from work last year, I thought that might change, but I found that having a familiar, non-sexual space where I could be naked was actually really healing for me."

"I'm super conscious of the way I smell. My first sexual partner commented on the smell of my genitals often, and made me shower before sex. I realize now that was abusive and not okay, on so many levels."

"I'm quite attractive by conventional beauty standards. I wish I wasn't, to be honest. Men come on to me a lot when I'm out with my mates. As a young gay man, I'm expected to be up for it, and be happy with all the sexual attention, but I'm ace and I just want to enjoy myself when I'm out and not get groped on the dance floor."

"I love play spaces that are just for Black folks and people of color. I can bring the whole of myself then, without having to navigate all the racism in the kink community, including how many comments I get by clueless white people about my light eyes and dark skin. I just want to be able to get off on what I enjoy: sensation and pain play."

"I love my job most of the time. I don't like how some of my potential clients comment on my body as if I were a piece of meat with no feelings because I'm a sex worker. I have a hard enough time with dysphoria and being a fat trans woman in my everyday life. I don't need random strangers commenting on my 'flaws' on the internet."

"I feel most connected to my body when I masturbate. I take my time and I've been exploring all the things that turn me on: touch, toys, smells, textures, sounds, even food. It's so fun and playful for me."

Bodymind, sexuality, and social landscapes

Let's think more about how the ways in which the social arena—or the wider systems in which we're embedded—relate to how we understand and experience our bodymind when it comes to sexuality.

We've mentioned that what we find attractive in our own and other people's bodies, and indeed minds, is influenced by what dominant discourses show us as being attractive. This is, of course, not neutral. The ways in which our bodies are gendered, racialized, classed, and categorized in relation to polarities such as healthy/sick, normal/abnormal, young/old, and so on usually determines the erotic capital that we have in the current social landscape in which we live. Erotic capital is the value that we have, as individuals or groups, on a social level, and it's determined by what is deemed sexually attractive according to dominant cultural norms.

Where we live, for example, Black and Brown bodies are exoticized and hypersexualized in dominant discourses, yet white bodies still have higher erotic capital and they're depicted as the dominant standard of beauty. Race, gender, size, disability status, and class cannot be neatly separated from one another when considering culturally dominant beauty standards.

To give one illustration of this, fatphobia is highly prevalent in Anglo- and western-dominant cultures. This includes the interrelated—highly damaging—myths that fatness is unattractive, unhealthy, and a sign of some kind of moral inferiority, as well as the commonly held belief that people should restrict their food intake and engage in a variety of physical practices in order to obtain and maintain thin bodies. Fatphobia is deeply rooted in anti-Blackness. Larger bodies were considered attractive in most western cultures until around the 18th century. At this point, linked to the ongoing transatlantic slave trade, racial categories begun to be redrawn to ensure that there was a more solid line between Blackness and whiteness. Fatness started to be equated with lack of self-control, lower levels of rationality, and as being less moral than thinness.

Protestant Anglo ethics viewed "the flesh" as mortal and sinful, so control and moderation around food and sex were promoted as superior. Given that fatness had been equated with lack of moderation and self-control, fat people were viewed as less moral, and also more highly—or problematically—sexual. Measures of size, such as the BMI (body mass index) were normed on white Anglo bodies, making it clear that white bodies are the standard for a number of things: health, morality, and attractiveness.

These issues are, of course, also inseparable from issues of class, disability, gender, age, and more. For example, fatness is read very differently on bodies gendered as male or female. There are highly classed stereotypes about fat people, similar to those around disabled people, as lazy or "scroungers." Please check out the further resources at the end of this chapter if you'd like to dig deeper into this topic. Of course, there are many other examples we could give to illustrate how erotic capital works, and how it is unjustly distributed.

Reflection point: Dominant discourses of sexual attractiveness and you

You might want to take a moment here to reflect on the ways in which these kinds of dominant discourses around sexual attractiveness and systems of erotic capital impact you, and how your various intersections come into play here. As always, please go gently as our relationship with our body and sense of attractiveness are loaded topics for most of us in a culture which puts such emphasis on physical appearance, and has such narrow standards for what is deemed attractive.

We just want to touch on one more thing before inviting you to engage with an activity. We're aware that all of our relationships with our bodymind are complex and heavily influenced by internal and external forces. This means that we might well struggle to be in touch, or present, with our body. It might mean that we don't even believe that we have a body, and that we truly think that our minds are what matters. If the bodymind model doesn't fit for you right now, that's okay.

We have centuries of ongoing colonialism, including Christian proselytism, racism, cisgenderism, and patriarchy to contend with. Whether you experience euphoria (that is unbridled joy in your bodymind), dysphoria (dissonance between body and mind), dysmorphia (distortion of your physical self-perception), or anything else, we hope that you find something interesting in this section and—if not—that you can focus on what works for you.

ACTIVITY: MAPPING OUR BODYMIND

For this activity, you need some paper, pen or pencil, and even colored pencils or markers, if you have any. You might want to ask a friend to help you if you'd like to draw a life-sized body map, as you might want to lie down on the paper and ask them to trace your outline.

As you approach this activity, please remember that all activities in this book are invitations that you can decline. If you choose to engage in this activity, as ever, please do so with as much kindness, curiosity, and non-judgment as you're able to, in this moment. This can be particularly challenging when dealing with our bodymind, as being mean to ourselves is so normalized in dominant discourses. If you need to, please get support from a trusted person or group of people.

Take some time to draw a map of your body on a piece of paper, large or small, or in your journal or notebook. You can also just use the shape provided below.

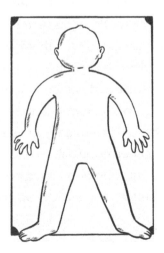

FIGURE 5.1: YOUR BODY MAP

Once you have a body shape on paper, take a few moments to think about how and where you experience erotic pleasure. For example, do you particularly enjoy feeling cool air on your skin, massaging your head, or touching or having a body part touched? Start annotating which areas of your body experience pleasure and arousal. You can do so by using different colors, shapes, words, or a combination of these. Use whatever works for you and feel free to experiment.

You might even want to create more than one map to explore different areas of pleasure, such as solo erotic or nurturing pleasures, partnered erotic or nurturing pleasures, and so on (remember section 4.4). You might also want to annotate how those pleasures change in different contexts, or how they have changed over time for you, or even create an ideal pleasure map.

Now pause and take in whichever map(s) you may have created. What do you notice in your own bodymind right now when considering the map(s) in front of you? Are there pleasure areas that you'd like to pay more or less attention to? What are the sensations, emotions, thoughts, and stories that come up when you take in your map(s)? Are there ways in which you'd like to give your bodymind more pleasure, care, or attention? If so, what would you like to do differently? Are there obstacles in the way of giving your bodymind more pleasure, care, or attention? If so, what support might you need to address these obstacles? Who might be good allies in this work? Allies could be green bloods (plants), other humans, such as therapists or support groups, ancestors, fictional characters, parts of yourself, and so on.

5.2 SEXUAL DESIRES

Now let's explore your erotic desires in more depth. In order to enjoy our sexuality fully—whatever it is—we need to know it well for ourselves, and we need to communicate it to others, whether that is those we want to be sexual or sensual with, those we get support from, or close people in our life who we need to understand us and mirror us well.

As we mentioned in Chapter 2, sadly there are many things that block our ability to be open about our desires with ourselves, and perhaps even more that block our ability to be open about them with other people. We'll say plenty about communicating about our sexuality with others in the next chapter. For now, let's focus on getting in touch with your desires and communicating with yourself.

After we've considered a little more about what blocks us in being open with ourselves about our desires, and how we might address those blocks, we'll take two different approaches to tuning into our desires. You may find that one of these works better than the other for you, or that both are helpful, or that neither works for you. For some people, the exploration needs to take a more embodied form, such as touching themselves or being touched by a partner or sexological bodyworker, for example. For others, it needs to be more relational, such as talking in a sharing circle about sexuality, with a sex therapist, or exploring with partners, friends, or hook-ups. We'll cover these kinds of options more in the next chapter.

For now, the two approaches we'll cover are creating your own personal sex manual, and tuning into your erotic fantasies. If you like these approaches, Meg-John has written a couple of zines with more suggestions about these with one of their other co-creators, Justin Hancock. The zines are listed in the further resources at the end of this chapter.

Blocks to being open with ourselves about our desires

So what blocks us from being honest with ourselves about our desires, fantasies, and turn-ons, or indeed about our absences of desire, nightmare sexual scenarios, and turn-offs?

Reflection point: Blocks

What blocks you from being open with yourself about your desires, and from tuning into what turns you on, or gives you pleasure?

Here are some common answers to this question:

— Not conforming to cultural rules about ideal, normal, or healthy desires.

— Having different kinds of desires from those my friends talk about having.

— Internalized queerphobia, acephobia, transphobia, whorephobia, or other forms of prejudice.

— Shame, if they relate to traumatic things that have happened to me.

— Not wanting to be seen as a "bad person" if my fantasies seem in opposition to my politics.

— Sadness, if they are things that I couldn't actually do in person due to physical or relationship limitations.

— Fear, if they are non-consensual desires about what this says about me, or whether I might act on them.

— Worry that my partner—or others in my life—wouldn't be okay if they knew I had these desires.

In response to these kinds of blocks we would emphasize that knowing, yourself, what your desires are does not mean that you have to share them with anybody else. We'll explore who you might want to share with, and how you might do it, in Chapter 6, but it's important to say that you never have to. Most of us have some desires that we keep to ourselves, some we share only with one person or a few people, and some which may be more generally known (for example, if we have a partner, it may generally be assumed that we're attracted to that person in some way, although of course even that isn't always the case).

However, knowing our desires ourselves actually makes us more, rather than less, likely to be able to act consensually and ethically with others and with ourselves. People often worry that acknowledging a taboo, politically questionable, or non-consensual desire will mean that they may act on it, or become somehow more oppressive in their thinking or behavior from having it. Actually, once the desire is something you're more aware of, there's more scope for you to reflect on what—if anything—you want to do about it.

Also, in a structurally non-consensual, racist, misogynist, and generally oppressive culture, we are all going to have non-consensual and oppressive thoughts and feelings sometimes, erotic or otherwise. Most of those who are engaged in social justice work emphasize that acknowledging those thoughts and feelings is an important step in anti-oppressive work, rather than repressing them or pretending to be completely non-oppressive.

Finally, people are anxious that having desires where they are treated non-consensually is a sign there is something wrong with them, or even—if they are a survivor—that it somehow means that what happened to them was their fault, or something they wanted on some level. This is absolutely not the case. As we explained in section 3.3, it is very common to eroticize the difficult and traumatic things in our lives; it can be an important form of survival, and it never means that it was in any way okay that those things happened to you.

We'll come back to how to decide which desires to act on, and how, with ourselves and others at the end of this section, and in the next chapter. For now, we'd just stress the need to balance kindness and honesty with yourself here. Kindness is essential to being open with yourself about your desires, and to not judging yourself for having them, whether that is for being "too" edgy or disturbing, or "too" boring or normative. As with all feelings, our desires are our desires, and neither we, nor others, should police or punish us for having them.

Creating your own erotic manual

One great way to tune into your desires is to create your own erotic manual, a kind of guide to you and what you're into.

This can be a living document, one which you keep adding to and editing as you learn more about yourself and change over time. You might keep it as a journal or a computer document, or make it into a zine, for example. You could even get creative and include Spotify playlists, Pinterest boards, and the like, obviously being careful about putting anything more explicit or personal out there in the online world.

You could start to build up your manual based on many of the activities in this book. For example, the river of experiences in Figure 3.6, the multiple levels of influence in Figure 4.1, and the body map you did in the previous section could all be great things to include. If making your own manual feels a little daunting, then the user guide zine in the further resources is full of activities you can just fill in. The spectrums at the end of the previous chapter also give you a lot of prompts.

Again, it's very much up to you whether you ever share this with anybody. Sharing user guides *can* be a great starting point for conversation with somebody you might be erotic with, but only if you trust the person and feel safe enough doing so.

Here are a few ideas for other things you might include in your user guide, and there are plenty more to come in the rest of the book.

Traffic lights of turn-ons

Start building up a list of your turn-ons, turn-offs, and "mehs." This can include anything: things you like thinking about, sensations you enjoy, things you find attractive in another person, practices you'd like to try, and more. They can either be words or phrases, images, or longer descriptions. You could color code them or put them in a table. You could first create a long list of all the things that somebody, somewhere might be turned on or excited by, and then read down the list and notice in your body which ones give you a feeling of excitement, aversion, or neutrality.

- Green = big turn-ons.

- Yellow = I can take it or leave it.

- Red = big turn-offs.

You might find this a helpful starting point when it comes to creating a "yes, no, maybe" list of sexual practices in the next section.

What does it mean to you?

To explore your desires in a bit more detail, you could take one of them and write a bit about what it means to you or why you find it so hot or pleasurable, if you know this. We often assume that the same sexual or sensual experience will mean the same thing to everybody, but actually they have very diverse meanings. For example, people can find orgasm powerful, vulnerable, cathartic, painful, shameful, neutral, transcendent, or irritating. People can get turned on by spanking because they like the sensation, because it feels fun and playful, because it helps them to let go of control, because it reclaims something traumatic that happened to them, or for many other reasons.

Hot dynamics

For some of us, what's exciting is not so much the activity we might do—or imagine doing—but the dynamic between the people. For example, some people would hate to orgasm except together with somebody they deeply trust. Others would only find it exciting if they were being told to do it by somebody taking a dominant role, or if they were being told *not* to do it. Similarly, some people would only enjoy spanking if it was done in a light playful way, and if they got to have a turn as spanker and spankee. For some, it would only be hot in one direction, with somebody who was kind and nurturing towards them throughout.

It can be good, in a user guide, to write more detailed descriptions of the dynamics you find exciting to imagine, or that you have enjoyed in the past.

Tuning into your erotic fantasies

Another great way of exploring your desires is through your erotic fantasies: observing what kinds of scenarios, events, and characters you imagine during solo sex; what kinds of porn or erotica you are drawn to; what fleeting erotic thoughts flash through your mind during sex or every day; what experiences you've had that you enjoy remembering; or what images or ideas stay with you from dreams, or from non-sexual media like books, movies, TV shows, and music videos.

There's no wrong or right way to fantasize. Some people don't do it at all. Some experience emotions, colors, or sensations. Some get static images or phrases. Some need external images, stories, or videos. Some run through stories or movies in their minds. All of this is okay as long as it's consensual and ethical with yourself and anybody else involved, including porn performers, and people whose images appear online. We'll come back to this at the end of the section.

Here are a few ideas for things you could reflect on about your fantasies, perhaps again towards a document, zine, or collection of brief stories. It's completely up to you if you ever share these (more on this in Chapter 6), and again you can check out the zine in the further resources if you want more prompts.

Go-to fantasies

Make a list of your go-to fantasies, erotic stories, porn clips, or similar. Perhaps give each one a brief title: "The one where I get pushed up against a wall and ravished," "The one where I'm a hobbit and Gandalf looks after me."

If you find this relatively easy, you could do a timeline of the different go-to fantasies you remember having at different ages. You could try writing one or more out in detail. If you find it more difficult, you could check out some of the collections of fantasies by authors like Nancy Friday and Emily Dubberly, or sexy stories online like those collected by Girl on the Net or on the Archive of our Own fanfiction website, and see which of other people's fantasies you find exciting.

What you get out of them

As with erotic desires, people can get different things out of fantasies or engaging with sexual media. Make a list of what it means to you. For example, it might be a way to release tension quickly, a way of connecting with others online, or a self-loving activity. You could also list what you personally find useful, and not so useful, about fantasizing.

Core erotic themes

In Chapter 3, we touched on Jack Morin's work about erotic

fantasies. He suggests that many of us have "core erotic themes" which we return to because they are meaningful to us, perhaps relating to those difficult or traumatic experiences we have eroticized. If you're finding it relatively easy to tune into your fantasies, reflect on whether any themes seem to come up regularly, or whether you're drawn to particular themes in the erotica or porn you seek out. You might also find it helpful to reflect on whether certain kinds of people (in character or appearance) crop up regularly. This links to the idea of plurality which we'll come back to towards the end of the chapter. The zine and book in the further resources give you more suggestions about how your fantasies can help you understand way more about yourself than just what turns you on. We'll return to this in Chapter 7.

Consent and ethics, desire and fantasy

When it comes to desire and fantasy there are two common schools of thought regarding consent and ethics. The first school of thought suggests that "anything goes" in the realm of desire and fantasy. It's fine to be turned on by anything you like, and to think about anything you like, so long as you only act on ones that can be done consensually and ethically (this would include only watching ethical porn, where those involved are well treated, and ensuring that you pay for it).

The other school of thought suggests that we shouldn't indulge non-consensual or oppressive fantasies, such as those drawing on things that were historically traumatic (see section 4.3) or those including misogynist or homophobic dynamics, disparity in age, and so on. The idea is that going over such narratives or images in our minds repeatedly could make us more oppressive or non-consensual ourselves. This is linked to the idea that fantasies and sexual media can be addictive, and we can end up drawn into increasingly worrying places for longer and longer periods.

In this debate we take a non-binary perspective (shocker!) along the lines of that of queer porn maker and writer Pandora Blake. They argue that these two schools of thought are a false polarization, and that we need to consider these things in a more nuanced way. They suggest that instead of an all-or-nothing approach to desires and fantasies with themes of non-consent, trauma, or injustice, we could engage intentionally with them, and in a way that involves ongoing consent with ourselves.

You could, for example, allow the fantasy and then give yourself time to reflect on what it means to you, and how it relates to wider cultural dynamics. You could plan what images you're going to look at initially and give a certain time period for it, instead of following where internet search terms lead you. You could pause several times while watching a video to check in with yourself: how you feel in your body, and whether it is going beyond what you're comfortable with. Instead of repressing your desire/fantasy, or acting it out unconsciously, you could use it as a way to learn more about yourself and your world. There is more on consent in the next chapter.

Of course, this won't prevent us from occasionally finding ourselves imagining something painful or disturbing, or stumbling across sexual media that troubles us. At such times, try to be very gentle and kind with yourself, maybe returning to the content later, after you've had a chance to self-care. If it continues to be difficult then an affirmative sex therapist can help (see Chapter 7).

5.3 SEXUAL PRACTICES

We mentioned that feeling sexually aroused, being attracted to someone, or having a particular desire does not necessarily mean acting on it. In fact, there are some things that we would never do that we might fantasize about. However, what about things we *do* want to do sexually? How do we go from desire to consensual sexual practices, with ourselves and others, if we so wish? Here we'll focus on how you can identify which sexual practices you might be interested in acting on, before we consider how to communicate this with others in the next chapter.

From desire to action

We've already shared several ideas to explore your desires, so we'll continue with the assumption that, at this point, you have an idea of at least some of your sexual desires, either from doing those activities or from existing knowledge.

There's no one way to practice our sexualities. The landscape is vast and so are the possible practices, and combination of practices! In a moment, we'll share an activity to guide you through this process, if you need a little support in figuring out your own erotic menu of possibilities. Before moving on to that, though, let's talk a little more about your felt sense of yes, no, or maybe.

Felt sense

Felt sense is a term coined by philosopher Eugene Gendlin and it means an internal sensory awareness, which is usually developed by practicing observing—and getting to know— our inner states. This highlights the relationship between our brain, nervous system, and the rest of our body, which, as we mentioned earlier, are in constant conversation with one another. Basically, it's a way of getting to know our bodymind more intimately.

There are many practices that encourage observing our inner states, and getting to know our bodymind better, including many Buddhist practices. If you already have a practice for this, please feel free to use that instead of the ones we suggest here.

No matter which practices we use, a felt sense of yes, no, or maybe helps us figure out what we want to do, what we're not sure about, and what's a definite no. This, of course, does not apply just to sexual practices. In fact, let's use a completely different example to illustrate what we mean by this.

Tuning into yes, no, maybe

Take a moment to think about three textures: one that you consider always pleasant and/or comforting, one that you find absolutely unappealing and that you try to avoid at all cost, and one that is either neutral or is sometimes pleasant, sometimes unpleasant. If textures do not work for you, you can think of food, weather, or anything else that can provide you with three examples along these lines.

Consider each of those things for a few moments, one at a time. First, sit with the thing you always consider pleasant and/or comforting. What information lets you know that this is a texture/food/weather state that you always find pleasant and/or comforting? Which sensations, images, emotions, and thoughts emerge to let you know that this is something you're likely to always say yes to, because you find it pleasant and/or comforting?

Now do the same with the other two, so that you get a clear sense of which sensations, images, emotions, and thoughts emerge with something you'd always say no to, because you find it absolutely unappealing, and something that you might say maybe to, as it may depend on a number of factors. You can repeat this exercise as many times as you like.

If you find it challenging to do this exercise, or to get a clear felt sense of yes, no, or maybe, please don't be discouraged. As we've already mentioned, in western-dominant cultures there's a deep wound of disconnect between our mind and body. You might need a little more support to figure this out, and that's okay. Try to be gentle and to view this as information, and not as a "personal failure." For some of us who resort to fawning, for example (remember those four Fs?), it can be extremely challenging, if not impossible, to figure out what we truly want, given that it wasn't safe enough for us to say yes, no, or maybe to anything growing up. If you struggle with this area, Chapter 7 provides details of the kinds of supporters who can help to guide you in these practices.

ACTIVITY: CREATING YOUR OWN EROTIC MENU

Now that you have some sense of what yes, no, or maybe feels like for you, let's consider which sexual practices you might be interested in. Take your time to create a list of sexual practices you might or might not want to try out, based on the desires you explored in the previous section. You might like to make multiple lists: one for solo and one for partnered activities; one for sex work and one for your own personal life; one for erotic and one for nurturing. You can make as many lists as you like, or just have one giant list. If you still need inspiration to identify sexual practices, you can check out lists of these practices online, such as this one by Heather Corinna and CJ Turett on the Scarleteen website (see further resources).

Write each activity on its own line, just like a shopping list, and leave enough space by each activity to write yes, no, or maybe. You might even want to leave a little more space so that you can jot down some other relevant information (such as details of how you'd like to do it, or contexts in which it would feel good). We'll come back to this in the following chapter to discuss if and when you might want to share this list with others.

Safety and sexual practices

One of the things that may come up for you, as you begin to consider which sexual practices you'd be interested in trying out or not, is the issue of safety. This can take many forms. For example, which sexual practices are safe in terms of infection transmission, what circumstances we find socially, physically, and/or emotionally safe, and so on. We'll do our best to address different aspects of safety, when it comes to sexual practices, but please know that this is not definitive and there may be many more aspects relevant to you that we've not considered here.

First of all, let's challenge the idea that we can ever be perfectly safe. Very few things, if any, in our lives can be considered 100 percent safe. However, we can certainly assess what is more or less safe for us. This is one of the reasons why most educators have shifted from *safe* to *safer* sex in their terminology.

Whether we consider sexual acts and/or relational dynamics, what is safer for us is dependent on a number of factors such as our gender, age, class, disability, and the ways in which our bodies are racialized. Remember, we are biopsychosocial, so our safety, when it comes to sexual practices, reflects all of these aspects.

When thinking about safety and sexual practices, you might want to consider these three aspects, based on the biopsychosocial model of sexuality:

- physical safety

- psychological/emotional safety

- social safety.

The kinds of sex education books that we shared at the end of Chapter 3 can be really helpful if you're trying to figure out what is safer for your own sexual practices. If this is something you haven't thought of before, we encourage you to start with some of the sex education books for younger children, such as *Sex is a Funny Word* by Cory Silverberg. These can be very helpful for those of us who did not receive much, if any, sex education growing up.

When considering physical safety, you might need to learn more about anatomy, sexually transmitted infections, the current risk of other infections, and the potential impact of them on your particular body, and so on. Like we said, no practice can be 100 percent safe, but you can figure out what is safe enough for you and your partners, if other people are relevant to your practices. Even practices like solo sex, which are often thought of as completely safe, need consideration. Plenty of people have put things that are not safe in their genitals, such as glass, porous stones, or lubricants with harmful components. Some people use toys for masturbating and this may or may not be legal where you live, which is relevant to social safety. Toys are also made with a wide range of materials, and some of them are toxic. Please take time to gather as much information as you need when considering safety, knowing that it's okay to keep learning and looking for trustworthy and relevant resources. As with the example of toys, different aspects of safety cannot always be neatly separated. It's worth considering all three aspects whenever assessing the level of safety for a sexual practice.

Psychological/emotional safety is both highly individual and closely connected to our own intergenerational patterns around sexuality, as well as our geopolitical, social, and cultural contexts. It can be tricky to assess this aspect of safety, especially if we have never considered it before. The yes, no, or maybe list you considered earlier can be helpful here. Do any of the sexual practices listed bring up an emotional reaction? If so, you might want to start from these activities, given that emotions are often easier to access when more intense. What does this emotional reaction tell you about whether those practices feel safe enough to you, or not, at least right now? This aspect of safety can also be closely connected to trauma—individual and collective—although we'd argue that we can never neatly separate the two. So take good care when addressing this, be gentle and kind with yourself, and seek support if you need to.

Social safety is very dependent on our intersections, as explored in sections 3.2 and 4.2. You might want to go back to activities and information from these sections and cross-reference them with your list of sexual practices. What is relatively safe or not for us socially is deeply dependent on how who we are is viewed in dominant discourse. Social safety includes learning what's legal or not when it comes to sexual practices where you live.

We want to highlight here that there is a difference between what is ethical and what is legal. Things that we might consider unethical could be legal where you live, and vice versa. For many of us with marginalized identities and experiences, it can be particularly important to be informed about what's legal where we live, given that this could easily be used against us. For example, if you like masturbating in nature, or walking around your house naked, could you risk being listed as a sex offender if somebody called the police on you? As well as being able to reflect on our own intersections, identities, and experiences, we want to be aware of how dominant discourse controls sexual practices in the legal realm, if we are to make informed decisions about our safety.

Reflection point: Boundaries and safety

When considering safety, in all its aspects, we're usually also identifying our own boundaries. Where is the line between the risk we would take and the risk we would not take? Make time to think about your own boundaries when it comes to sexual practices and safety. What are your physical boundaries around sexual practices and safety? For example, are permanent marks on your body acceptable or not? What are your psychological and emotional boundaries? What actions (your own and other people's) and environments help you feel safe? What are your social boundaries? Would you risk being persecuted legally for practicing your sexuality or not? If anyone disclosed your sexual practices to others, would that be and feel safe for you? Remember that safety is always relative; however, you get to have your own boundaries around what feels safe for you or not, knowing that these might change throughout your life, or in different circumstances.

Multiple experiences: Practicing our sexualities

"For a long time, I felt as if there was something wrong with me because I'm definitely not interested in penetrative sex. As a cis man I'm supposed to want it and enjoy it. Now I have a partner who is really accepting of the fact that oral sex is my main partnered sexual practice. We both enjoy it and I don't feel pressured to perform in other ways."

"I really like cuddling and occasionally enjoy parallel masturbation with others. People assume that, because I'm ace, I don't have a sex life and they're surprised if they find out I went to a sex party. They don't get that I love cuddle parties, some forms of sensation play, and even enjoy watching other people have sex sometimes."

"I consider trees my main sexual partners. I love going outside and sitting with a tree, connecting. As I breathe, I know we're in a mutually beneficial relationship: they take in carbon dioxide to nourish themselves, and I take in oxygen to nourish myself. I love sitting with my back to trees, or hugging them, or lying down next to them to just be there, breathing together. That's the sexiest thing for me."

"I prefer having sex with other trans and/or non-binary people. It's easier for me as I don't feel I need to explain when I'm feeling dysphoric or not. I love getting fucked in my front hole but when I say that to cis men, I feel they look at me differently, and sometimes they misgender me because of it. So I just stick to fucking with other trans people and keep it simple."

"I have different sexual and safety practices for my sex work and my everyday sex life. With clients, I'm clear that my boundaries are no contact with my genitals, only me touching theirs, and more general erotic massage. Also, I ensure that I have a buddy who knows where I am and checks in afterwards. With my partners, I'm all about genital contact, and we all use condoms and get regularly tested."

"My sex life is entirely with myself, so you might assume I don't have to think about practice and safety much. Actually, I found it really helped to apply the concept of safer sex to my solo sex life. I realized I was very goal-oriented towards coming, and sometimes felt bad if I couldn't come. Taking the pressure off orgasm and just enjoying my body felt way better. Also, I tended to do pretty much the same thing every time, which got a bit dull. Now I include different vibrators, sometimes anal penetration, really tuning into what I fancy each time. Finally, I would always get on with my day quickly afterwards. Now I ensure I give myself the same kind of afterglow time that people often do in partnered sex."

Let's take a little break.

It can be a lot to think about our bodymind,
desires, and things we might want to do sexually.

Take all the time you need to slow down.

If you want to, you could try this activity to help
you connect with yourself in a pleasant way.

If you can, be outside for this activity, but don't
worry if you're not able to do that right now.

Take your time to connect with an element
around you, that might be the air we breathe,
water, the warmth of a fire, or a plant,
tree, or the soil underneath your feet.

Choose an element that seems pleasant and
easy to connect with for you, in this moment.

Once you have chosen an element,
take your time to experience it.

If it's air, for example, how does air feel going
into your body as you breathe in, and out as
you exhale? If you're outside, can you sense
air all around you, touching your skin?

Take all the time you want to connect
with the element you chose, or to repeat
this exercise with another element.

Make sure you've chosen something that
feels pleasant, comforting. or neutral.

Then, when you're ready, come back
to this book, and read on...

5.4 IDENTIFYING OUR SEXUALITIES

In addition to considering which sexual practices you might engage with, once you've got a sense of what your erotic desires are, this opens up the possibility of identifying accordingly. What we mean by identifying our sexualities is giving them a label through which we understand them, and can perhaps describe them to others.

So, for example, if you recognize that you rarely experience sexual attraction, or only under certain circumstances, you could just acknowledge this aspect of your experience, or you could consider identifying somewhere on the ace spectrum, perhaps as gray-A or demisexual. If you realize that you have erotic fantasies about people of more than one gender, you could explore whether a bi, pan, or queer identity label feels right to you. If you find that you enjoy practices involving strong sensations and power exchange, you could consider a kink identity, or delve deeper into whether you're a submissive or a dominant, a masochist or a sadist, a switch, a service top, a bratty bottom, or any number of further options.

There are heated debates both in sexuality studies, and in LGBTQ+ activism, about the value—or otherwise—of identifying our sexualities, genders, or other aspects of our experience with labels or categories.

Certainly not everybody across time and place has identified their sexuality in these ways, as we saw in Chapter 2. Up until quite recently in Anglo and western cultures, sexuality was more about the kinds of sex that you had, than it was about you as an individual. The idea of having an individual identity, which makes us a certain kind of self, is linked to the neoliberal capitalist model we discussed in section 4.1, so there are certainly good reasons for questioning it. For example, acknowledging gayness as an identity, and a gay man as a type of person, brings with it marketing to the "pink pound," the sense of what it means to be the kind of "good gay citizen" who is acceptable to the heteronormative world, and a lot of policing of what it means to be a successful gay man on the "gay scene," which—at its worst—involves body shaming and privileging of "straight-acting" guys.

We might also recognize that generally those expected to label their sexuality, and come out about it, are those who deviate from the assumed cultural norm, sometimes even employing labels which have been used in the past to categorize them as abnormal. So we might question the idea of identifying strongly with any sexuality, given that this can be seen as part of a rather individualistic culture that's not very good for us. Queer theorists also argue that identifying with a sexuality is a problem because it implies that our sexuality is a fixed, unchanging, essential part of who we are.

However, scholars like Gayatri Chakravorty Spivak have pointed out the importance of identity in battling for rights in a world which is currently very identity-based. LGBTQ+ rights have historically been fought for on the basis of being oppressed identities, and we now have much greater sexual equality in many areas. Spivak suggests that, for marginalized people, it's often necessary to obscure the inevitable differences between us and to present a united front, in order to gain rights in a way that the wider world understands.

**Reflection point: Closing
down and opening up**

Let's get more personal and think about this from a
non-binary perspective. Pick a sexuality identity term
that you use, or might consider using. Rather than trying
to decide whether it is right or wrong for you to use this
term, think about what using this word might open up
for you and what it might close down. What things might
expand or become more possible if you start using this
word yourself, or with other people? What things might
get constricted or feel less possible?

What does identifying our sexuality close down? What does it open up?

Here are two examples of people thinking through what
sexual identity labels open up and close down for them.

Claiming the label "bi" was really important to me. As
soon as I did so, a whole world of bi community opened
up for me. I realized that there were people out there
talking about the things I'd always thought were "just me,"
like my mates being excited when I was dating a guy, but
not when I was dating a girl, and feeling frustrated at the
terrible bi characters on TV shows. I felt like I'd found
my people. When I attended a bi event though, I was
disappointed. It seemed like everyone there was middle
class. Plus, people seemed very focused on getting off with
each other. Feeling left out hit harder because I thought

I'd found where I belonged. I feel more at home now in lefty politics and there most of us use the word "queer" instead. I do use "bi" when talking with politicians about our rights though.

I felt so ashamed about watching so much porn, especially after my girlfriend found out. Realizing that there's a thing called a "sex addict," which I might be, was a huge relief. It was something she could understand, and it wasn't my fault. Also, I could find a support group of people who really got how tough it is. I'm anxious though that now I say I'm a sex addict I'll be stuck with that for life. Also, I'm not sure I buy all of the things we have to do in our group. Like maybe it can be okay to enjoy porn if it isn't taking over your whole life, rather than having to completely abstain from it.

A bit of politics

There are political issues involved here of course, around who gets to define themselves as queer, ace, a sex worker, and so on. It would not be respectful of all of the people who have suffered greatly through being marginalized in relation to their sexuality, if a whole bunch of folk suddenly started claiming those identities who've really never had to struggle in the ways those people have, living in such a queerphobic, acephobic, whorephobic world. For example, there have been debates about people adding terms like "sapiosexual" to the list of queer sexualities, given that nobody is marginalized or oppressed for being attracted to intelligence. Also, there are similar issues around the cultural norms of what is deemed "intelligent" as there are with the cultural norms of "physical attractiveness" that we discussed at the start of this chapter.

However, politically, there can be something valuable about expanding the categories of queer, kinky, or sexually non-monogamous, for example, until so many people fit into them that we're clearly talking about majorities rather than minorities. A lot of LGBTQ+ rights have been fought for, over the years, on the basis of being an oppressed minority that deserves equal rights. Some of that has been immensely helpful, of course. But there are limitations on what can be achieved if we present ourselves as a small group outside the norm who are different in this one way but just as normal as everybody else is really. Sometimes it may be more radical to point out the following:

— Most people shift in their sexuality, in some way, over time.

— If you add together all of the people who are attracted to the same gender, or more than one gender, at some point, who experience periods of no sexual attraction, who have some kinky fantasies or practices, and whose relationships are sexually non-monogamous some or all of the time, then suddenly heterosexual, allosexual, non-kinky, monogamous people are the ones who seem pretty rare!

— Most people fall off the cultural expectations of a heteronormative life course at some point in their lives, even if they are not queer as in same-gender attracted. For example, those who choose not to marry or have kids, those whose bodies don't conform to ideals of heterosexual attraction, or change this over time, and those who move away—through choice or circumstance—from the ideal of becoming more "successful" over time by buying property, raising a family, and so on.

We'll come back to the question of how we identify our sexuality to others—if at all—in the next chapter, and to political issues in Chapter 7.

Multiple sexual identities?

By now in this book you'll be clear that, if you are considering identifying your sexuality, one term is probably not going to capture it! Culturally, people tend to assume your sexual identity means whether you're gay, straight, or bi, but we have seen that there is a lot more to it than that. So probably you're considering multiple sexual identity terms that you might use, in relation to where you are on the ace spectrum, gender of attraction, number of partners, solo versus partnered sex, erotic versus romantic attraction, desires, practices, and more.

There's a further way in which sexual identities may be multiple, for the same person, and that's if we experience ourselves as plural rather than singular.

Many different therapeutic approaches suggest that it can be useful to understand ourselves as having many parts, rather than being one coherent unified self. You might have heard of people having an "inner child" or an "inner critic," for example. Some people have a very vivid experience of their plurality, moving between different selves or states, and describing themselves as a "plural system," rather than a "singlet." For others, it's a more muted experience, but they might still notice, for example, that they have a vulnerable childlike part who comes out when they're with a partner, a busy organized part who comes out at work, and a nurturing part who comes out with their kids.

Some authors, like Janina Fisher, have mapped such plural parts onto the four F trauma survival strategies which we covered in the last chapter, suggesting that we all have parts whose go-to mode of relating is freeze, flight, fight, fawn, and also attach. We may also have parental parts and/or parts who get on with our everyday lives. For most of us, some of these parts will be foregrounded and quite accessible to us; other parts will be disowned and harder to contact.

How does this relate to sexuality? First of all, for many of us, we learn as we grow up to foreground parts which are approved of by others, and to disown parts which are disapproved of. Often the disapproved-of parts will be parts that are sexual in ways that are regarded as unacceptable by our families or wider cultures.

One of the reasons that it can be great to tune into the characters who show up in our erotic fantasies, and the people we desire out there in the world—as we did in section 5.2—is that this can give us useful information about the parts of us which we might have disowned. Often we're attracted to things in others that we can't contact so easily in ourselves. For example, Meg-John has written about how they eroticized a dynamic between a nurturing femme top and a vulnerable masc bottom for ages in their thirties, assuming that they wanted to "be" the woman and "have" the guy. Only later did they realize that a part of them *was* that guy, which enabled them to get to know that part of themselves which had been disowned at an early age.

It's an intriguing way to think about our erotic desires and attractions: to consider whether they are informing us about something that we might want to find in ourselves rather than look for in another person, or even in sexual practices with others. Might attraction to solid, steady, protective partners suggest that you could cultivate a relationship with your own inner father-figure (of whatever gender)? Might desires to be treated cruelly by a harsh mistress speak to a need to embrace your inner critic and the fiery protective energy she holds? If these ideas resonate for you, there are resources for how to explore this more at the end of the chapter.

In addition to this, the concept of plurality can help us to understand and articulate the different aspects of our sexuality, and how they change over time, to ourselves, and to others if we want to. We've seen that sexuality is fluid for most people—with some aspects of identity, attraction, desire, and practices, changing over the years. For many of us there is also some fluidity and flux day to day, or moment to moment, too—generally, or perhaps depending on things like mood, circumstances, how our body is doing, or who we are with. Terms like "abrosexual" and "resexual" have been coined to capture experiences where we change between sexualities frequently; for example, having asexual and allosexual days, times when we're attracted to different genders, or being more or less kinky, dominant or submissive on different occasions, or shifting in this during an encounter. The word "abromantic" captures such fluidity in relation to romantic or nurturing experiences. Plurality is one way of understanding how we might encompass multiple sexualities and be in very different places sexually at different times.

ACTIVITY: MAPPING OUR SEXUAL SELVES

If you do experience yourself as plural and have a sense of some of your parts, try writing a list—or sketching—some, or all, of them, and describing their sexualities. You might note down identity terms that fit for each of them, or chart them on some of the spectrums we gave you in section 4.4. Meg-John found it helpful initially to chart theirs on spectrums of masculine to feminine, and submissive to dominant, although these days they might add asexual to allosexual, and giving to receiving.

If this is a newer concept for you, reflect on the parts of yourself that come out in your erotic interactions, if you have them. Is this relatively consistent, or are there different parts you can identify there? For example, the lazy, loving sex part and the feisty, rough sex part; or the pleasure-giver and the pleasure-seeker; or parts that are more or less sexual, or more or less kinky, or more or less queer. If you identify distinct parts then, again, you might try describing them, and their sexualities, in more detail. Recognizing that these are different parts of you can be helpful in communicating with partners about what space you're in, why you sometimes like some things and sometimes others, or sometimes feel sexual and sometimes don't, for example.

If fantasy or media is more your thing, then try listing all the kinds of characters who turn up regularly in your fantasies, or who you're drawn to in sexual media or mainstream TV shows, books, and movies. Might these characters represent more known and unknown sexual selves for you? What do you know about them already? What would you like to find out? You can always try undertaking an imaginary interview with them—spoken or written—to get to know them better.

> **REMEMBER:** Whatever you discover about your sexuality—desires, attractions, experiences, or identities—it's always up to you whether you share this information with others. In the next chapter, we'll consider things you might like to share, and how you might do that, but nobody should ever pressurize you into sharing anything you're not comfortable with. You don't owe anybody that information, whatever kind of relationship you are in, or whatever the politics around "coming out" are in your communities.
>
> Trust yourself if your sense is "not now," or "I'm not ready," or "not with this person." It's always okay to go slowly and get more information if you're at all uncertain. It's also okay for what you discover to change over time, and for you to update people accordingly.

FURTHER RESOURCES

A great book on sex and disability is:

— Silverberg, C. and Kaufman, M. (2016). *The Ultimate Guide to Sex and Disability: For All of Us Who Live With Disabilities, Chronic Pain, and Illness.* Jersey City, NJ: Cleis Press.

If you want to read more about the intersection of gender and race, check out:

— Schuller, K. (2018). *The Biopolitics of Feeling: Race, Sex, and Science in the Nineteenth Century.* Durham, NC: Duke University Press.

If you're interested in knowing more about how fatphobia is rooted in anti-Blackness:

— Strings, S. (2019). *Fearing the Black Body: The Racial Origins of Fat Phobia.* New York, NY: New York University Press.

An incredibly useful resource to look at racialized trauma in our bodymind is:

— Menakem, R. (2017). *My Grandmother's Hands: Racialized Trauma and the Pathway to Mending Our Hearts and Bodies.* Las Vegas, NV: Central Recovery Press.

And if you want to learn how to love your bodymind better and celebrate it, we recommend:

— Taylor, S.R. (2018). *The Body Is Not an Apology: The Power of Radical Self-Love.* Oakland, CA: Berrett-Koehler Publishers.

The two zines mentioned in section 5.2 on sexual desire are:

— Barker, M-J. and Hancock, J. (2017). *Make Your Own Sex Manual.* https://megjohnandjustin.com/product/make-your-own-sex-manual

— Barker, M-J. and Hancock, J. (2018). *Understanding Ourselves Through Erotic Fantasies.* https://megjohnandjustin.com/product/understanding-erotic-fantasies-zine

The book on fantasies mentioned in section 5.2 is:

— Blake, P. (in press). *Unspeakable Fantasies.* pandorablake.com.

There's some good advice about finding an appropriate, affirmative therapist at the following links:

— www.them.us/story/how-to-find-a-queer-therapist

— https://megjohnandjustin.com/you/should-i-go-to-therapy

And more great stuff about this and about the impact of gaslighting and trauma on our sexuality in this book:

- Bisbey, L-B (2021). *Dancing the Edge to Reclaim Your Reality: Essential Life Skills for Trauma (and Gaslighting) Survivors*. Lightning Source. https://drloribethbisbey.com

If you're interested in finding out more about Eugene Gendlin's work on the felt sense and other work inspired by him, check out the website for the International Focusing Institute:

- https://focusing.org

You can find an example of a "yes, no, maybe" inventory here:

- www.scarleteen.com/article/advice/yes_no_maybe_so_a_ sexual_inventory_stocklist

There's much more about the whole idea of plurality here:

- www.rewriting-the-rules.com/plural-work

There is also more on focusing and plurality in our book:

- Iantaffi, A. and Barker, M-J. (2021). *Hell Yeah Self-Care!* London: Jessica Kingsley Publishers.

CHAPTER 6

SEXUALITY AND RELATIONSHIPS

Over the last couple of chapters we've focused on your experience of your sexuality and how you want to identify and express that. In this chapter, we'll consider the various ways in which you might do that in relationship with others.

First, we'll explore how you might share information about your sexuality with the people in your life, considering questions about coming—or being—out, and how much you want to talk about the details of your sexuality, and with whom.

After that, we'll focus specifically on relationships in which you might want to be sexual or sensual. What relationship contexts are there in which erotic contact can happen? Which of these work best for you? Then we'll explore how to ensure that the relationships in which you are erotic—and the contact itself—is as consensual as possible. Finally, we'll end the chapter by thinking about sex as a way of being intimate with others, and how erotic intimacy relates to other forms of intimacy that we can have in relationships.

6.1 SHARING YOUR SEXUALITY WITH THOSE AROUND YOU

We hope that by now you have an idea of your sexual identities, if any, and of your desires, attractions, and preferred sexual practices. If not, that's okay too. This exploration takes time, and you might find that you end up understanding your sexuality in different ways to the ones we've described here.

We do believe that it's important for us all to reflect on what happens *when*—and *if*—we share our sexuality with those around us. We might also think about *how* we want to share this information, with *whom*, and *why*.

In section 5.2 we wrote:

> In order to enjoy our sexuality fully—whatever it is—we need to know it well for ourselves, and we need to communicate it to others, whether that is those we want to be sexual or sensual with, those we get support from, or close people in our life who we need to understand us and mirror us well.

We'll address this in this chapter and also in the next one.

So, one of the reasons we might want to share our sexuality with those around us is that we're interested in engaging sexually and/or erotically with them, in some way. That's definitely a valid reason to share our sexuality, but it's not the only one. We might also want to share our sexuality with others because we're close to them and we want them to truly know us. Or we might want to share our sexuality for political reasons, such as using some of our power and privilege to be visible, to educate, or to advocate for the rights of one or more of the communities we belong to. We might also want to share our sexuality because keeping parts of ourselves hidden from others is tiring or feels "wrong" in some way.

Whatever our reasons for doing so, it's okay to want to share our sexuality with others—or not. Nobody has an automatic right to any parts of our stories. Whether we want to share these parts of ourselves, or not, can depend on a number of factors, including whether our sexualities are viewed as acceptable in dominant discourses, and how intimate we are with someone (more on intimacy later in this chapter).

Coming out

This process of sharing our sexualities is sometimes called "coming out." However, this term is generally only used when people who are bisexual, lesbian, queer, gay, kinky, asexual, and so on, share their sexualities: in other words, people whose sexualities fall outside those considered "normal" by dominant discourse. The term "coming" out seems to indicate that we're moving out of what is included in dominant discourse—that is, legitimate and generally acceptable sexualities.

This concept of coming out is problematic in a number of ways. First, it's often assumed or implied that coming out is a one-time event. In reality, those of us who have sexualities outside the ones considered legitimate by dominant discourses usually come out multiple times throughout our lives, either voluntarily or involuntarily. Coming out also implies choice and agency, whereas often we might be "outed" by others—that is, our sexualities might be disclosed without our consent—or we may feel pressured to be out because of other people's expectations.

Reflection point: What is coming out?

When we disclose our sexualities, what are we coming out of and into? When is it considered coming out, and when is it not? Can we imagine a world in which there are no assumptions made about our sexual identities, attractions, desires, or practices? What if we were all free to share our sexualities whenever—and with whomever—we wanted, because it was a given that any of us could have any combinations of identities, desires, attractions, or practices? It seems a bit utopian, doesn't it? But what if we let ourselves dream a little here?

We'd love to live in that world, because that would mean that all sexualities were considered legitimate. However, right now we live in a world where the concept of coming out exists because only straight, allosexual, monogamous, and normative sexualities are viewed as legitimate. This means that those of us who have sexualities that do not fit within dominant discourses can feel pressured to come out for fear of being accused of being deceitful if we don't.

No straight person would be viewed as deceitful for not telling their families or potential partners that they're straight! However, someone being depicted as deceitful for not disclosing a non-normative sexuality is a common trope in popular media. At the same time, sharing our sexualities in a world where what is acceptable is so narrow can make us incredibly vulnerable.

In our previous book on gender we called the pressure of disclosing identities and experiences outside cultural norms "enforced vulnerability." This term can also apply to the pressure that many people with marginalized sexualities might experience around disclosure. Much of what we've written about enforced vulnerability, passing, and pride in our book on gender applies to sexuality as well, so we invite you to refer to that if you're interested in delving a little deeper into this concept. For now, let's turn to examples of sharing our sexualities with others in a range of contexts.

Sharing our sexualities: Some brief examples

Despite the pressures we may experience around sharing our sexualities with those around us, we might also really want to share who we are with people for all kinds of reasons. This makes sense, given that to be human is to be relational, as we're interdependent with nature and with other humans. Let's take a look at a few examples of common environments in which you might want to share your sexualities with others.

Family of origin

Our families of origin—that is, the people we grew up with— can be one of the groups of people we might want to share aspects of our sexualities with. Our families are, of course, not just one homogeneous block of people. We might want to share some aspects of our sexualities with some family members and not with others. We get to decide what we want to share and with whom. Unfortunately, we might often feel pressured to share our sexualities with our family of origin due to societal expectations, rather than because we truly want to.

Please know that we're not saying that you have to disclose your sexualities to your family, just that this is often a common scenario for people. Our families of origin do not automatically have the right to all aspects of our identities and experiences, including sexuality. In fact, just like with everyone else, we encourage you to evaluate whether your physical, emotional, and social safety will be at risk if you decide to share your sexualities with your family of origin. Here are some examples of people reflecting on sharing their sexualities with their family of origin:

> I'm a sex worker and, for a long time, I didn't tell anyone in my family about my work. I was really afraid of their reaction. But I was also getting anxious about them finding out from someone else. When one of my exes threatened to tell my family, I decided it was time to tell them myself. I didn't want to be afraid anymore. My brother was great, but my parents took a little while to come around. We had to go a few rounds of family therapy with an affirming therapist for them to understand my choice. I'm glad we did, as I feel much more relaxed around them now.

> I've decided not to tell anyone in my family that I'm asexual and kinky. They know I'm fluid in my attractions, and they're okay with that, but I decided that they didn't need to know whether I have sex with my partners or not, and what kind of erotic dynamics I have with others. I don't want to have to educate them about these things.

I don't care if they make assumptions; that's just where I'm at and what I'm comfortable with.

Everyone in my family is some kind of queer so having to tell them I was straight, monogamous, and vanilla was a thing. My mom kept thinking this was some kind of "rebellion" to their sex-affirming upbringing and it took her a while to accept that this is just who I am. They still poke fun at me sometimes and it can get uncomfortable at family reunions.

Work

It seems odd to consider work here, when sexualities are viewed as something private in dominant discourse. However, it's not uncommon for people to talk about dating, relationships, and sexualities at work. After all, many of us spend a great deal of time at work in order to survive under capitalism, and some of our closest people may be our colleagues or the people we work with. We might also find ourselves pressured to at least come out to Human Resources (HR) if we're in a same-gender relationship, for example, as this might have implications for issues such as health insurance, pension, life insurance, and other benefits.

Disclosing our sexualities to co-workers, supervisors, managers, clients, or HR/personnel departments can feel particularly vulnerable as it's usually people with marginalized sexualities who're expected to disclose relevant aspects of their identities. Straight people generally don't need to worry about disclosing their sexualities, and they openly and freely talk about their partners without fear of consequences, such as harassment and discrimination.

The intersections of our sexualities with other aspects of our identities and experiences might mean we're particularly vulnerable when it comes to sharing our sexualities at work. For example, if one or more intersections mean that you're viewed as hypersexual, or objectified, it can increase the risk of sexual harassment. Once more, nobody has an automatic right to our stories, but sadly we're sometimes pressured or forced into sharing our sexualities. We might also genuinely want to be able to be ourselves around people we see almost every day and spend significant amounts of time with. Here are a couple of examples of people reflecting on sharing their sexualities at work.

I'm a pretty private person but when same-gender marriage became legal in my country it was a huge deal. I never thought I would see this happen in my lifetime. I really wanted time off to celebrate, connect with my community, and also to go and get married to make sure my partner and I would have the same protection under the law as any other married couple. I had several conversations at work with my boss, HR, and even with colleagues to sort all of this out. It was exhausting honestly.

When the #MeToo movement started to gain momentum, it was exciting to witness as a survivor and also really hard on my mental health. I ended up being hospitalized as my suicidality went up again. I could have made some excuse but I decided to share with my supervisor at work that I'm a survivor, and was really struggling to see stories of other survivors all around me in the news and on social media. He was actually great about it and shared that he had been sexually abused as a child, and was also having a rough time. I was surprised and I think it was healing for both of us to share that moment.

Friends and partners

We might, of course, also want to share our sexualities with people we're interested in nurturing intimacy with. When we say intimacy, we don't just mean sexual intimacy, and we'll talk more about this in section 6.4, but for now let's just say we mean close friends as well as people we might date, potential sexual play partners, people we're romantically interested in, and so on.

This can feel especially vulnerable as it might involve sharing aspects of our sexualities that we would usually not share in the other contexts considered in this section. For example, we might share fantasies, desires, and practices with close friends or potential partners in a way that's different from what we would share with family members or co-workers. Again, nobody has an automatic right to know every aspect of our sexuality, not even partners.

Intimacy often thrives through communication—and communication is also essential for consent—so we might choose to share quite a bit more with those close to us, especially if we're interested in engaging erotically and/or sexually with them. Talking about our attractions, desires, fantasies, and sexual practices can be challenging though, given that in many dominant discourses, sexuality is closely connected with shame. Again, it can be harder to communicate such things for those of us who have sexualities that don't fit well within normative discourses.

We hope that in the previous chapters we've given you

some useful tools to explore any attractions, desires, fantasies, and practices you might be interested in. How do we communicate those to others though? One way can be to invite potential erotic partners to engage in the same activities that you have. For example, you might share your erotic user guide with someone and invite them to create and share their own. Or you might ask them if they'd be interested in doing some of the activities in this book about exploring desires together. You could also ask someone if they'd be interested in sharing erotic or sexual fantasies verbally, or in writing, before engaging sexually. There are so many ways to share our desires and fantasies, as covered earlier and in the resources sections of this book.

However, such sharing can feel vulnerable. What if they not only reject your attraction but also who you are? What if they feel "deceived" when you reveal something they didn't previously know? Once more, we encourage you to assess your physical, emotional, and social safety before disclosing any aspects of your sexuality. It's a vulnerable risk to open up with someone in this way, so it's okay to take your time, and to really tune into your yes, no, or maybe, as we outlined in the last chapter.

There's no rush, and if you feel pressured by someone to open up before you're ready, it's okay to move back and notice whether this might be a red flag. The desire to share quickly can be due to having experienced trauma and wanting to "rush intimacy" because of a survival response, or fear of abandonment. None of us is immune from the cloud of historical, social, and cultural trauma around sex and sexuality. We don't expect any of us to be "perfect" at this.

Slowing down can be helpful in navigating communication,

which it's why we invite you to do so throughout the book. If you're finding that it's hard for you to assess safety around disclosure of your sexuality, it's okay to seek support from a therapist, trusted friend, or group of people (see Chapter 7). In the next section, we'll also address building safe-enough relationship containers in more depth. For now, here are some examples of people navigating disclosure around sexuality with friends and partners.

Multiple experiences: Navigating disclosure

"I was in lesbian community for several years so, when I fell in love with a man, it was really hard to come out as bisexual to my friends. I mean, many of them knew this in theory, but it was still news to them that I could be in a relationship with a man. I lost some close friends. It was all rather painful and I almost broke up with my partner over it. I felt I had to choose between my friends and community, and my relationship."

"When I'm interested in playing with someone, I try to figure out if they're kinky as well. I might drop hints to see if it's safe to even tell them I'm into BDSM. For example, I might talk about a favorite movie, *Secretary*, and see if they know about it. Or mention *Fifty Shades of Grey* and see their reaction. That one usually tells me a lot!"

"Writing erotic fiction is a big part of my life so I like to be able to share it with my friends. However, it can be complex territory to navigate, given that they might be turned on by what I share. I need my close people to know their boundaries around what feels okay or not around this, as well as honoring mine."

"Before having sex with someone, I like to ask if they'd be interested in sexting. To me that feels like a safer way to explore
if we're sexually compatible or not. Not everyone is up for it,
and that's okay. Then we figure other ways of exploring our
sexualities together. I find I need that before getting physical
with someone."

6.2 RELATIONSHIP CONTEXTS FOR SEX

Now that we've explored how you might share your sexuality
with the people around you, let's think about the relationship
contexts, or containers, in which you might be sexual, erotic,
or sensual.

There are some important things to emphasize up front
here:

1. It is absolutely fine to need the relationship context
   that you require for erotic things to happen, whatever that is, however many people are involved, whatever
   depth of connection that entails. So long as everybody
   involved is on the same page and consents to this, it's
   absolutely fine.

2. What is seen as sexual, erotic, or sensual within that
   relationship context can be whatever it is, whether or
   not that conforms to wider cultural understandings
   of what "counts" as sex, however frequently or infre-
   quently it happens, however much it differs or stays
   the same over time. Again, this is as long as everybody
   is aware that what is happening *is* an erotic, sexual, or
   sensual thing for at least one of the people involved,
   and consents to that.

We'll talk about how to ensure that everybody is informed and consenting more in the next section of this chapter. In this section, we'll focus on tuning into the relationship contexts—or containers—that you need for sex, play, erotic sharing, or intimate touch to feel good enough and safe enough. Let's start with some multiple experiences to get a sense of the diverse needs that people can have for this, and then we'll help you to explore what works for you.

Multiple experiences: Diverse relationship contexts for sex

"The only relationship contexts for sharing my erotic self that I want right now are my relationship with myself, and group contexts where we do solo sex in the same space. I've had some pretty traumatic experiences of one-to-one erotic relationships so it feels really good to be clear with myself and others that this is what feels safe right now."

"I'm a sexological bodyworker and I have a clear contract with my clients about what this means, and what is and isn't on offer in our sessions. I need partners to respect my career and my polyamorous relationship style. They need to be good with the fact that I will be sexual with multiple people: both clients and other partners. I'm also only really interested in partners who have the same sense that I have of sex as a shared spiritual experience."

"I feel comfortable having sex in a monogamous relationship where we've built a lot of trust between us over time. Sex is a very vulnerable, intimate thing for me to share, and I need someone who gets that and can meet me there."

"Sex is an easy way of connecting for me. It feels on a similar level to sharing a conversation. I often hook up with people I've just met. I go to gay clubs and saunas where we all know that's what we're looking for, and we can read the codes that say if somebody is interested or not. The only thing I wouldn't want would be to get with somebody who thought that having sex meant more than that."

"My partner and I never have sex as in genital contact, but our whole relationship is erotic to us. We're in a 24/7 kink dynamic. I'm her domme and every exchange we have involves her surrendering power to me, whether that's her giving me a massage or washing the dishes. We have a detailed contract for our relationship which we continually revisit, and several other people in our BDSM family who support us, to ensure that it remains a good, consensual dynamic for us both."

"I'm ace and my partner isn't. We started off monogamous but over time we realized that we both needed a relationship model where he had sex with other people. Otherwise I felt pressure to meet that desire even though he never put it on me. Now we're primaries, but he has other secondary relationships for sex, and I have similarly close relationships with people in my faith community, which he isn't part of. We need other people in our life to respect our relationship style, and to understand that our connection, and the intimacy that we share, is just as valid as sex is for allosexual people."

Reflection point: How you do relationships

What is your current way of doing relationships, and your relationship status? How does that work for your sexuality and how you like to express it? You might want to think about aspects of your sexual attractions and desires that get met in your current relationships, and ones that don't.

In the rest of this section, we'll describe the various sexual relationship models that are available to help you tune into those that might work for you, if you don't already know or are considering a change. Then we'll explore what kind of relationship container works best for you for sex. This includes things like levels of closeness, trust, shared understandings and experiences.

Meg-John has written a whole zine—with Justin Hancock—to help you make your own relationship user guide, which could go well together with the sex user guide we introduced in the last chapter. Creating a document where you outline the ways in which you like to do sex, and the ways in which you like to do relationships, can be a great starting point for tuning into your own needs, wants, limits, and boundaries, and expressing these to others so that you can figure out together whether sharing sex, or a relationship, can work for you. Here we'll offer a couple of the key ideas for such a user guide, but feel free to check out the whole zine—listed in the further resources—if you want more suggestions about what you could include.

Tuning into your preferred relationship model

There are many different relationship models in which people have sexual or erotic contact, and/or romantic or nurturant forms of contact. Remember from the last chapter that some people want both of these, some neither, and some want one but not the other. Some who like both sexual or erotic contact, and/ or romantic or nurturant forms of contact, prefer to get them in the same relationship, and some in different relationships.

Here's a brief list of some of the main consensual relationship models that are out there which sex happens in. It's not a complete list because new models are coming in all the time, and everybody tailors their model to their specific preferences and values, so probably there are as many relationship models as there are relationships.

We'll get into way more detail about all of this in our next book, *How to Understand Your Relationships*, but for now, consider this list and whether each would be a yes, no, or maybe for you. Are there several models you'd consider or just one or two? Would everybody involved need to share that model or could there be a relationship where people had different models? What tweaks would you want to make for them to be the bespoke relationship model which worked best for you?

— *Hook-up:* You get together with strangers or casual acquaintances for sex, perhaps ones you meet online or on a night out.

— *Friends with benefits:* You have friendships where sex is one of the things you do together.

— *Dating:* You see a few people for romantic and/or sexy time together, often on arranged dates.

— *Monogamous:* You commit to one person with whom you have a sexual, and often romantic, relationship. This might be a lifelong bond or it might be serial monogamy where you have one monogamous partner after another.

— *Monogamish:* You and a partner have a monogamous partnership, but it's somewhat open to eroticism outside that relationship. For example, it might be agreed that you can flirt with other people, kiss other people, have certain kinds of sexual contact, or under certain conditions, such as when you're in another city.

— *Don't ask, don't tell:* You and a partner have an implicit arrangement that you can be sexual with other people, as well as each other, as long as you don't ask each other—or tell each other—about the other ones.

— *Open relationship:* You have a main relationship, but it's open for you both to have sex with other people. This might be something you always do separately, or always together, or together and separately. It might be with the same people—like another couple who you regularly get together with for sex—or with different people each time. Swinging is one version of an open relationship form.

— *Hierarchical polyamory:* You have multiple relationships which can be both sexual and romantic, but some are more committed, close, or important than others; for example, primary, secondary, and tertiary relationships.

— *Egalitarian polyamory:* You have multiple relationships which can be both sexual and romantic, and they are all on a similar level of importance to you, even though they might take different forms. Kitchen table polyamory is a version of egalitarian polyamory where it's also ideal for all the people in the cluster—or polycule—to be friends, communicate, or even live together.

— *Polyfidelity:* This is a version of polyamory where a group of people are all committed to each other, and don't have other romantic or sexual relationships outside that group. Group marriage is one form of polyfidelity.

— *Self-partnership or solo polyamory:* Your core relationship is your relationship with yourself. You might be open to another partner, or partners, beyond this.

— *Relationship anarchy:* You are open to multiple close relationships in your life and do not see romantic/ sexual relationships as any more important than other kinds of relationships such as friendship. You emphasize the freedom of all involved, and ongoing honest negotiation of how the relationships work.

If you want to read more about these different models, check out Jonathan Kent's book—and his podcast with Zayna Ratty—in the further resources.

What relationship container do you need for sex?

There's more to creating the right relationship container for you, for sex to happen, than just agreeing on a relationship model. Two people could have a shared model of monogamy, or egalitarian polyamory, for example, and still need very different conditions to be met in order to feel good about erotic contact happening.

For example, one person might be up for sex on the first date; the other might need to get to know each other for a year before sex feels possible. One person might only feel good about having sex if they know that they're free to talk about it with close friends afterwards; the other might need to know that it would be kept private. For one person, having sex might come with a lot of expectations about what level of commitment they now have; for the other, it might be very important that having sex doesn't change anything.

As with relationship models, it is vital to emphasize here that all conditions that you need for sex to feel good enough and safe enough are valid. Nobody should ever shame you for your relationship model or your conditions; and if they do, that's probably a pretty good indicator they're not a great person for you to have a relationship—or sex—with.

These considerations are perhaps particularly important if you're a trauma survivor, as so many of us are. If you've experienced non-consensual sex and/or relationships, then it is particularly vital to know that this relationship is a safe enough place for you. Unfortunately, for trauma survivors, that can be more difficult to determine because we've often been gaslit around our experiences and taught not to trust our sense of danger and safety, and we can even be erotically drawn to dynamics which are similar to past traumatic ones, because they feel familiar. Also, intense sexual attraction, and new relationship energy, can dampen down our fear responses, making it easy to get into situations which we only later realize weren't safe enough.

To be cautious around this, you may want to:

— slow down the pace of new relationships

— have up-front conversations with new people about your needs and boundaries and tune into whether these are being respected or not

— get friends to meet any new potential partner

— get support in tuning into your feelings about potentially moving towards erotic content (more on this in the next chapter).

It's also worth thinking about the connection between your erotic contact and your everyday connection in relationships. It can be risky when these lines get blurred; for example, if important decisions get made during—or right after—sex, if somebody witholds or offers sex in order to get other needs met, or if erotic dynamics play out between you in everyday situations, unless that's something you've explicitly negotiated, with clear agreements about how you'll navigate it, and you have support around that.

ACTIVITY: YOUR RELATIONSHIPS AND THE PLACES FOR SEX

Who (or what) are your closest people (or other beings)? You might like to list them as they come to mind, or perhaps to write them into something like the diagram in Figure 6.1, with yourself in the middle, your most intimate relationships at the next level out, then the other relationships you have close contact with but which are perhaps not quite as intimate, and finally the relationships in your life you wouldn't describe as that close or intimate.

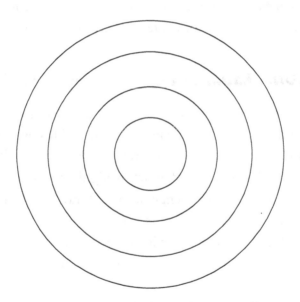

FIGURE 6.1: CONCENTRIC CIRCLES OF CLOSENESS

— What defines the relationships in your closer levels? For example, it might be time spent together, trust, how shared your life is, what kinds of feelings you have for them, or other things.

— On what basis do people move to a closer level from a further away one, for you?

— Which of these levels feel like places that you would be up for erotic, sexual, or sensual contact happening?

— What relationship conditions do you need to be met for erotic, sexual, or sensual contact to feel good enough and safe enough?

Agreeing on the relationship models and containers for sex is a big part of ensuring that sex is consensual. In the next section, we'll explore how else you might ensure consensual sex, and that it happens in the context of a consensual relationship.

6.3 CONSENSUAL SEX AND RELATIONSHIPS

Throughout this book, we've stressed the importance of only acting on our sexuality in consensual ways. However, this is not as straightforward as it is often made out to be. This is because we live in a world which is highly non-consensual, where non-consensual behavior of all kinds is normalized from childhood onwards, and where there are few models—and little support—for learning how to communicate consensually in our sex lives, or in our lives in general.

ACTIVITY: MULTIPLE LEVELS OF CONSENT/NON-CONSENT

If you want to explore this for yourself in more detail, you might find it useful to return to the concentric circles model we introduced in Chapters 3 and 4 and reflect on the messages that you received growing up about consent at all these levels, as well as the messages you receive about it now. This might include both what kinds of consensual and non-consensual behaviors you saw modeled around you, and how you, yourself, were treated in consensual and non-consensual ways.

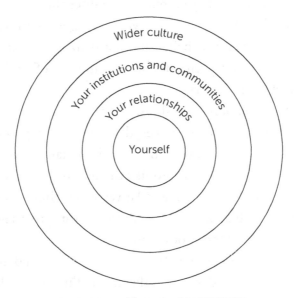

FIGURE 6.2: MULTIPLE LEVELS OF INFLUENCE

At the level of wider culture, you might consider, for example, how society is based on a capitalist model—at least where we live—that treats some lives, bodies, and labor as if they are much more valuable than others. Also, countries and organizations are measured on the basis of how much money they make rather than how well people are doing or whether they are looking after the local and global environment. You might also think about the ways non-consensual behaviors are depicted as normal, or even romantic, in mainstream media, like people making declarations of love when they have no idea whether it's reciprocated, stalking somebody they don't know but have decided they're in love with, or running across airports trying to stop their partner getting on a plane to follow their dream job.

At the level of communities and institutions, you might reflect how most workplaces and educational settings require people to do tasks they're told to do, rather than tuning into what they're interested in or what engages them, valuing productivity over well-being, and normalizing pushing people beyond their capacity, despite this amount of work being completely unnecessary.

At the level of relationships, you might think about how non-consent infuses our everyday lives, from pressuring friends to do what we want them to do socially, to trying to shape partners into who we'd like them to be, to telling kids to eat food they dislike, hug relatives when they're uncomfortable with that, or express enthusiasm for gifts they don't want or activities they don't enjoy.

The non-consensual nature of the systems and dynamics that we're embedded in means that most of us struggle hugely to be consensual with ourselves. We may find it very difficult even to tune into what we want and don't want, let alone feeling able to articulate that to others. Think about your everyday life. How often do you stop to check in whether what you're about to do next feels good to you? Do you tune into yourself when deciding what to eat, which show to watch, or who to spend time with?

Cultivating the conditions for consent

The first step in ensuring that sex, and the relationships in which sex happens, are as consensual as possible, is recognizing how difficult this is within non-consensual culture. We need to get serious about learning how to treat ourselves consensually if we're going to learn how to treat other people in this way. And we need to develop systems and structures around us to support us in practicing consensual relating.

Throughout this book, we've introduced various ways in which you can develop self-consent, particularly across our slow-down pages. It's about tuning into your body, and emotions, learning what a yes, no, or maybe feels like to you. This can help you to know what it feels like when you want to try something, when it's not feeling great for you, or when something is getting close to a boundary or limit.

It's a great idea to practice self-consent in solo sex, solo touch, fantasy, and when engaging with sexual media. Can you slow down and be very present to what you are doing? Can you keep checking in with yourself whether it's still feeling good or not, perhaps making pauses to do so? Can you keep giving yourself multiple options for what you might do next? Can you remind yourself that there's no particular goal here, other than curiosity and doing what feels good to you, and notice when you've fallen into judging yourself or assuming you should be feeling something you're not, or having a particular experience?

If feeling your emotions, being present, or knowing your boundaries, is hard for you, perhaps due to trauma responses like overwhelm and dissociation, it may be helpful to access support to learn how to do this. There will be more on that in the next chapter.

In the next chapter, we'll also say more about how to develop consensual communities, so that we get to practice consensual relating, feel well supported by those around us to do so, and also get support when we struggle to be consensual, or when something non-consensual happens to us.

Consent and communication

We've just said a lot about consent, but what exactly are we talking about here? The dictionary definition of consent is "agreement to do something." Being able to agree to something requires everyone involved feeling free enough and safe enough to tune into themselves, and to communicate openly with others about who they are, what their capacities are, what they want and don't want, and what they're willing to do and not willing to do.

When it comes to sex, in particular, people clearly struggle a lot with this. Research has found that in long-term relationships people generally only know about 60 percent of what their partner likes sexually, and only 20 percent of what they dislike. It's very hard to be consensual when you don't feel able to communicate your desires and boundaries, or don't know what somebody else's are.

We hope what we've covered so far in this book about how diverse sexuality is, and how valid your sexual desires and boundaries are—whatever they are—will help with this. If communication about sex is difficult in relationships where you have—or want—sexual or erotic contact, then it can be good to start with meta-communication—that is, communicating about communicating. You could make time to talk about your history of talking about sex: how it was dealt with in your families, education, and previous relationships, for example, and the blocks that come up for you around talking about sex now. Talking about why communication might be hard, and what you might do to make it easier, is a great way of lifting some of the shame and fear around talking about sex, without actually going there yet. You can ask for—and offer—reassurance about the fears and insecurities you might have.

Then you might open up the topic of consent and talk about how you could go about making both the sexual or erotic contact itself—and the whole relationship in which it happens—consensual. The following criteria, adapted from Meg-John's "consent checklist" zine, are some of the main ones that are important to consider. For each one, we've said a bit about how they apply to sexual or erotic contact, and how they apply to the rest of the relationship.

Checklist for consensual sex and relationships

1. *Make consent the aim*

   Often people approach sex as if a successful outcome—of an evening with a partner, or a hook-up, for example—is that sex happens. This puts us under pressure and makes it more difficult to be consensual. It's better to agree that your aim is for consent to happen, whether or not sex happens, not the other way around.

   We could similarly make mutual consent the aim of the whole relationship, and of each encounter with a person, not getting what you want from them, or trying to be what they want.

2. *Everyone knows that they don't have to do it (now or ever)*

Sex can't be consensual unless we know that we absolutely don't have to do it, that there's no kind of duty or obligation around it, and that no kind of punishment will occur if we don't do it. It's also helpful to keep affirming with each other that it's fine for each of you to have the erotic desires and practices that you have, and that you only want to do things together that are a big "yes" for each of you, rather than putting anyone under pressure to do things they don't like because the other person does.

The same is true for the whole relationship. We need to know that we are free to *not* be in this relationship, or in this particular way, without fearing that we'll be punished or suffer significant loss. Here it can be useful to keep affirming with each other that our whole relationship (and our home, community, security, etc.) isn't contingent on, for example, having sex regularly, continuing to cohabit, feeling romantic towards this person, our body staying the same, doing certain things together, earning a certain amount.

3. *Consent is informed*

In sex, informed consent means knowing what's on the cards before the encounter, rather than being surprised with activities we weren't expecting. It means knowing what's being suggested, asked for, and offered, and why. Of course, sometimes we're exploring unknown territory together, which is where the next point—ongoing consent—also comes in. That involves continuing to provide more information as the situation unfolds.

In relationships, informed consent means having enough information to be able to make a decision about whether a relationship with this person is a good idea for us, and what kind of relationship container might work. It's important not to hide vital information that we know might make a person think twice or want to go slower. With each new step in a relationship, people need enough information in advance in order to make a consensual choice.

4. *Consent is ongoing*

In sex, ongoing consent means checking verbally and/ or non-verbally during the encounter that everyone is enjoying it, and pausing or stopping if not.

In relationships, this means also continuing to check whether it is working well for everyone, and taking whatever kinds of pauses, breaks, or step-backs are necessary on aspects of the relationship—or the whole relationship—if it isn't working (if it's not working for everyone, it's not working for anyone).

5. *There is no default script, but multiple options*

In sex, there's often a default script of first to fourth base (or similar), with a sense that "success" means penetration and/or orgasm, and not being able to "achieve" those things is "failure." It's really hard to communicate what we want and don't want when there's a default script like this, but much easier if we're working with multiple options. For example, we could go to bed and snuggle, we could explore touching each other's bodies, we could stay here watching TV. It's vital to know that all erotic, sensual, or sexual activities—and none—are equally valid, so choose what works best for everyone.

In relationships, there is a similar cultural "escalator" model where it is seen as good to get closer over time, checking the points on the relationship checklist (e.g. dating, having sex, becoming exclusive, moving in together). If, instead, we can affirm that all ways of doing relationships are equally valid, then we can find what works—and doesn't work—for this particular relationship. It's important that the person or people whose ways of doing things are the closest to the normative script maximize the agency of those whose ways of doing things are further away, to articulate their preferences and to have them respected.

6. *We're all mindful of power imbalances and how they constrain consent*

Sexual consent is way harder when one person has a lot of power over the other. For example, it is hard to say "no" if you feel at risk in some way (career, money, care, emotional or physical safety) if you don't respond to another person's sexual advances.

Similarly, those with more power in a relationship, in various ways, need to recognize that those with less may feel far less able to say what they need and where their boundaries are. It's good to be open about power imbalances—for example around gender, class, race, age, disability—and to do what you can to enable those with less power in each area to identify and articulate their needs and boundaries and have them respected.

7. *We try to be accountable*

It's important to recognize that we won't always be perfectly consensual and to acknowledge—as soon as possible—when full consent hasn't happened, and to be accountable for that, both in sexual and erotic contact, and in the wider relationship. Micro-moments of non-consent can be fairly easy to repair, and the more we make a habit of doing that, the easier it can become. For example, we can make a habit of checking in the day after sex, or a conversation, or a date, and naming anything that happened where we weren't as present with the other person as we might like to be, or where we felt we might have let our needs and desires override theirs, or where we were left with an uneasy feeling. Even if the other person reassures us that it wasn't non-consensual, we've let each other know that we're up for naming and addressing non-consent when it happens.

Bigger non-consensual moments can be much harder, and this is where it's really good to have a network of support around you to help each person to process what has happened, to enable them to take as much space as they need in order to be ready to address it, and to support them coming together to hear and be heard, and repair if possible. There is more on this in the next chapter.

Reflection point: Your consent checklist

Take a moment to look back over this checklist now that you've read it. You might want to reflect on how one or more of your relationships is doing on these seven points. Which do you find easier? Which are more of a challenge? Are there any other points you would like to add? A personal version of this checklist—saying what is important for you—could go into your user guide, if you make one of those.

In the next section, we will go into more depth about how you can explore erotic intimacy consensually with others.

6.4 INTIMACY AND SEX

Our desire to share our sexuality with others can often stem from seeking intimacy. In fact, sometimes people talk about intimacy as if it were synonymous with sex. However, intimacy and sex are two different things, although one type of intimacy can be sexual intimacy. Let's start by defining intimacy.

What is intimacy?

Intimacy is described in most dictionaries as a state of closeness and/or familiarity. This closeness can be with another person or people, ourselves, or even a place, history, and so on. Intimacy seems to include a deep knowing and relating that shortens the distance between self and other, or even the distance we sometimes place between different parts of ourselves.

When it comes to sex, people often think of intimacy as related to sexual intercourse. While this is one type of intimacy, there are many more types of intimacy, including, but not limited to, erotic intimacy. If you're interested in reading about other types of intimacy, we've included an intimacy assessment in our previous books, *How to Understand Your Gender* and *Life Isn't Binary*. There we included types of intimacy, such as intimacy with colleagues at work with whom we might share much of our day, or recreational intimacy—that is, who we share our time off with. For the purposes of this book, we're going to focus on erotic intimacy.

We're using erotic intimacy as an umbrella term to indicate all types of intimacy that bring us closer to a sense of aliveness, presence, and connection with ourselves, the world around us, and others. Different types of intimacy are not necessarily disconnected from one another though. For example, someone might only be able to experience sexual intimacy if they also feel they have emotional intimacy with someone—that is, the closeness that comes from sharing our emotions openly and vulnerably.

Reflection point: Intimacy

Before we move on to addressing erotic intimacy a little bit more, take a moment to think about what you know about intimacy already. How would you define intimacy? Where did you learn what intimacy is? Who are you close to in your life? Would you say you have intimacy with the people close to you? If so, what kind of intimacy do you have with them? You can, of course, experience

more than one type of intimacy with a person. Is intimacy important to you? If so, what types of intimacy
are most important to you? If intimacy is not important
in your life, why not? As always, please be as kind, curious, and non-judgmental as you possibly can be as you
engage in these reflections.

Erotic intimacy

We said earlier that erotic intimacy is an umbrella term, so
what are the types of intimacy under this umbrella? One type
of erotic intimacy is definitely *sexual intimacy*, but even this
is so much larger than simply sexual intercourse, however
we might define that. Sexual intimacy includes a feeling of
closeness with someone, and touch is often involved That
might be sexual physical contact, such as kissing, caressing,
petting, intercourse, but sexual intimacy can also include
mutual masturbation, watching somebody be sexual, sexting,
sharing sexual fantasies, and so on.

Another type of erotic intimacy is physical intimacy.
Physical intimacy can be sexual, but does not need to be.
For example, cuddling, an ease with physical touch, and
being naked around other people can all be types of physical
intimacy that are not necessarily sexual. Intimacy is also not
just a private affair but, like everything else we address in this
book, a cultural one. For example, Alex comes from a culture,
Italian, where there is generally more physical intimacy in
day-to-day interactions, especially in the south. Where Alex
grew up, people greet each other by kissing cheeks and there is

much more casual touch than in Anglo middle-class culture. Just like other aspects of our sexuality, intimacy is also closely connected to—and mediated by—culture, class, education, language, disability, religion, spirituality, and so on.

A form of intimacy that, for some, closely relates to their spirituality, is *ecological intimacy*. This could be described as closeness with land, green bloods (plants), non-human red bloods (animals), and elements such as water, fire, air, and earth. Ecological intimacy is about feeling a sense of kinship and close connection with the world around us. This is more often found in Indigenous cultures, compared to settler-colonial cultures. This is because colonialism, as an ideology, requires us to feel separate from land, so that we can "own" it or "conquer" it. We cannot have ecological intimacy if we view ourselves as separate from the ecosystems around us.

If eroticism is about our sense of aliveness in—and belonging to—the world, then *creative intimacy* is another type of intimacy that we need to consider here. By creative intimacy we mean the sense of closeness and familiarity that we derive from engaging in creative endeavors together, such as writing a book or making music with others. Creating something together generates its own type of connection with others. What is being created does not need to be permanent, or necessarily artistic. You might have experienced creative intimacy when cooking an elaborate meal with someone, doing a puzzle or crossword together, taking care of a garden, or dancing together.

Another form of erotic connection *is kink intimacy*. This might or might not be sexual for people, although kink activities are often considered to be inherently sexual in dominant discourse. For some people, kink connections are more spiritual than sexual and/or much more focused on the relational power exchange. This is why we include kink intimacy as its own distinct type of erotic intimacy. Kink intimacy is the sense of closeness we might experience when engaging in sharing our kinks with others. This could happen through play but also by belonging to communities with whom we might share fantasies, desires, and behaviors that we might not share with others outside that community. For example, we might engage in kink sexual play at a party, or in a dungeon, and experience kink intimacy with everyone around us, rather than just our play partner(s). We might feel a sense of closeness with those who can both witness our kinks and share theirs in play spaces, or through vulnerable group discussions.

Erotic intimacy can also be about getting to know ourselves better through *self-pleasuring intimacy*. People often think about intimacy as something we do with other people, or perhaps in relationship to spirituality, or with the world around us. However, we can also derive a sense of aliveness and closeness with ourselves by exploring what brings us pleasure. Once more, this might be sexual or not. We might experience self-pleasuring intimacy through masturbation or fantasy, but also by simply being more present and intentional when we shower, or massage lotion into our skin, or soothe ourselves in tough emotional states, or notice which food brings us more or less pleasure. Self-pleasuring intimacy is literally about a deep knowing of what brings us pleasure, and the ability to give this to ourselves, when possible.

Vulnerability and presence

All the types of erotic intimacy described above and, we would argue, all types of intimacy beyond these, require vulnerability and presence. Vulnerability is about being able to be open, authentic, and not guarded about our soft and tender parts. Presence is about our ability to be in the here-and-now, as much as possible. Both of these qualities make it possible for us to experience intimacy, in all its forms.

However, vulnerability and presence can be incredibly challenging for many of us, especially those of us with marginalized identities and experiences, as well as any of us with a history of trauma, particularly developmental trauma (trauma that happened early on in our lives). People with marginalized identities have often experienced their vulnerability being used against them by people with privileged identities; for example, in the form of bullying, ridicule, or discrimination. We are also usually subjected to enforced vulnerability—a state of vulnerability generated by the fact that we have identities and experiences that do not fit within dominant discourses. This all means that vulnerability with ourselves and others can be challenging.

This is really all rooted in trauma: not just in our individual trauma, but also forms of collective trauma such as historical, cultural, and social trauma. It's only really possible to be vulnerable when we feel somewhat safe from danger. If there is no safety in dominant discourse, then it can be impossible to fully embrace vulnerability, and it can, in fact, be downright dangerous to do so. Our capacity for presence is similarly impacted by trauma. Safety—even relative safety—is a requirement for presence too. This is why sometimes people might seek spaces with others who share similar identities and experiences to theirs. Those spaces can offer the relative safety needed to be vulnerable and present with ourselves and one another.

Mia Mingus names the importance of this relative safety

and knowing for disabled people as *access intimacy*. Access intimacy is about knowing that someone, other than you, understands what your access needs are, so that explaining, justifying, or even defending them is not necessary. There are similar types of intimacy when we experience connection with others because they share similar experiences of how our bodies might be gendered, racialized, classed, and so on. This sharing enables us to let down our guard and to be more present and vulnerable with one another, enabling easier access to intimacy.

Exploring intimacy

Erotic intimacy is often assumed to happen automatically in relationships, yet it is a capacity that needs to be understood and cultivated both by ourselves, and by those with whom we're in relationships. Fortunately, there is an increasing number of resources available to people who want to explore and cultivate intimacy.

If you're interested in better understanding sexual intimacy, for example, you might choose to work with a sex therapist or counselor, as they have specialized training in these areas. You might also find some of the tools used in sex therapy, such as sensate focus exercises, available online or in books for the general public. We have included some of these in the resources at the end of this chapter.

If you're interested in exploring erotic intimacy more generally, working with a sexological bodyworker is another way to receive support for this. If you're looking to deepen your understanding of kink intimacy, there are also sexological bodyworkers and sex therapists who specialize in this area. You can explore erotic intimacy by yourself, or you might negotiate doing so with casual sex partners, or with committed partners, or with a group of friends who are interested in exploring similar types of intimacy.

Erotic intimacy can be pursued in so many different ways, and it does not need to be limited to sexual partnerships. You can also have support in this process. We don't automatically know how to do erotic intimacy, especially in a world in which dominant discourses often suppress our capacity for eroticism. It's okay to be curious, to explore, to play, and to look for help! There's more on cultivating supportive relationships and community in the next chapter.

ACTIVITY: EXPLORING DIFFERENT TYPES OF EROTIC INTIMACY

For this activity, you might want to use your notebook or a larger piece of paper. You can also use the grid below if that is easier for you. Take time to consider all the different types of erotic intimacy described in this section: sexual, physical, ecological, creative, kink, and self-pleasuring. You might want to take some time to journal, sit with, dance, or explore, in whichever way you choose, each one of the different types of erotic intimacy we've described. Guiding questions for your exploration might include:

— Do you experience this type of intimacy? If not, would you like to, or is it simply not important for you?

— Are there other types of erotic intimacy you experience? Do they fit into these categories or not?

— Are there things that block you from experiencing some types of erotic intimacy? If so, what are they?

— Are there opportunities to explore erotic intimacy in your life? If so, what are they?

Once you've reflected on the different types of erotic intimacy, you might want to spend some time mapping them out. For example, are your needs met for each type of intimacy? If so, who meets these needs, including yourself? Is there anything you want to change around this type of intimacy? Below is a grid that might help you map this out. For the first two questions, you could use a scale of 1–10, where 1 is least important and 10 is most important, or reflect on its importance in a more qualitative way (maybe writing down words or drawing). However, you don't need to use this grid format if it's not helpful. Please feel free to represent your reflections in any way that feels comfortable to you.

Type of erotic intimacy	How important is this type of intimacy for you?	Are your needs met in this type of intimacy?	Who meets your needs in this area, including yourself?	Is there anything you would like to change around this type of intimacy?
Sexual				
Physical				
Ecological				
Creative				
Kink				
Self-pleasuring				

REMEMBER: The most important thing about sharing our sexuality with others is that we feel free enough and safe enough to do so. That is consent. If you're not sure, then it's always fine not to share yourself in these ways, whether that means not being sexual, or not telling people about your sexuality. Nobody should ever put you under pressure to share your sexuality in ways that don't feel good and comfortable to you.

In the final chapter of the book, we'll explore more about how you can access support around your sexuality in the form of role models, professionals, and communities, which also might help you to ensure that the sex and relationships you have are as consensual as possible. We'll also get into how you might take your learnings about sexuality and apply them much more widely.

FURTHER RESOURCES

Meg-John and Justin's relationship user guide zine can be found here:

— Barker, M-J. and Hancock, J. (2016). *Make Your Own Relationship User Guide.* https://megjohnandjustin.com/publications

Jonathan Kent's book on non-monogamous relationships is:

— Kent, J. (2021). *A World Beyond Monogamy.* Portland, OR: Luminastra Press.

The accompanying podcast is:

— *Beyond Monogamy* (with Zayna Ratty and Jonathan Hancock)

If you want to learn more about how you might navigate the rules or agreements within your relationships, Meg-John covers this in:

— Barker, M-J. (2018). *Rewriting the Rules: An Anti-Self-Help Guide to Love, Sex and Relationships*. London: Routledge.

You might also find the Hot Love and Slow Relating blog posts on their website helpful:

— www.rewriting-the-rules.com/love-commitment/hot-love-being-and-having

— www.rewriting-the-rules.com/self/slow-relating

Meg-John's consent checklist can be found here:

— www.rewriting-the-rules.com/wp-content/uploads/2019/10/Consent-Checklist-1.pdf

There's more on how to navigate sex consensually with others in:

— Barker, M-J. and Hancock, J. (2017). *A Practical Guide to Sex*. London: Icon Books.

Other useful resources on consent include:

— Hancock, J. (2020). *Can We Talk About Consent?* London: Frances Lincoln.

— https://consentculture.com

— www.consentcollective.com

There are helpful resources to explore consensual and erotic intimacy practices here:

— https://bettymartin.org

— body-curious-sexcoach.co.uk/quintimacy

— https://wellcelium.org

Find out more about access intimacy on Mia Mingus's blog:

— https://leavingevidence.wordpress.com/2011/05/05/access-intimacy-the-missing-link

It can be challenging to think about relationships, consent, and intimacy. So let's take as many moments as you need to slow down, and maybe even find some time to resource yourself.

If you want, take some time to be with yourself and notice what's coming up for you. You don't have to be quiet or meditate to do this. You could go for a walk and notice what emotions come up as you do so.

Or you could draw, or simply use crayons on a piece of paper and see what colors you feel drawn to. As you run the crayon across the paper, what emotions do you notice?

You could also dance, or listen to music, and notice what comes up for you.

Are there emotions, needs, and desires that are trying to get your attention in some way? If so, try to notice them with as much curiosity and non-judgment as you're able at this moment.

You might want to record those emotions, needs, or desires in some way so that you can get back to them, if you want or need to.

Take all the time you need and, when you're ready, come back for the next and final chapter in this book.

CHAPTER 7

TAKING YOUR SEXUALITY OUT INTO THE WORLD

Here you are in the last chapter of our book! In this one we'll explore a number of ways in which we might move beyond ourselves, and our erotic relationships, into the wider world. First, we'll consider how you might find role models and professionals who can support you on your sexuality journey. Then we'll reflect on sexual communities: why these are important, as well as some of the tensions and troubles that can be involved in engaging with a community. Finally, we'll explore the ways in which your erotic life might relate to your everyday life, and how the erotic can inform how you engage with the rest of the world.

7.1 FINDING ROLE MODELS AND SUPPORTERS

In the dominant cultures where we live, we've noticed some mixed messages around authenticity and sexuality. For example, in self-help books and popular psychology, there's an emphasis on the importance of authenticity and vulnerability. The popularity of Brené Brown's books, TED talk, courses, podcast, and now Netflix special, seems to highlight just how much people are yearning for these ideas. On the other hand, sexual identities, desires, attractions, and practices that fall outside societal and cultural expectations are often viewed as far less desirable—or even as intolerable—within dominant culture.

We believe that to be able to be authentic and vulnerable when it comes to sexuality, especially if our sexualities do not align with societal expectations, we need both role models and supporters, which it's why we've dedicated an entire section to these.

We'll start with role models—those people who've opened up the doors we've walked through, or even shown us that the door was there. This could be people in our lives, activists, community organizers, fictional characters, celebrities, educators, content creators, and so on. We'll get started by introducing some of the role models who've accompanied us on our own journeys.

ALEX WRITES:

My sexuality was pretty dormant until my teenage years. I grew up Catholic and was probably one of the most devout people in my family. From about nine years old, and studying for my first communion, I was really into hagiographies (biographical accounts of the lives of saints). This shaped my early understanding of sexuality as total surrender, given that so many of the saints I admired had completely surrendered to God.

As I entered my teenage years, things got a little more complicated as I started to experience attractions and desires. It was hard, for me to reconcile my love for God and my budding sexual feelings. Some of the role models during this stage of my life were lay people who lived their marriages as part of religious communities, such as the Focolare movement inspired and started by Chiara Lubich, and the Secular Franciscan Order.

At the same time, some of my own beliefs did not match those of the Church I was brought up in. For example, one of my close friends—and dance partner—was gay and he was subjected to conversion efforts in his own family. I believed that he was perfect as he was, and that efforts to turn him heterosexual were absolutely wrong. He was definitely one of my early role models of what it meant to be authentic to oneself. The first time I saw two people of the same gender kiss was in my early twenties in London. Those two feminine-presenting people at a random bus stop in Trafalgar Square were definitely early role models for me, as they opened up a portal for attractions and desires that I previously had no blueprint for.

As I grew in my understanding of my own sexuality, writing by queer, feminist writers became my possibility maps. The work of Audre Lorde, Rita Mae Brown, Alice Walker, Patrick Califia, James Baldwin, and so many more became the staple I needed to better understand myself and my own identities, attractions, and desires. On the threshold of 30, I came across BiCon, a large bisexual convention in the UK. Activists and community organizers in this space, especially Jen Yockney, became my inspiration and role models. In these bi spaces,

I also began to feel more freedom to explore my gender and how this intersected with my sexuality.

There are so many more people I could mention here, including friends like somatic sex educator and coach Dr. Pavini Moray, who constantly models centering the potential of the erotic for creative and spiritual growth; or Barbara Carrellas, sexologist, sex educator, and author, whose writing continues to open up possibilities for deeper connection; or Staci Haines, co-founder of generative somatics, whose work on healing from sexual abuse has been foundational for me, both personally and professionally.

MEG-JOHN WRITES:

Until I was in my twenties I didn't really think about my sexuality as being anything other than normative, and kept all my non-normative desires secret. An unlikely early influence on my sexuality was James Bond! I borrowed my dad's James Bond books, and later watched the films, and incorporated this character into my fantasies. I imagined him training me to become able to endure the kinds of things he did, as my life was so frightening at the time. I remember buying *The James Bond Movie Poster Book* furtively, without letting anybody know. I kept it hidden under my mattress and would get it out and leaf through it when I was drawing and fantasizing about James Bond.

Another important early model for me was finding Armistead Maupin's *Tales of the City* books in the college bookshop. While I couldn't put into words, yet, why those books spoke to me, the kind of queer community described in them felt huge. Following the break-up of my first long-term relationship, I met Grant Denkinson, a UK bi activist, who was part of the same online comic discussion group as me, and happened to live in the same city. Grant told me about bi, poly, and kink communities, and took me to my first BiCon event where I attended workshops about all of these things and realized how deeply I connected with them.

At a Buffy the Vampire Slayer conference a few years later (I'm just releasing quite how geeky all of these examples are!), I heard a paper which referenced an article by US activist and theorist Gayle Rubin. Reading her essay, "Thinking Sex," was another lightbulb moment as I realized that it wasn't so much about finding specific identities, for me, but about a whole different way of approaching sexuality beyond the normal/abnormal binary.

Audre Lorde's essay, "The Uses of the Erotic," landed in a similar way when I read that some years later and realized that the erotic was much wider for me than simply sex. Authors whose ideas expand the concept of sexuality in ways that encompass and affirm my own experience have been the most important thing for me in coming to understand my own unique sexuality, and giving myself permission to express it in the ways which feel congruent.

As I've mentioned elsewhere in the book, lately a significant feature of how I experience myself, and my sexuality, is plurality, and I've enjoyed returning to those old James Bond fantasies and reclaiming him as part of that. My James is very different from the deeply problematic character in the books and films. Although also tough, passionate, and full of dignity, my James is queer, fights for social justice, and is a nurturing father figure! It's been great to connect online with David Lowbridge-Ellis, whose project, Licence to Queer, brings together other queers who connected with these books and films in some way in their early lives, and now find different ways to read Bond queerly or to reclaim him for our purposes.

We hope that these snapshots illustrate what we mean by role models in this section, and why we think it's important to identify who these might be in your own life.

Different kinds of role models and their importance

In our own accounts, we've tried to highlight how varied role models can be, from people met on the street once, to friends, spiritual leaders, authors, activists, and community organizers. Role models can also include ancestors, or fictional characters, such as Willow Rosenberg and Tara Maclay in *Buffy the Vampire Slayer*, or Captain Raymond Holt from *Brooklyn Nine-Nine*, or Elena Alvarez in *One Day at a Time*, Blanca Evangelista in *Pose*, Kurt Hummel in *Glee*, Randall and Beth Pearson in *This Is Us*, Rose Nylund in *The Golden Girls*, Callie Torres in *Grey's Anatomy*, Chloe Decker and Lucifer Morningstar in *Lucifer*, Eric Effiong in *Sex Education*, Bette Porter in the *L Word*, Justin Suarez in *Ugly Betty*, David Rose in *Schitt's Creek*, Annalise Keating in *How to Get Away with Murder*, Theo Putnam in the *Chilling Adventures of Sabrina*, or Lafayette Reynolds in *True Blood*. We're glad to notice that our list of role models from TV characters grows more extensive and inclusive of all kinds of sexualities every year.

Whoever your role models might be, and wherever you might be drawing from, be it TV, your ancestral web, or community, we believe that role models can be important for the following reasons:

- Through their work, or conversations with them, they can help us think about sexuality in new and helpful ways.

- Through their lived experiences, they can provide us with examples of how to navigate our own sexualities.

- They can provide us with terminology to describe our own sexual identities, attractions, desires, and practices.

- They can give us a sense of what is possible beyond our own lived experiences and imagination.

- When their identities, attractions, desires, and practices are different from our own—in whatever aspect—they can broaden our understanding of sexuality and help us be better allies and accomplices to those who have different intersections from ours.

- They can give us comfort, support, and hope either directly, or through their work, when we're experiencing oppression or hardship.

FIGURE 7.1: ROLE MODELS

ACTIVITY: YOUR SEXUALITY ROLE MODELS

You may already have a clear idea of who your sexuality role models are by this point. In this activity, we invite you to do something to honor this. For example, you could write them a letter, which you could just keep for yourself or send, as long as you think that sending and receiving it would feel consensual to all involved. You could express your thanks, if it's someone in your own social circles, or highlight their work in a blog post, zine, or book, if you think that they'll feel that this is okay.

If you can't think of anyone for this activity, you could do some research. For example, you could explore some of the people, authors, or characters we have mentioned, or follow up on some of the further resources in this or other chapters of this book. Who has inspired your journey so far when it comes to sexuality, and who might inspire your journey moving forward?

In a moment, we'll talk more about supporters, who are different from role models. However, before we do so, we want to notice that role models and supporters, just like anything or anyone in our lives, can both open up and close down opportunities for us. We've already mentioned that one of the patterns we might struggle with, because of trauma and dominant discourses, is all-or-nothing thinking. In this case, we might notice a tendency to put role models on a pedestal, to view them as either completely good, or—if they fall from grace in some way—as completely bad. The truth is that most humans—and human-created characters—are complex, fallible, and make mistakes and mess up. It's important to remind ourselves, especially when dealing with actual people, that our role models and supporters are flawed, imperfect humans, who are likely to be full of contradictions, and may disappoint us at some point. It can be helpful to practice moving to more "both/and" thinking which embraces everyone's capacity for strength and struggle, kindness and harshness, wisdom and ignorance (there is more on this in our book, *Life Isn't Binary*).

It's also worth remembering that when we consider someone a role model, we might be much more focused on them than they are on us. This is one of the reasons why we mentioned consent in the activity above. For example, if we reach out to a favorite author, public figure, or community organizer, we might feel disappointed if they don't reply, but they might well receive too many messages and not have enough resources to be able to address every message. Or we might receive a reply and feel upset by it, in which case it can be helpful to remember that we might have caught them on an off-day or maybe—if our intersections are different—we might have communicated in a way that was oppressive for them; for example, if it felt to them like a request for unpaid labor. We encourage you to hold your experiences kindly and with open hands if you decide to reach out to one of your role models and they don't respond, or if they respond in a way that is unexpected.

Reflection point: Inspiration or comparison

As you think about role models, we invite you to reflect on whether you compare yourself to them, or whether you feel inspired by them. Notice the difference: inspiration tends to uplift us, whereas comparison tends to make us feel lesser ourselves. Sexuality role models are really about us feeling more expansive in, and present to, our sexualities. If they become a measuring stick to compare ourselves against and beat ourselves with, it might be time to let them go.

Comparison is very appealing to our trauma brain, which might be looking for ways to make us feel bad about ourselves, but it's really not so conducive to our own psychological and emotional health. So please remember, if you feel uplifted and inspired by your role models, that's great; but if they become another way to feel bad about yourself, or less than someone else, then it might be time to become your own inspiration, and let go of external references.

Sometimes we might want to reach out to our role models for support. That's often not appropriate. For example, an author or actor doesn't usually have the capacity to support all their readers or followers. If we're looking for support, we might want to take a moment to evaluate what we need support with, and then decide who might best be able to support us. It's to this need for support—and what might be available in relation to sexuality—that we turn next.

The role and importance of supporters

As we mentioned earlier, it can be challenging to authentically express our sexual identities, desires, and attractions if they differ from those considered legitimate within dominant discourses. In fact, it can be challenging even when these align with dominant discourses but we've run into an obstacle of some kind. Role models can offer inspiration and a sense of possibility, but we often need more than that: we need support. Support can take many forms and come from many sources, including friends and family. Here we'll focus on what support might be available to deal with sexuality beyond our social and familial circles.

Depending on what we're struggling with, we might consider hiring a professional. Below are details of types of sexuality professionals who might be helpful to you and others around you. We've included some links to useful online directories of such practitioners in the further resources at the end of this chapter.

Sex worker

A sex worker is someone who works in the sex industry.

This work can take many forms, including administrative and managerial work within the industry, acting, and direct sexual services, either via online platforms or in person. If you watch sexually explicit materials—commonly referred to as porn—you're already using the services of sex workers. People choose to hire a sex worker for a number of reasons, including not having a current sexual partner and wanting sex. Please note that sex work is different from human trafficking, even though these are often undifferentiated in media reports. Sex work is work that is consensual, and therefore only includes adults who are able to consent to this type of work. In order for consent to be possible, sex work also needs to be free of coercion, including coercion from clients. Please note that different forms of sex work may or may not be legal where you live.

Surrogate

Surrogates usually work alongside a sex therapist (see below) and some prefer the term "partner surrogate." A partner surrogate is someone who, usually in collaboration with a sex therapist, supports a client in achieving their goals around sex, sexuality, and intimacy, through the use of touch, sometimes including intercourse. Surrogates offer clients the opportunity to learn and practice intimate and sexual touch in a supportive and affirming environment. This work might or might not be considered legal where you live, and might be viewed as falling under the purview of sex work by some, and within the criminal justice system in some areas.

Sex therapist

Sex therapy is a specialist branch of psychotherapy focused

on human sexuality. Usually sex therapists are also licensed therapists who have additional training to be able to address issues related to sex and sexuality. However, in many countries, the designation of sex therapist is unregulated, which means that anyone could claim this title. Sex therapists support clients in achieving therapeutic goals around sex and sexuality, such as self-acceptance, dealing with genital pain, or inability to achieve and/or maintain an erection, inability to orgasm, either by oneself or with partners, and so on. Some sex therapists will work alongside a partner surrogate, as this can offer clients touch-based services which are not provided by sex therapists who are also licensed therapists.

Systemic therapist or family therapist

Systemic or family therapists are trained in working with more than one person in the room. They can be very helpful when there are issues involving partners or family members. For example, if a child discloses their sexuality to a parent who is having issues dealing with this, a systemic or family therapist can provide appropriate support. Or if someone is having difficulties in their romantic as well as sexual partnership, a systemic or family therapist might be a good option for support. Some therapists are trained in both systemic/family work and sex therapy.

Sex educator

Sex educators are trained to provide education on sex and sexuality in a range of contexts, from classrooms to families and individuals. They have usually received specialist training in human sexuality and might offer their services through online or in-person classes. Sex educators often also spread information by writing books or creating other materials, such as curricula for schools. Some sex educators might also work as coaches and offer individual services.

Sex and relationship coach

Sex and relationship coaches are similar to—but different from—therapists. They are usually not trained therapists and are more focused on providing advice and solutions to clients. They might also offer online or in-person classes, as well as one-to-one sessions. Unlike therapy, sex coaching does not involve diagnosis or treatment, but rather it provides insights, education, and solutions for specific issues. Some coaches focus on both sex and relationships, while others focus on one or the other.

Sexological bodyworker/somatic sex educators or coaches

Sexological bodyworkers are trained to work with client's bodies (soma) to address issues around sex and sexuality. They might do so through education or hands-on bodywork, including techniques such as genital mapping, pelvic release, and masturbation coaching. Sexological bodyworkers are sometimes known as somatic sex educators or somatic sex coaches as well, depending on the country they work in, and where they have trained. They are trained in bodywork, somatic approaches to healing, and sexuality. Some of their work might or might not be considered legal where you live if there is genital touch involved.

Somatic sex therapist

Somatic sex therapists are sex therapists with additional training in somatic approaches to healing. Often, somatic sex therapists have additional trauma training as many somatic approaches are designed to address trauma responses in the body.

You may already be aware of some of these kinds of professionals, while others may be new to you. Whether this list is new or familiar to you, we encourage you to evaluate what your needs might be and what support you might benefit from, if any.

We can, of course, receive support from people other than professionals, such as family members and friends, and from the communities we're part of. We'll address the role and importance of finding a community in the next section. We'll also talk about consent in this section, and please note that some of these issues apply to working with professionals as well.

7.2 FINDING A COMMUNITY (IF YOU WANT TO)

Like role models and pioneers, it's important to remember that communities can be extremely useful for helping us to understand and affirm our sexualities, and that they can also be limited in various ways. It's helpful if you can go into relationships with both individuals and communities with an awareness of this. It's easy to get hurt if you're looking for a person to be a perfect role model or to rescue you, or if you're looking for a community to be the family you've always yearned for, or the place where you finally belong completely, and everyone sees things exactly the way you do.

When we approach individuals or groups in this kind of way, we risk giving up too much of our own power and putting them on a pedestal, which they will inevitably fall off at some point, often harming both us and them in the process. Individuals and groups who want to be seen as perfect or wonderful are also often not the safest ones to put our trust in, compared to those who know that they are imperfect and limited, and are up for being open about—and addressing—their issues. It's better for everyone to recognize that we're all human, which means that we're vulnerable and will make mistakes.

Sexual communities can take many different forms. A community can be for all the people who share a particular sexual identity, like LGB, queer, or ace communities. A community can be for people who share particular desires, often with more of a sense that sexual things will happen within that community. Kink communities and communities for writers of erotic fiction would be examples of those kinds of communities. There are also communities for people who have gone through similar experiences; for example, survivor networks or groups for disabled people or trans folks around sexuality.

A community can be a very wide term for everybody who shares a particular aspect of sexuality. For example, the gay community could be a term for all the people who are gay in a particular city or country, and the survivor community refers to everyone who has ever survived abuse or assault. Alternatively, community can be a more specific term for a particular online or offline space, or set of spaces. For example, when we were both part of the bi community in the UK back in the early 2000s, most people who would have seen themselves as part of this community attended the annual BiCon event and were linked together via a particular online platform. Community can be even more specific than this, just referring to the members of a specific club or online network, or folks who have undergone a particular training, or live in a particular setting, for example.

Here are some of the things that finding a community of people who share some aspect of your sexual identity and/

or experiences can open up, and some of the things it can close down.

Opening up

— Finding a community can help you to feel far less isolated: there are people out there who share this important aspect of who you are and are also interested in talking about these things.

— If your sexual identity or experience is marginalized or stigmatized, then it can be hugely normalizing and affirming to find people who share it and are comfortable talking about it.

— Accessing a community can expose you to language and ideas which help you to make sense of aspects of your experience because others have navigated similar territory already.

— A specific sexual community can be a great place to find partners with similar desires, or those who will understand your particular body or past experiences without you having to explain them and risk rejection.

— Some communities can particularly draw in folks with a whole cluster of interests and experiences in common, beyond that particular aspect of sexuality, which means they can be a great place to find like-minded friends.

— Communities based on marginalized sexualities can often be somewhat more clued up than the mainstream about other intersecting identities (e.g., gender, disability, race). These days there are also many smaller sub-communities for those who share multiple identities or experiences.

— We need communities for mutual aid and support, and if we are to effectively fight wider systems of oppression in solidarity with others. Colonization, consumer capitalism, and white supremacy all operate in ways that isolate us from each other, and communities are an important corrective to this.

Closing down

— Communities often end up with norms and ways of doing things which can make you feel pressured to fit in with these, or isolated if you don't.

— Sexual communities, in particular, can lead you to feel that you have to be sexual in certain ways, take part in certain activities, or express your sexuality in certain ways in order to belong, which can be constraining or even lead to damaging sexual experiences.

— Becoming identified with a particular community can lead you into "us-and-them" thinking, whereby you see your community as inherently better than other communities, potentially becoming quite isolated from people outside that community.

— In communities, we can become blinkered to the ways in which we might actually connect really well with people beyond that community, as well as with problematic behaviors and dynamics within that community.

— If something tough—like a break-up or conflict—happens, then we can end up losing our whole community and support system over it if people "take sides" or if we now feel uncomfortable in that community.

— Many sexual communities end up perpetuating norms and oppressions which are present in wider culture; for example, structural racism, or ideas about who is deemed most sexually attractive. It can be particularly hard if you think you have found a community "home" and then find that the same marginalization or injustice you experience in the wider world also happens there.

— Communities can also end up reproducing the toxic dynamics of dominant culture, such as dividing into in-groups and out-groups, appointing problematic leaders, scapegoating certain individuals, or allowing non-consensual behavior to go unchecked because "everybody knows about it."

For these reasons, we'd suggest holding the concept of community lightly, rather than either desperately trying to find your "one true" community or rejecting a community—or the whole idea of community—because it turns out to be imperfect. It can be wise to be part of more than one community and to question the idea that "your people" are particularly going to be the ones who share a feature of your sexuality—rather than other aspects of your interests or lived experience.

It can be useful to ask yourself what you are looking for from the communities you are part of, and what the best ways of finding—or building—communities that meet those needs might be.

Reflection point: Communities

Take a moment to think some more about the social networks and communities you belong to which relate to your sexuality in some way. Which communities are you part of? How does your sexuality impact your participation in those communities? Are there communities you would like to be part of or create? If so, what are they? How would being part of, or creating, those communities impact your life moving forward? Are you happy with the communities in your life? If so, what do you appreciate most about them? If not, what would you like to change?

Here are some examples from different people of the kinds of communities which are important to them, and how they have found them or built them.

Multiple experiences: Finding and building community

"I've had both very negative and very positive experiences of community. When I got involved in the conscious sexuality world, I went along to workshops and events where I often felt pressured to go beyond my limits. I was assaulted more than once by this one leader who everybody said was wonderful, so

I doubted my own experience and left the community. Some years later, other people began to speak out about their similar experiences. Joining that group of survivors was really important to me, and led me back into that world in a much safer way, attending events which were now committed to being consensual and trauma-informed."

"When I moved to this city, I tried leaping into the queer community and it did not work for me. It all seemed to be focused on dating and partying and that's just not me. Gradually I met a few friends who I had more in common with, and eventually we started to realize our dream of developing a housing collective with a veggie garden and everything. It's a queer community, but of a very different kind."

"Ace community was the game-changer of my life. Before, I thought there was something wrong with me, the friends I'd had had bullied me, and the partners I'd had had tried to pressure me into sex. Suddenly I was welcomed and I was accepted, I had a language that made sense of everything, and I found a supportive friendship network and eventually a partner."

"My faith community is far more important to me than the LGBT+ community, I have to say. The stereotype is that religious communities are intolerant of diverse sexualities and genders, but I have found the opposite to be true. I regularly experience ignorance and microaggressions towards my faith in LGBT+ spaces, whereas I experience real fellowship in multifaith groups and in my specific spiritual community."

"In my everyday life, my community is my family, my neighborhood, the people round here who are bringing up their kids together, and that feels great. But I also have an important community online who are completely separate: the fellow authors who I share my erotic fanfic with."

"I like to see myself as a bridge between communities. It's never made sense to me to have just one community in the same way as it doesn't make sense to have one partner. I'm somewhat involved in polyamorous communities, eco activist communities, and leftie politics communities, and I like to bring them into dialogue and get people talking about different ways of relating with each other and the world."

Consent and communities

We mentioned in the last chapter that communities are important when it comes to sexual, and other forms of, consent. Given that wider culture is so non-consensual, if we are to practice engaging in more consensual forms of behavior, we really need systems and structures around us to support that. Also, a great deal of non-consensual behavior happens within private relationships, families, and groups, so it's important to cultivate community support and cultures of greater openness in order that people get used to spotting the signs of non-consensual sex and relationships, and supporting those who are in such situations to recognize it and to address what's happening.

Sexual communities can operate in ways that enable greater consent, and in ways that foster—and obscure—non-consensual behavior. The consent culture movement which we mentioned in the last chapter grew out of people realizing the extent of non-consensual behavior that was happening within kink and sex-positive communities, and recognizing that the only way to change this was to create a whole culture of consent within those communities.

There has been a tendency in many communities to allow the non-consensual behavior of some individuals to continue unchecked. Sometimes this is because those people are leaders who are well regarded in communities and nobody wants to believe it of them, or people fear being rejected if they mention it. Sometimes it is because there's a shared community understanding that a particular person behaves in this way and "everybody knows" to avoid them, the way the members of a household know to avoid the "missing stair" on the staircase. It also may well be the case that other people in the community are also involved in non-consensual behavior which is perhaps less obvious to them or to others, but which leaves them feeling uneasy about raising the issue of non-consent.

There has also been a tendency—once non-consent in a community is acknowledged—to focus on getting one particular individual removed from the community, rather than recognizing non-consent as a systemic issue, and non-consensual behavior as something most of us have engaged in at times. Sometimes the tactics for addressing non-consent can become non-consensual themselves, such as insisting that survivors speak out, or using shaming tactics to call out or cancel certain individuals.

While it is vital that communities do address consent violations, and work to build cultures of consent, it's important that this comes from a place of acknowledging that we're all capable of non-consent, of various kinds, within a non-consensual wider culture. It's the system that needs to be addressed rather than individualizing the problem, and ways of addressing non-consent need to be developed which are transformative rather than using the tools of non-consent, such as policing and punishing. For example, the Bay Area Transformative Justice Collective developed the concept of "pods" to refer to the relationships that we might build around us with people who can turn to each other for support around violent, harmful, and abusive experiences, whether as survivors, bystanders, or people who have harmed.

When you are entering a new community, it's worth asking about the understandings of consent, and consent practices, which are present there. When developing a new community, consent is something useful to consider in terms of how you might build it into the foundations. And it can be helpful to all of us to think about who the people around us are to whom we might turn for support when we are hurt, or find that we've hurt others, or when something of this kind unfolds in our community. We've included some resources at the end of this chapter where you can find out more about these ideas.

In the next section, we'll explore how the things we learn from our sexual lives and communities—like how to do consent—can apply beyond our sexuality and to the rest of our lives.

7.3 FROM SEXUALITY TO THE REST OF OUR LIVES

Reading through this book you might well have found yourself questioning where the dividing lines are between sex and other aspects of life. For example, we've included activities under the broad definition of sexuality which could be regarded as forms of sport, play, art, or spirituality, as much as they could sex. Tying people up in intricate forms of rope bondage, role-playing being a pony, puppy, or other animal, writing or drawing erotica, and developing ecosexual relationships with land and plant life would be good examples to reflect on here.

We've also considered how sexuality can be divided into erotic and nurturing types of contact, as well as solo and part-nered contact, and you may well wonder about what makes a certain kind of touch or intimate connection erotic rather than nurturing, or vice versa.

As we've mentioned, one of our key influences—Audre Lorde—deliberately defined the erotic in a much broader way than what we often think of as sex and sexuality, referring instead to a feeling or force of aliveness, creativity, and vitality that can be present in all kinds of solo and relational activities.

In her essay, "The Uses of the Erotic," Lorde also makes the suggestion that tuning into the erotic can enhance our lives, way beyond our sexual or intimate lives. She says:

> Once we begin to feel deeply all the aspects of our lives, we begin to demand from ourselves and from our life-pursuits that they feel in accordance with that joy which we know ourselves to be capable of... This is a grave responsibility...not to settle for the convenient, the shoddy, the conventionally expected, nor the merely safe.

In this section, we'll return to some of the specific aspects of sex, sexuality, and the erotic which might be helpful to apply to our life more broadly, as well as how we might turn to sexuality to help us to understand and navigate aspects of our wider lives. In the final section of the chapter—and the book—we'll pick up the further thread in Lorde's essay where she suggests that the erotic can also inform what we do in the world: the personal as well as the political. This is both because we would want to demand this same capacity for joy for all people, and because we can use the energy of the erotic in this way. As Lorde says, "Recognizing the power of the erotic within our lives can give us the energy to pursue genuine change within our world, rather than merely settling for a shift of characters in the same weary drama."

Briefly, here are four ways in which we might use the practices that we develop in our sexual or erotic lives to enhance the rest of our lives. These are followed by four ways in which we might bring the rest of our lives into our erotic practices in order to help understand ourselves better, process our feelings, and address things we're concerned about. For the first four we've included reflection points to explore how they might apply in your life. For the second four we've given multiple experience examples so you can get a sense of the kinds of things that people do, given that these may be less familiar.

From sexuality to the rest of our lives

Being present

One feature that most authors agree is important for enjoyable sexual or sensual experiences is being present. This means being able to be in the here-and-now of what is happening to you as it unfolds, rather than drifting off into memories of the past, or planning for the future, or being distracted by thoughts, phone messages, or whatever else is going on in the room, or in your life. Being present means being grounded in your body, your feelings, and your immediate environment. The capacity to be present is also something that's emphasized by many therapists, mindfulness practitioners, and healers of various kinds, as an important practice for mental and physical well-being.

So we could see sex—with ourselves and with others—as a place where we could specifically practice being present: noticing when we have drifted off or disconnected, and gently bringing ourselves back to the present moment. In some ways, this can be easier during sex—than in the rest of our lives—because we're engaged in a focused activity, and because the physical arousal and/or sensations and/or specific headspace that we may feel can make it easier to be in our bodies and in the immediacy of our situation. Of course, it can also be particularly challenging to be present during sex because of the strong self-criticism, fears of "getting it wrong," and desire to be "normal" in this area that many of us have, along with the impact of sexual trauma.

Reflection point: Presence

Which situations, sensations, headspaces, and so on make it easier—and more difficult—for you to be present? Might practicing being present in a sexual, sensual, or erotic context work for you?

Tuning into ourselves, our aliveness, and our creativity
Another important feature of sexuality which we've emphasized throughout this book—and particularly in Chapter 5—is the capacity to tune into your needs, desires, attractions,

and so on. Again, we could use our sexual or erotic times as a way to practice being more in touch with what we want and don't want, in ways that enable us to be more in touch with this in our everyday life. Approaches like Betty Martin's wheel of consent and three-minute game particularly help us to learn how to tune into what we want and don't want erotically, and what we are and aren't willing to do.

As Audre Lorde suggests, if—through the erotic—we become more able to get in touch with that sense of aliveness or vitality that we are capable of, we might start to become more able to tune into that in other, or all, areas of life. We might become more able to be guided by what gives us that kind of feeling; for example, in the types of work, relationships, creativity, leisure pursuits, or activism, we engage with.

Reflection point: Aliveness

In which kinds of erotic practices, relationships, or scenarios do you find it easiest to tune into yourself or to get in touch with that kind of alive feeling? How might you approach your everyday life, or specific areas of life, in a similar way?

Consent

Tuning in relates strongly to the theme of consent, bcause tuning into these things in ourselves makes it much easier for us to articulate our needs and desires, as well as our limits and boundaries. It is to be hoped that if we're guided by this sense of sexuality as being all about inviting that sense of aliveness, then we'll also want the same things for all those we connect erotically with.

As we explained in Chapter 6, we live in a highly non-consensual world way beyond the problems with sexual consent which the #MeToo movement and consent culture movement have highlighted. If we get used to practicing deep, careful forms of consent in our erotic lives, then this will ripple out to the rest of our lives. This involves being mindful of the power imbalances, social scripts, and traumatic experiences which make consent so difficult, and cultivating explicitly consensual practices to maximize everyone's capacity to consent, in sexual contexts, social contexts, professional contexts, and more.

Reflection point: Consent

Think about the most consensual erotic experiences that you've had. How might the things that the people involved did there apply to situations and relationships beyond erotic ones?

Connecting with ourselves and others

As we explored in the intimacy section of the last chapter, erotic intimacy is one way—or a set of ways—in which we can connect with ourselves and with other people. Again, perhaps there are things to be learned from the ways we connect erotically which apply to all ways of relating with ourselves and others.

For example, when connecting erotically with ourselves or others, we might build in practices of connecting, creating space, and negotiating what will happen beforehand, and making time for afterglow, aftercare, or debriefing afterwards. We might also build in ongoing check-in practices to see how we're doing. These could be useful practices to bring into our daily lives and work, as well as into social or professional meet-ups with others.

We might also endeavor to welcome all feelings into our erotic lives, being present to ourselves and others whatever our emotional state, and perhaps tailoring the kind of sensual, nurturing, erotic, or sexual contact that we engage in to that. It can be possible—and even wonderful—to connect erotically with ourselves and others when we are feeling sad, scared, angry, or lonely, as much as when we're in more joyful, excited, transcendent, or peaceful emotional states, so long as everybody involved feels good about it and about how their feelings are being met.

> ### Reflection point: Connection
>
> How might you use your erotic life to practice ways of connecting with yourself and others? How might you use it to practice welcoming yourself and others in all emotional states? How might these things apply to the rest of your life?

From the rest of our lives back to sexuality

Fantasies for self-exploration

Picking up on our exploration of fantasies back in Chapter 5, you might remember that we suggested that our erotic fantasies—like our dreams—are a rich place for coming to a better understanding of ourselves. If we come up against things in our life which we struggle with, we could turn to our fantasies to understand them better, to process them, and to explore how we might engage with them.

Multiple experiences: Fantasies

"I keep a journal where I write about my daily life and my erotic life side by side. I often notice that where I go to erotically is a reflection of what I'm currently going through. For example, when I'm feeling too much responsibility, I want to watch porn where people are controlled, and I identify very much with them. When I'm feeling scared of 'getting it wrong,' I engage with erotica where people get looked after and babied. Taking these themes to therapy has been very helpful in addressing my patterns, and I recently paid a porn performer to create customs for me which helped me to personalize it more."

"I explicitly use my fantasies to process tough stuff that happens in my life. For example, in a situation of workplace bullying I went to a similar scenario in my fantasies and imagined it playing out in a bunch of different ways, embodying different parts of myself to deal with it. That helped me to get in touch with my feelings about what happened, and it did actually inform how I dealt with it."

Sexual healing
Many people implicitly or explicitly use sexual activity as a therapeutic or healing practice. This might be as simple as engaging in solo or partnered sex as a form of soothing when

you're distressed, or because you know that orgasm will help you to release pent-up feelings. Or it might be as complex as creating a specific scenario to revisit painful past situations in the form of an erotic scene, where you reclaim what happened as something hot, or give it a happy ending. It's important to be careful in this territory, of course, as going to painful or traumatic places erotically also has the potential to retraumatize or hurt us. You might usefully consider engaging in self-consent practices during solo sex (see Chapter 5), and ensuring contexts for healing partnered sex where you have developed deep trust in the people involved (see Chapter 6), as well as accessing some of the kinds of professionals discussed earlier in this chapter to support your journey if you want to use erotic practices in this way.

Multiple experiences: Healing

"I regularly visit a sex worker who helps me to revisit the abuse that I received from teachers and older boys at boarding school when I was younger. Finding arousal and joy in what was once so painful feels healing to me. In addition to acting out the scenes, we chat about how common this theme is in her clients, and about how much she feels for us all. That helps me to feel less alone."

"I really struggle with confidence in my life, and found that sex was somewhere that I could develop a part of myself who is much more able to feel competent and sure of themselves. Initially this just came out sometimes with partners, surprising us both, but now I've developed a sexual relationship with a friend who gets it. We explicitly play with me being in that role."

Intimate engagement

We can use erotic or sexual contact to deepen intimacy with specific people, or to practice certain kinds of intimacy which we'd like to cultivate more in the rest of our lives. For example, sex can be a place where we practice being vulnerable around another person and are seen in that vulnerability, or express certain emotions which we struggle with, or ask for what we need, or allow ourselves to be taken care of, if we find those things difficult.

Multiple experiences: Intimacy

"I have a real thing from my upbringing that conflict just isn't okay. When I've got heated with somebody, I often have a massive vulnerability hangover and a lot of shame. My current partner is really into make-up sex, and clearly feels both tender and desiring towards me when we've been through a conflict and resolved it. Connecting in that way afterwards is doing a lot to teach my body that it's really okay to have a conflict."

"I've always felt a lot of fear about getting emotional in public. I used to dream about it happening and how I'd lose control and everyone would be disgusted with me. I decided to address it in the conscious sexuality event that I go to, with a group of people I've developed very trusting relationships with over time. We crafted a scene together where I'd have a beating which reduced me to tears and then everybody would come round and hold me as I cried. Since then I've cried in public a couple of times and it felt okay."

Sacred sex rituals

Many people weave sexual or erotic practices together with their faith or spiritual practices. Through our sexualities we can access peak or transcendent experiences, we can commune with guides or spiritual beings, and we can create rituals around aspects of our lives that we'd like to accept or change, or which relate to ways in which we'd like to engage with the wider world.

Multiple experiences: Rituals

"Ecosexuality and paganism were such an obvious click for me. I love being out in the wild doing rituals alone or with others which draw in the environment around us and our erotic energies. For example, we've done a group climax during the eclipse, and a number of outdoor rituals where we've embodied different aspects and connected sexually through those. I have an altar at home where I keep objects taken from the places I've done these things."

"Buddhism is often thought of as not being particularly sexual, given the history of monks and nuns with celibacy. Personally, I see it as an easy fit though. I bring a solo erotic element into the Tibetan practices of meeting your demons, and a regret ritual that takes place on the full and new moons. It feels an important way for me to welcome the 'demonic' feelings back in, or to release those emotions of regret and remorse."

In the last section of the chapter we turn to the ways in which our sexuality can inform how we relate to the world out there, particularly in a more political or activist sense. But before that, let's have one final slow down...

Breathe in... Pause for a moment... Breathe out...

Feel free to focus on your breath for as long
as you want, it's okay to take a break.

In this moment, we'd like to invite you to
nourish yourself through your senses.

What does this mean?

Maybe there's a smell, a texture, like a favorite
blanket, or a sound, such as a favorite song,
that you find pleasant or comforting.

If so, take time to give yourself this
comforting or pleasant experience.

Smell an essential oil you love, snuggle with a blanket or cuddly toy, listen to that song, eat that favorite snack or drink your most delicious cup of tea, coffee, or hot chocolate.

You could also nourish yourself through touch.

You can hug yourself, or gently squeeze your arms and legs, or put your hands on your heart or belly and just breathe.

Self-touch can be so nourishing, and, of course, you can also nourish yourself through touch by masturbating, if that's something you find pleasurable.

Whatever you choose to nourish yourself, through whatever senses are most available to you, make sure it helps you stay present and connected.

7.4 CHANGING THE WORLD!

In the previous section, we talked about how the erotic—which as Audre Lorde teaches us is so much broader than sex and sexuality—can impact, heal, and change so many parts of our lives. Here, we conclude the book by discussing how an intentional relationship with the erotic has the potential to change the world.

We want to make it clear, from the start of this section, that we're not talking about a specific way of having sex or specific sexualities—being queer, for example, or practicing relationship anarchy. While those things can change the way we relate to ourselves and others, they're not always inherently revolutionary, although they might, at times, feel that way and be a part of our own activism. We want to address the ways in which our sexuality—whatever it is—is in relationship to the world around us and vice versa. What do we mean by this? Let's start with some examples.

Urban Tantra

In the 1980s, a global pandemic—HIV—which is still one of the largest global pandemics, began to sweep across the globe. One of the communities most impacted by this virus was, and is, the queer community, with gay men and trans people, especially trans feminine people, and people of color, being the most affected. Given that one of the modes of HIV transmission is through sex, people in our gay and trans communities were not only grieving the loss of too many, too soon, but also trying to figure out how to keep connecting with one another safely and intimately.

During this time, a young performance artist, Barbara Carrellas, alongside others, became interested in broadening our understanding of what sexual and intimate connection could be. Drawing from traditional tantric approaches, while acknowledging that those cannot be simply taken from another culture and adapted to an Anglo context, she began what would become her Urban Tantra approach, in which so many sexuality professionals have now trained. Nowdays, it seems obvious to many sex therapists, counselors and educators that there are ways to connect intimately and erotically beyond sex, but this understanding did not emerge fully formed and separate from a specific historical, geographical, and cultural moment.

Ecosexuality

Another global crisis which we've been aware of for at least as long as we've known about HIV, is the climate crisis— global warming, climate change, and its consequences, such as droughts, floods, and tsunami affecting people and animals across the globe.

You might wonder what sexuality has to do with the climate crisis. However, if we draw the dots between the ongoing settler-colonial project, the transatlantic slave trade, and capitalism, we can understand that once we start treating the land as something that can be owned—and people as property—we begin to lose relationship with the source of our nourishment, the land, and with ourselves and others through the dehumanization of some for the benefit of the few. Of course, this is something that Indigenous people and cultures know intimately, as do most Black and Brown people who continue to be highly impacted by these unjust systems.

For some of us who might have been displaced from direct relationship to more Earth-based spiritualities, ecosexuality has been one way to recognize and reconnect with the Earth as a sacred source of nourishment and erotic connection— connection to the cycles of life and death. As Beth Stephens and Annie Sprinkle declare in the *Ecosex Manifesto* (point iv):

> *We are ecosex activists.* We will save the mountains, waters, and skies by any means necessary, especially through joy, love, and our powers of seduction. We will stop the rape, abuse, and the poisoning of the Earth. We do not condone the use of violence, although we recognize that some ecosexuals may choose to fight those most guilty for destroying the Earth with public disobedience, anarchist and radical environmental activist strategies. We embrace the revolutionary tactics of art, music, poetry, humor, and sex. We work and play tirelessly for Earth justice and global peace.

Ecosexuality is, of course, only one approach to environmental justice and it is specific in its geographical, historical, racial, and cultural positioning. This is not a unique movement, and many Indigenous activists, scholars, and organizers, on a global level, are fighting for similar ideals. Our movements, just like us, are immersed in and influenced by the dominant discourses, and our own historical and societal positioning influences how we engage with the world around us. In relation to ecosexuality, here are the reflections of Dr. Kim TallBear—who we introduced in Chapter 2—on the notions of "sex" and "nature" as she writes about Beth Stephens and Annie Sprinkle's activism:

> With the rise of scientific authority and management approaches, both sex and nature have been rendered as discrete, coherent, troublesome, yet manageable objects. Both sex and nature are at the heart of struggles involving ideas of purity and contamination, life and death, but which only scientifically trained experts or rational subjects (read historically white, Western men) are seen as fit to name, manage, and to set the terms of legitimate encounter.
>
> Annie's and Beth's art and activism disrupts these dominant ideas. Sexual practices and identities do and should be allowed to take multiple, shifting forms over time as our needs for different kinds of intimacies change. Thus the transformation of Beth and Annie from queer to also ecosexual. Practices and identities are fluid. This is good, something to be open about and celebrated. Likewise, we are in nature. Nature is us. We have close intimate everyday relations with nonhumans, and they do not always accord with the dominant, heteronormative, scientistic view of things. Sex is both nature and culture, both instinct and art. As Annie told my surprised undergraduates at UC Berkeley this past spring when she passed around a flower in full bloom for them to smell: "You put your nose in to smell that flower's sex organ. You just had sex with that flower." The seemingly mundane can be revelatory.

The erotic and activism

We hope these examples illustrate what we mean when we say that our sexuality is in relationship to the world around us and vice versa. Our sexuality and sex lives are not neutral, as we've pointed out again and again throughout the book. Rather, they're shaped by history, societal structures, and culture. This means that once we start to question what we've been taught about sex and sexuality within dominant discourse, one of the possibilities that opens up is to go further upstream and to become more aware—if we're not already—of how power and oppression operate, not just in our individual lives but also on a systemic level.

If we become more present, more connected to our own aliveness and creativity, more capable of intimacy with ourselves and others, and better at consent in all aspects of our lives, we can often become more interested in changing the world. This could involve addressing those wounds of separation, disconnect, dissociation, and violence at their sources, including colonialism, racism, anti-Blackness, classism, ableism, and patriarchy. If our own bodies, other people's bodies, and the body of the Earth are no longer non-consensually treated as commodities, our politics often cannot help but change.

adrienne maree brown is one of the contemporary authors and activists whom we admire and who expresses some of these sentiments much more eloquently than we can in one of her latest books, *Pleasure Activism: The Politics of Feeling Good*. In this collection of her work, she writes:

I believe our imaginations—particularly the parts of our

imaginations that hold what we most desire, what brings us pleasure, what makes us scream yes—are where we must seed the future, turn toward justice and liberation, and reprogram ourselves to desire sexually and erotically empowered lives. (p.157)

She also writes:

I touch my own skin, and it tells me that before there was any harm, there was miracle... Pleasure activism is the work we do to reclaim our whole, happy, and satisfiable selves from the impacts, delusions, and limitations of oppression and/or supremacy. (p.303)

This is very much what we're trying to communicate at the closing of this book. To be in deeper relationship with ourselves, with our sexual, erotic selves, and with others is indeed not a superficial self-indulgence, but rather the compass that can guide us to a more engaged, present, consensual, honest, and connected life. This too has the potential to change the world.

ACTIVITY: GUIDED BY PLEASURE TO CHANGE THE WORLD AROUND US

Take a moment, or two, or three, right now, to track how the work you've already done, or maybe are doing through reading this book, has been guiding you, or could guide you, in your activism. Please note that we're using "activism" as a broad umbrella term, which can include direct political action, such as protests, as well as living your daily life in joyful resistance to systems of oppression that never meant for you to survive.

You can write down, dance, draw, or record your reflections in whatever way feels comfortable to you. First of all, take time to notice what brings you pleasure in the broader sense of the erotic—that is, the sense of aliveness, power, and creativity that is our birthright. If you like, you can write this down in a few key words or pictures in the center of the concentric circles below. Then reflect on how this pleasure radiates out and impacts those closest to you. You can jot this down in the second circle out from the center of the concentric circles below. Then take time to think about the ways in which this pleasure impacts the communities around you—that is the third circle out from the center below. Finally, take some time to think about how all of this connects with activism, or cultural changes in the wider world—that is the fourth circle out from the center in the diagram below.

Finally, take a few moments to notice your reflections, with as much curiosity, compassion, and non-judgment as you're able to, in this moment. Please try to hold all of this, including this whole book, with open hands, knowing that this too is a process in constant flux, rather than being any kind of definitive answer to close our fists around.

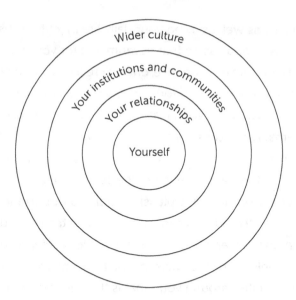

FIGURE 7.2: MULTIPLE LEVELS OF INFLUENCE

REMEMBER: Sexuality can seem like such a personal and private matter to us, especially if this is what's promoted in dominant culture all around us. This can feel isolating and—if our sexual identities, desires, attractions, and practices do not fall within what is considered normative—we might also struggle with shame and the fear of being "found out." However, we don't need to explore or live our sexual lives in isolation.

We can access—and are deserving of—human connection and support. This connection and support can take many forms, from trained professionals to communities, and we can choose any of these forms of connection and support at different points in our lives. Whatever our own sexual identities, attractions, desires, and practices might be, being present to and connected with our own erotic agency has the potential to heal ourselves, our relationships, and the world around us.

We can hardly wait to witness the world we can co-create together if we're committed to our own and one another's liberation in all aspects of our lives, including our sexualities. Thank you for being on this journey with us!

FURTHER RESOURCES

- American Association of Sexuality Educators, Counselors, and Therapists—Directory: www.aasect.org/referral-directory
- Certified Sexological Bodyworkers—Directory: www.sexologicalbodywork.com/doku.php?id=directory
- American Association for Marriage and Family Therapy—Directory: www.aamft.org/Directories/Find_a_Therapist.aspx
- Association for Family Therapy and Systemic Practice: www.aft.org.uk/page/findatherapist
- RAINN US National Anti-violence organization: www.rainn.org
- International Professional Surrogates Association Referral Program: https://internationalprofessionalsurrogatesassociation.wordpress.com/referrals-2
- Sex Workers Outreach Project, USA: https://swopusa.org
- The survivors trust: www.thesurvivorstrust.org. Survivors UK: www.survivorsuk.org

— SWARM, Sex Worker Advocacy and Resistance Network: www.swarmcollective.org

— Pink Therapy: www.pinktherapy.com

— The Licence to Queer project: www.licencetoqueer.com

For more on building consensual cultures check out:

— Stryker, K. (ed.) (2017). *Ask: Building Consent Culture*. Portland, OR: Thorntree Press.

Mia Mingus's worksheet on developing consent pods can be found here:

— https://batjc.wordpress.com/pods-and-pod-mapping-worksheet

For more on Betty Martin's approaches see:

— Martin, B. (2021). *The Art of Receiving and Giving: The Wheel of Consent*. Eugene, OR: Luminare Press.

The Audre Lorde essay, which we've referred to several times in this book, is:

— Lorde, A. (1984). "The Uses of the Erotic: The Erotic as Power." In A. Lorde (2012). *Sister Outsider: Essays and Speeches*. Berkeley CA: Crossing Press.

You can read about Barbara Carrellas's work in:

— Carrellas, B. (2007). *Urban Tantra: Sacred Sex for the 21st Century*. Berkeley, CA: Ten Speed Press.

— Carrellas, B. (2012). *Ecstasy is Necessary: A Practical Guide*. London: Hay House.

You can read about Beth Stephens and Annie Sprinkle's work at:

— Sexecology.org

Kim TallBear's essay mentioned here is:

— TallBear, K. (2012). *What's in Ecosexuality for an Indigeneous Scholar of "Nature."* Retrieved from: https://indigenoussts.com/whats-in-ecosexuality-for-an-indigenous-scholar-of-nature on 12/14/2020 adrienne maree-brown's books include:

- maree-brown, a. (2017). *Emergent Strategy: Shaping Change, Changing Worlds*. Chico, CA: AK Press.

- maree-brown, a. (2019). *Pleasure Activism: The Politics of Feeling Good*. Chico, CA: AK Press.

- maree-brown, a. (2019). *We Will Not Cancel Us: And Other Dreams of Transformative Justice*. Chico, CA: AK Press.

Index

Page numbers in *italics* refer to figures.